Globalchild
Multicultural Resources for Young Children

Maureen Cech

Addison-Wesley Publishing Company
Menlo Park, California • Reading, Massachusetts • New York
Don Mills, Ontario • Wokingham, England • Amsterdam • Bonn • Sydney
Singapore • Tokyo • Madrid • San Juan

Acknowledgments

I would like to thank Health and Welfare Canada for their financial assistance through the Child Care Initiatives Fund, and TESL Ottawa for supporting this project.

Many other groups and individuals have contributed generously to the content and form of this book through their reviews, field tests, and searching questions; in particular, Joan Weller with her literary expertise, and Karin Leslie-Fairless with her artistic input. I am especially grateful to my committee — Diane Blenkiron, Barbara Cummergen, Karin Leslie-Fairless, and Wendy Magahay-Johnson. These women gave unselfishly both their ideas and their support to this project.

Finally I would like to thank my husband, Denis, for his invaluable technical assistance and his unending patience, and my home field testers, Alexandra and Jeremy, whose enthusiasm made GLOBALCHILD a reality.

The opinions expressed in this book are solely the author's and in no way express the policy or opinions of Health and Welfare Canada.

This book is published by the Alternative Publishing Group.

Editing: Elizabeth Driver, Lois Fowkes, Wendy Magahay-Johnson
Illustrations: Josephine Wang
Photographs: Justin Wonnacott
Design: Wangs Graphics

ISBN 0-201-29822-8

7 8 9 10 - EB - 95 94 93

CONTENTS

Multiculturalism is a sharing of
cultures. It empowers individuals who
then share that strength among groups.
It expands cultural consciousness
into global consciousness.
As essential as literacy, multiculturalism
is no longer an option in education.
It is an integrated part of any
well developed program.

Welcome to Globalchild

At the center of each program is the child, and at the center of each child is culture. The choices the child makes form the "language" of that culture. The very young child decides what smells good and what is strange and stinky, develops a taste for certain foods, and eats them with fingers, or chopsticks, or silverware. This cultural language may begin as early as conception, long before the child can say the word "culture."

By the age of five, the child has also learned the cultural score — which ones are good, which ones are not, and how cultures are rated against each other. Knowing the score gives a child with a high cultural score a sense of self-esteem based on privilege. On the other hand, a child with a low score may lose that chance for self-confidence and self-esteem.

Educators cannot change society's score card completely, but they can help to even the balance. With more and more children in full-time day care, early childhood educators feel increasingly responsible for nurturing and developing the child's culture. Accordingly, their deep, personal commitment to multiculturalism is critical.

Educators have taken many approaches to multiculturalism:
- the "uniculture" approach relating all cultures to the dominant one
- the "information" or "museum" approach offering globes, maps, and fact sheets
- the "tokenist" approach with food, fashions, and festivals to show the exotica of culture
- the "colonizer" approach that evokes sympathy rather than empathy for minority cultures and races.

The GLOBALCHILD approach sees culture as ever-changing rather than static and fixed. As people change, so does culture, and no one activity or adjective can epitomize a nation. So-called national activities are inevitably linked with activities originating half a world away. The parents, volunteers, refugees, and ethnocultural groups who suggested Globalchild activities confirmed this sharing. Each activity was personal rather than national, just as sugaring-off may mean spring for some North Americans but not for all.

Throughout the text background information draws many cultural parallels; others wait to be discovered. One field tester who labelled an activity as Italian was reminded of this by a Pakistani child who said, "No, it isn't. We do that too."

The GLOBALCHILD approach stresses commonalities rather than confrontations. Similarity among cultures helps both adult and child to experience multiculturalism without feeling alienated or threatened by it. The choice of a familiar seasonal format rather than more abstract anti-racist themes eases this transition from the known to the unknown.

Activity is the second GLOBALCHILD strategy. Direct experiences are used to change perspectives and attitudes. Both adult and child can learn multiculturalism by doing it: making a game, playing an instrument, or eating a snack. Communal activity reinforces the learning experience, reminding us that we all have much to learn.

Developing global consciousness is challenging. When presenting the material remember:

- Some children are delighted to recognize their own culture and rush to bring in supplemental material.

- Other children may want to forget their culture. They may also have little knowledge of it and show little initial interest.

- A homogeneous group with high self-esteem (usually a dominant culture group) may not see the need for multiculturalism and may show antagonism, overt racism, or boredom.

- Past experiences of racism, length of stay in the United States, fear and anger may deter a child from participating at all.

The same applies to the child's family. They, too, may react with suspicion, disinterest, or enthusiasm. Members of the dominant culture may not want to share ideas with a minority group, and vice versa. Over time, however, the educator's interest and respect for culture will inspire trust, and on this trust a GLOBALCHILD program can be built.

Share your difficulties and successes with parents, staff, and volunteers. Ask them for feedback. Read the suggested resource books, and establish a liaison with local ethnocultural groups. Use the checklists to monitor biases and assumptions. Remember that you are not alone. There are many others who also believe in the GLOBALCHILD perspective. They join me now in saying to you, "Good Luck!"

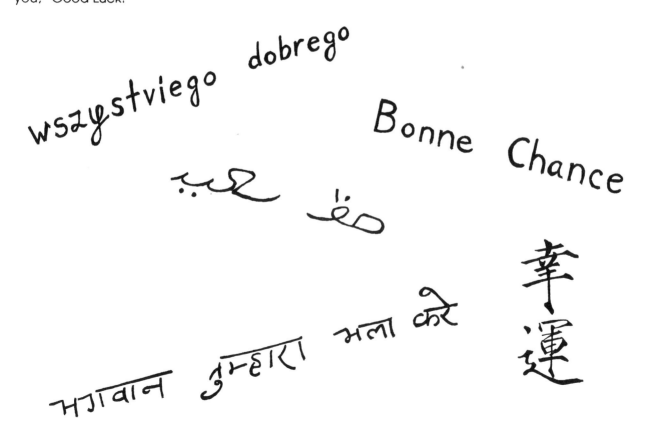

CHAPTER ONE

Creating the multicultural experience

Creating the multicultural experience

Share cultures in each of the six familiar areas of a program:
1. **Setting the mood**
2. **Music and movement**
3. **Art**
4. **Discovery**
5. **Group time**
6. **Food to share**

The overlap between areas is intentional: musical instruments are used at group time, dress-ups are worn at snack. This frequent repetition reinforces new vocabulary and concepts and results in greater group participation. Children will naturally create their own variations within the comfort of repetition.

Discussion of each of the six activity areas begins with a checklist to help educators assess cultural bias. Check through the props, materials, and visuals of a play area, then examine body language, parent interviewing techniques, and the use of volunteers. Cultural bias is evident in program planning too. Principles of child rearing, play, and social behavior reflect cultural norms just as do rules about playing in the snow, daytime napping, and speaking freely to elders. This does not imply that other norms are "wrong" or "right", but it does recognize their equal validity within a multicultural United States. Educators who recognize this validity can plan activities that meet the cultural needs of all the children.

Read over each checklist, comparing your responses with those of other staff members, and talk about possible strategies for change. Ask questions relevant to your program. Update the checklists and ensure that new staff have copies. In this way each area's multicultural content can be continually assessed and improved.

Practical suggestions and sample activities follow the checklists. Adapt these to the children and the program. These direct experiences of a culture can change the attitudes of both adult and child. To emphasize global similarities, activities have been linked with parallel ones. Background information is included to use with parents and volunteers, and to adapt in response to children's questions.

A pronunciation guide for many of the non-English words is on pp. 238-239. Try to pronounce these words correctly and to use them in the program. This validates our multi-lingual community in a very direct way. Once again, ask parents and volunteers for their help with longer phrases, stories, and songs.

By concentrating on global activities, the educator helps the children to develop a global consciousness. It won't happen in a day or a week, and may not be sudden or dramatic. But little comments, tentative first friendships, and physical expressions of sharing will show the educator that the children are on their way to developing a multicultural perspective.

1. Setting the mood

Look at your own classroom. Start with the arrangement, design, and use of the space. While the basic equipment may be the same every day, its position and its function can make a statement too. Look at your visual props, your everyday living center, and your dramatic play materials, and think about the statement they make or the mood they convey.

Checklist 1: Setting the mood

1. Does the arrangement of space encourage co-operative group learning?
2. Do the cultures presented visually reflect the multicultural reality of the world rather than your classroom reality?
3. Are some groups over-represented?
4. Are some groups under-represented?
5. Are minority cultures presented as an integral part of American society?
6. Are members of minority groups shown as individuals with distinct features rather than stereotypes?
7. Are all of the visual props equally aesthetically appealing?
8. Are games played with some of the visuals so that the children begin to look at them more closely?
9. Do the props in the everyday living center reflect the multicultural reality rather than the dominant culture only?
10. Do the props stretch the child's flexibility by suggesting alternative methods of cooking, eating, or cleaning?
11. Do they support a variety of lifestyles — briefcases as well as handbags, toolboxes as well as typewriters?
12. Are some of the props contributed or made by the children or their families?
13. Are there enough props and dress-ups to allow for and encourage co-operative play?

Having considered these questions, turn back to the room and think about the arrangement of space. In American early childhood settings we are accustomed to having five or six learning centers in the room. There is intermingling, but generally the messy art area is separated from the quiet area, the everyday living from the psychomotor, and so on.

In many countries of the world, space is neither so abundant nor so compartmentalized. A co-operative group learning approach rather than an individual approach is stressed. An activity is started together and is directed by the educator. Everyone cuts out the paper or makes the snack together. If one child cannot do the task, the other children or the educator will help the child keep pace with the group. The activity ends when everyone is finished.

Both settings reflect the influence of Pestalozzi, Piaget, Comenius, Montessori, and Froebel. Both also reflect cultural norms. There are no "wrongs" or "rights" here, and the sensitive educator realizes this when talking to parents accustomed to other educational settings. The space can be changed and the methods modified to reaffirm the validity of each child's culture.

Visual props

Young children read pictures just as older children read books. If the visual props are appropriate, accessible, and attractive (clean, clear, and orderly rather than merely beautiful), children will read their multicultural message every day. Suggestions follow.

- Hang the wall visuals at the child's eye level.

- Group several visuals together to make a photo collage on the wall.

- Surround them with artwork produced by the children themselves.

- Put drawings and photographs in a classroom album and leave it out for the children to read.

- Hang pictures on strings from the ceiling.

- Label and laminate photographs and hang them over a matching activity area.

- Use drawings and photographs to illustrate stories or to explain situations in folktales.

- Mount pictures on a folding wooden screen, then fold them away for later use.

- Glue pictures to a roller blind and unroll a few each day. When the unit is complete and the pictures are no longer needed, simply roll up the blind, unhook it at the top, and put it away.

Using a roller blind

This does not mean a major outlay of funds! There are many sources for both no-cost and low-cost visual props. Remember to mention to the distributor why you need these and how they will be used. This may prompt more free posters and brochures as new materials are produced.

- The artwork of parents, volunteers, children and educators is free and often the most relevant.

- Back copies of magazines such as **International Wildlife, China Pictorial, Japan, Equinox** and **National Geographic World** can be bought from secondhand bookstores or thrift shops. Preview pictures for bias and relevancy; for example, one family living in the rain forest of Brazil does not represent all Brazilians.

- The Canadian International Development Agency (CIDA) offers posters with beautiful photographs of children and families from many backgrounds. Free poster kits are available by writing to CIDA, 200 Promenade du Portage, Hull, Quebec K1A 0G4. Use these judiciously to depict children in both urban and rural settings.

- Multiculturalism Canada publishes a series of resource guides for educators on Multi-culturalizing through Play, Physical Education and Recreation, Parent Involvement, and Children's Literature. This series and the Together We're Better kit are available free from Multiculturalism Canada, Ottawa, Ontario K1A 0M5.

- Inuktitut alphabet posters and posters of Inuit children are available free from the Department of Northern Affairs, Ottawa, Ontario K1A 0H4.

- Embassies and consulates offer pamphlets, magazines, and posters from their countries. Consult the telephone directory for individual listings. Again, check pictures for bias.

- Books with difficult text sometimes offer beautiful illustrations. Create a new story to suit the pictures. One example is **Who Hides in the Park?** (Warabe Aska, 1986).

- The United Nations High Commissioner for Refugees, United Nations, Grand Central P.O. 20, New York, NY 10017 offers low-cost poster sets, wall calendars, and a monthly magazine, **Refugees**. Donations are welcome.

- Office for Civil Rights, U.S. Dept. of Education, 330 C St. SW, Washington, D.C. 20202 offers a wide selection of free pamphlets on multiculturalism.

- The National Association for the Education of Young Children produces low-cost posters depicting inter-racial friendships. For a free catalogue write to NAEYC, 1834 Connecticut Avenue NW, Washington, D.C. 20009-5786.

Alphabet books

Written language is seen everywhere in early childhood settings. Shelves are labelled, welcome signs are on the door, and books are on the shelves, almost always in the language of the dominant culture. It is important for young children to recognize that theirs is not the only language, and that there are, in fact, many alphabets at the base of many languages. Part of this realization comes through seeing words from many languages.

Labels can be translated by parents. The alphabet frieze can be Arabic, Hindi, or Inuktitut. Rather than buying it, make it with the help of volunteers and the books listed below. Remember that the goal is not to train young linguists. It is to increase global awareness by validating all cultures, and language is the key to culture!

Use these alphabet books as visuals. A full listing of multicultural books is on pp. 36-40.

Aubin, Michel. **The Secret Code**. Toronto: James Lorimer, 1987.
In this amusing urban story children substitute pictures for letters of the alphabet.

Ehlert, Lois. **Eating the Alphabet: Fruits and Vegetables from A to Z.** New York: Harcourt Brace Jovanovich, 1989.
Brilliant collages depict fruits and vegetables from artichoke to zucchini.

Feelings, Muriel. **Jambo Means Hello: Swahili Alphabet Book**. New York: Dial, 1974.
Pictures by Tom Feelings illustrate African animals and locations. Children love the word "jambo" and will incorporate it easily into everyday language.

Feeney, Stephanie. **A is for Aloha**. Honolulu: University of Hawaii, 1980.
Photographs depict everyday life for families in Hawaii.

Harrison, Ted. **A Northern Alphabet**. Montreal: Tundra, 1982.
Colorful pictures depict life in Canada's North.

Moak, Allen. **A Big City ABC**. Montreal: Tundra, 1984.
This is a detailed illustration of urban life; a filmstrip based on the book is also available.

Musgrove, Margaret. **Ashanti to Zulu.** New York: Dial, 1976.
Detailed drawings by Leo and Diane Dillon depict everyday African lives.

Pachano, J. and J. Rabbitt Ozores. **James Bay Cree ABC in Songs and Pictures**. James Bay, Quebec: Cree Cultural Education Center, 1983.
Singing this alphabet to the tune suggested makes some of the difficult words easier to say.

Roache, Gordon. **A Halifax ABC**. Montreal: Tundra, 1987.
Good urban pictures complement this localized ABC. This book is available in French too.

Zendrera, Concepcion and Noelle Granger. **Mi Primer Diccionario Ilustrado**. Barcelona: Editorial Juventud, 1984.
This Spanish alphabet book connects bright colorful objects to each letter.

First five letters of the Arabic alphabet

Everyday living

More happens in the everyday living center than simple housekeeping. Children act out their lives and those of the adults around them, trying to make sense of the world. That is why it is so important to provide culturally appropriate props and materials to help them. As always, ask the children and their families for help so that the area really becomes their own. Some suggestions for props follow.

Parenting

- Offer a variety of dolls to reflect the diverse American/global population. Black-skinned dolls with Caucasian features are just as inappropriate as the sexual features of a teenage Barbie. Children may enjoy playing with them, but what do these dolls say about our own bias? Instead, look for dolls that are facially accurate, then dress them appropriately too.

- Use futons, cribs, head rests, sleeping bags, and hammocks for sleeping dolls. Some Latin American babies sleep in highly decorated baskets or moises, similar to those used in Europe.

- Provide backpacks, slings, snugglies, and cradleboards for carrying the dolls. Carrying a baby on your back rather than in a stroller is now more commonplace throughout the United States, and has always been the custom in much of the world. From the picken of Nigeria to the rebozo of South America, the fabric differs. But the style of the backpack — fabric wrapped around baby, then around mom's waist — remains the same. In the North of Canada a type of parka called an amauti lets the mother carry her baby on her back all day.

Cradleboard

The cradleboard was designed to make the baby feel secure. With its traditional inner moss lining and its tight laces, the cradleboard kept the baby snug and immobile yet able to watch and hear the surrounding family. It was often made by the father as his preparation for the birth of the child. Cradleboards are still used by some Native American families.

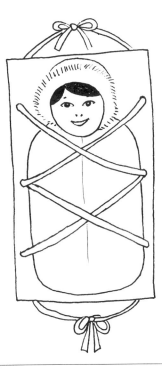

Materials: 1 piece of heavy cardboard 12 by 20 in.
  hole punch
  glue
  1 large paper or cloth bag
  2 strips of bias tape or stretch fabric,
    2 by 80 in. each

Method: 1. Punch 3 holes as indicated on each long side of the cardboard.
  2. Glue the paper or cloth bag to the board.
  3. Lace the strips through the 6 holes, crisscrossing them over the bag to secure it to the board.
  4. To carry the cradleboard, tie the top 2 ends together to make a loop for the forehead. Tie the bottom 2 ends together around the waist.

Cleaning

- For clothes scrubbing use a washboard or a large stone and water in a big washtub. Taking the program dress-ups or blankets to the laundromat is another way to experience alternative methods of washing clothes.

- In Central and South America a bar of soap is often used to wash dishes. In rural Africa a stump of fibrous wood may be a scouring pad. Campers in the United States may use sand, lichen, or leaves to clean pots. Experiment with these materials in your dishwashing activities.

- Give the children a palm leaf duster made with large real or artificial leaves. Feather dusters, often made from ostrich feathers, are also used for cleaning.

Preparing and eating food

- Put out a variety of cooking and eating utensils such as a wok, rice cooker, tortilla press, pasta maker, mortar and pestle, bamboo steamer, hibachi, expresso coffee maker, tongs, decorated wooden utensils, pasta fork, garlic press, and ulu (Inuit chopper).

- Offer a selection of Japanese, Chinese, and Korean chopsticks. Japanese chopsticks are more tapered at the end than the Chinese, and Korean ones are often stainless steel as opposed to bamboo. Chopsticks also come in a variety of sizes — long ones for cooking, short for eating, and very short for children. They can be plain or decorated, and made of plastic, metal, or wood.

- Put large plastic soup bowls and simulated lacquerware dishes on the tables. Use cushions and low tables; a board on bricks works well. Eating on a canvas rug is fun too: sew one out of old potato bags and you won't have to worry about juice spills.

- To act out mealtime, collect a wide variety of plastic vegetables and fruit. For extra durability and weight fill each one with a sawdust and glue combination and allow to harden. Put the produce in rice bags, baskets, clay pots, and bins.

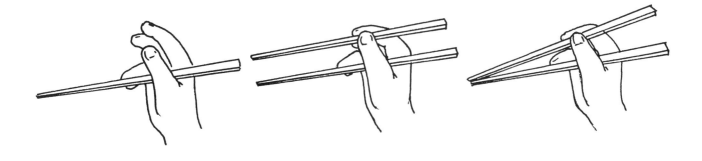

Holding chopsticks

Dramatic play

Dramatic play gives children a chance to become someone else, if only for a moment. Young children enthusiastically enter into the spirit of their props, inventing dialogue and acting out situations appropriate to the costume they are wearing or the new setting they create. What a wonderful opportunity to imagine life in another culture! This is a time when an educator can instill global consciousness through choosing appropriate props and addressing misconceptions and false assumptions as they arise.

Why do some children rush to try on dress-ups, while others never do? The answer lies in individuals and their need for fantasy, as well as in the dress-ups that are available. Assess the variety and balance of your dress-ups, then become a collector! For further information on dress-ups see pp. 107-110. Here are some suggestions for enriching dramatic play props.

- Learn a little about the clothes children wear every day, not just costumes or holiday wear. Ask parents for advice, use resource books, and scour import and thrift shops until your collection is globally balanced.

- Invite parents to bring in a special outfit to show the children, then make a durable duplicate for everyday use.

- Look for adult clothes that can be adapted, A flannel shirt without sleeves or collar can look like a child's vest. An adult's embroidered blouse can become a child's dance dress.

- Look also for large pieces of material for the children to use as wraps, ponchos, saris, or jubbas. Smaller fabric pieces can be used as dolls' clothes, headscarves, or turbans. A triangular piece of woven fabric worn over the shoulders doubles as a gutra. Worn on the head with a headband it becomes a gubytra (kaffiyeh).

- Let the children make their own ponchos and vests from big paper bags, earrings from plastic curtain rings, and hats from cardboard. Let them sew button designs on blankets to make a Salish wrap. Making the dress-ups gives the children another reason to cherish them.

Kente

Materials: 3-ft square of colorful cotton fabric
2-in. strip of velcro (optional)

Method: 1. If the fabric is plain, hand print or block print it with a tempera paint and detergent mixture. Allow the fabric to dry overnight.
2. Hold a corner of fabric to 1 shoulder.
3. Wrap the fabric around the body under the arms.
4. Either tie the corners of fabric together, or sew on velcro tabs to keep them together.

Poncho

Materials: 3-ft square of blanket cloth or heavy fabric
scissors
waterproof fabric markers

Method: 1. Fold the fabric in half.
2. Cut a V-shaped slit in the middle of the fold. The slit should be large enough to let a child's head push through it.
3. Cut fringes at the bottom of the poncho.
4. Draw geometric designs on the bottom edge.

Six ways to wear a scarf

2. Music and movement

Music and active games involve the whole child. By pretending to carry a heavy basket, or by dancing to a new rhythm, the child enters into the life and games of another child, another culture. When children put on overalls they become plumbers, not simply acting out the role but really entering a new reality.

Psychomotor games and exercises for young children are strikingly similar from culture to culture. Materials and names change, but the essence of a game — fun, excitement, and the joy of movement — remains the same. Look for simple ball or skipping games that are easily mastered in crossing cultures. Try to use the original name of the game and a facsimile of the authentic equipment.

Co-operation and acceptance are important in music and movement activities. Rhythms or melodies that at first seem uneven or discordant may, on closer listening, develop new musical insights. It is important for children to have the chance to listen to and perhaps even play a variety of instruments such as the balalaika, the sitar, and the steel drums. Approach local ethnic organizations and folklore centres to recruit volunteer musicians willing to share their art. Through this direct personal experience children can begin to see other music as familiar rather than as different or weird.

Checklist 2: Music and movement

1. Are the games drawn from many cultures rather than just one?

2. Do the props and materials used in the exercises and games reflect these cultures?

3. Are handmade materials used in the games and are the children given the chance to make these?

4. Are there visual props in the room that show children playing these games, and do they meet the criteria for visuals outlined earlier (see p. 11)?

5. Is meditation, yoga, or a quiet relaxation time a regular component of the movement program?

6. Is co-operation rather than competition the basis for group games?

7. Is music used with movement on a regular basis?

8. Is the music selection varied in rhythms, instruments, language, and composition?

9. Are musical instruments accessible to the children and do they reflect the multicultural reality?

10. Is spontaneous dance encouraged as well as group dancing?

Props and materials

Start your collection of props and materials by borrowing them or buying them at local craft shops. Others can be made with the children, providing the basis for a multicultural music and movement area. Consider the following suggestions.

Stilts

Stilts can be made of tin cans with rope loops (Canada/Italy/Spain) or coconut shells with string loops (Malaysia/Indonesia).

Materials: 2 short, fat tin cans of the same size
hammer and nail
one 6-ft string
scissors

Method:
1. Fill the cans with water and freeze them. This makes the cans easier to punch.
2. Use a hammer and nail to punch a hole on either side of the closed top of each can. Empty out the ice.
3. Cut the string in half. Put one 3-ft length of string through the 2 holes, then pull it up to make a loop. Repeat this for the other can.
4. Adjust the length of the loop so that the child can walk comfortably on the cans, holding the loops taut for balance.

Pois (Argentinian, Native Canadian, New Zealander)

Pois (New Zealand), Boleadoras (Argentina), or Papassi Kawan (Canada) are all versions of the same equipment: two balls joined with string. In New Zealand this is a child's game orginating with the Maori. In Argentina the balls were made of leather and were swung to herd cattle. Papassi Kawan is a woman's game, played with leather bags full of sand.

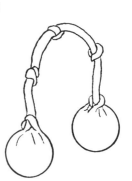

Materials: 1 pair old pantyhose
2 soft tennis balls

Method:
1. Put a tennis ball into each foot of the pantyhose. Tie a knot in the pantyhose to hold the ball in place.
2. Knot the middle section of the pantyhose several times to make the length between the two balls shorter.
3. Holding the pantyhose in the middle, try to swing both balls in the air together. Alternatively, swing one ball around your waist to strike the other ball.

Badminton (Chinese, English, Japanese, North American)

Battledores (Japan), shuttlecock (England), or hanetsuki (China) are all versions of a game known in North America as badminton.

Materials: 1 durable paper plate (or 2 glued together for strength)
1 craft stick
masking tape
several sheets colored tissue paper
elastic band

Method: 1. Tape a craft stick to the back of a paper plate for a handle. This makes a racquet. Alternatively, use an old ping pong paddle.
2. Crumple tissue paper into a ball, then wrap the ball in a tissue paper circle. Wrap securely with an elastic band. Fringe the loose ends to make a birdie.

Ribbons (Chinese, Korean)

Ribbons help children develop co-ordination skills and a sense of rhythm.

Material: two 2-by-3 ft lengths of ribbon
Method: 1. Tie one end of a ribbon around one wrist. Repeat with the other ribbon.
2. Make big arm movements to music so that the ribbons follow the arms.

Simple play materials

- Hollow balls are made of rattan in Malaysia and Indonesia, and of banana leaves in Burundi, India, and Zambia. Imitate this by making papier mâché balls, using a small balloon as a form (see p. 131). Younger children can make newspaper balls by crumpling up newspaper into a ball and holding it together with a wide elastic band.

- Thin elastic bands are held tightly in rectangles or triangles by children in Australia, New Zealand, the United States, and Vietnam, so that other children can jump in and out of the elastic shape. Imitate this by using thin elastic or string loops.

- Kick the can is a game played everywhere. It reminds adults that simple, found objects are often the most fun. Encourage young children to kick snowballs, used cans, or other materials through obstacle courses, up hills, down paths, or around the play yard. Children should be wearing proper footwear (running shoes, snow boots) for all of these outdoor activities.

Hand-clapping games

Hand clapping is done with infants, toddlers, and young children. It becomes more complex and acquires sophisticated language when the child reaches school, but the appeal remains the same. Later, the child may use the same rhythmic hand clapping when folk dancing.

"Change hand clap" is played by Egyptian children in much the same way as "Pat-a-cake" is played in the United States. It is the same game in Germany, Italy, and Spain, but the words are different. Try one of these versions with the children, and invite a parent who speaks German, Italian, or Spanish to play the game. Four language versions (English, German, Sicilian, Spanish) of the game follow.

Pat-a-cake, pat-a-cake, baker's man,
Bake me a cake as fast as you can,
We'll roll it and prick it and mark it with B,
And put it in the oven for baby and me.

Bake, bake a cake,
The baker called.
Who wants to bake some cake?
You must have seven things:
Eggs and salt,
Butter and lard,
Milk and flour,
Saffron to make the cake yellow.
Put it right in the oven.

Hand little hand, breads and figs.
Here he comes bringing candy.
We eat it all up,
And to baby give none.

Little cakes and more little cakes,
For mother the prettiest,
Round loaves and more round loaves,
For the baby the littlest.
And for father the biggest piece.

Backe, backe Kuchen,
Der Bäcker hat gerufen.
Wer will schöne Kuchen backen?
Der muss haben sieben Sachen:
Eier und Salz,
Butter und Schmalz,
Milch and Mehl,
Safran macht den Kuchen gelb.
Sheib, sheib in´ Ofen ´nein.

Manu, manuzzi, pane ficuzzi,
Vieni lu tata porta ´ti cusuzzi.
Nua tri nn'i manciamu,
Al bambino noi nocendiamo.

Tortitas y más madres tortitas,
Para madre, las más bonitas,
Roscones y más roscones,
Para niñitos los más pequeños,
Y para padre, los coscorrones.

Yoga, a quiet activity

Children can benefit from quiet activities as well as from more active ones. Hatha yoga, or "yoga for health", originated in India as a healthy exercise for both body and spirit. Today it is practised throughout the world by people who use rhythmic breathing for relaxation. Dimmed lights, incense burning, and soft background music or sound effects can create a soothing atmosphere for these exercises.

The butterfly

1. Sit with a straight back.
2. Bring the soles of your feet together, and hold your feet.
3. Gently move your knees up and down like wings.
4. Straighten out your legs. Breathe deeply and relax.

The bow

1. Lie on your stomach and bend your legs so that you can hold your ankles.
2. Lift your head and hips and balance on your stomach.
3. Holding your ankles, rock gently back and forth. Try to keep your arms straight.
4. Stop rocking, let go, and relax.

Great listening

Bibliographies of music for young children can be frustrating. They may suggest multicultural content, but often the songs are poorly translated or adapted for children beyond any cultural authenticity. In addition, many ethnic recordings are out-of-date or unavailable. The following is a list of exciting, multicultural records for young children, all of which are currently available in major North American music stores. Use these to build an authentic base for your own music collection.

Dario Domingues, **Tupac Amaru: Awakening in Rhythms** (AMOK, 1987).
Enya, **Watermark** (WEA, 1988).
Messenjah, **Session** (WEA, 1984).
Raffi, **One Light, One Sun** (Troubadour, 1985).
Bob Schneider, **Listen to the Children** (Capitol, 1982).
Bob Schneider, **When You Dream a Dream** (Dr. Charly, 1982).
Bob Schneider, **Having a Good Time** (Capitol, 1983).

3. Art

Art mirrors society and its culture, and can be a first step to understanding and appreciating other cultures. Art encourages creativity, experimentation, flexibility, and involvement — the same qualities needed for living in a multicultural society.

Art activities in GLOBALCHILD reflect the cultures of many groups. Although the name of an activity may differ from group to group, its essence remains the same. It is this essential common quality that we want children to experience.

Art is a means of communication, a language. It can be used to make an anti-racist statement, particularly through color. Light colors have traditionally been associated with positive values and dark colors considered negative. "Brown and dirty" is a familiar phrase that can slip out before its hurtful implication is even considered. How many children have been told to "Wash that grimy black off your hands"? How many others have been handed white paper day after day and told to add some color (preferably not black for that would make a dirty grey!). Art can be used in another way, however, to instill positive associations with black and brown. Think about these questions when developing your multicultural art program.

Checklist 3: Art

1. Are examples of art drawn from various cultures rather than just one?

2. Are practical art projects a regular part of the program?

3. Is art made by the children used in other areas of the room?

4. Are group projects a regular part of the art program?

5. Is the selection of brown materials as wide as the blue or white?

6. Are brown and black paper used as often as white?

7. Are recycled materials used regularly?

8. Are natural rather than synthetic materials used?

9. Is conservation of material stressed during and after the activity?

10. Are art materials saved and recycled rather than thrown away when the activity is over?

New materials

To enhance your regular art program, consider the following ideas:

- In addition to using a variety of colors of playdough, use black playdough for its richness and luster.

- Put out brown or black paper with colored chalk.

- Put out the primary colors and let the children mix them to make interesting shades of brown.

- Add cinnamon or nutmeg to brown playdough so that it smells delicious.

- Use phrases such as, "rich brown", "chocolate brown" or "spicy brown" to enhance the visual flavor of the word and its associations.

- Add anise to black fingerpaint for a wonderfully scented experience.

- Offer just as many hues of brown markers as you do the blue ones.

- Look at the color of paper you use for face or body pictures; offer enough brown and black eyes to stick on the faces, and offer black yarn for hair too.

- Use aromatic coffee grounds, used tea leaves, shiny black mica, or soft brown fur as collage materials.

Art activities are also an important source of income in many cultures. To allay costs, natural materials are preferred. Not only is this environmentally sound but it also encourages an appreciation for the art around us. Suggestions for natural (and cheap!) art supplies follow.

- Paint brushes made of coconut hair scraped from the coconut then twisted together, sticks with frayed ends, feathers, pine tree branches, or corn silk (hair)

- Paint rollers made of discarded corn cobs, small branches, or bamboo

- Paint made of natural juices of puréed berries, boiled onion skin, or grass

- Newsprint, flour, and water to make papier mâché for modelling

- Mud rather than playdough or clay

- Pressed leaves and wildflowers as natural stickers

Use these natural art supplies to make usable art that can be added to the dramatic play area or the everyday living center. Children can help to make props and will proudly show them to their parents. Art does not need be taken home each day but can be enjoyed in the day care "home" instead!

Clay beads

Beads and earrings are worn by young children everywhere for adornment and sometimes for their symbolic value. Let the children make, paint, then string their own clay necklaces and bracelets. Leftover beads can be used in wind chimes, tambourines, or group weaving.

Time: 2 sessions: making, painting and stringing
Materials: 1 C cornstarch
             11/2 C baking soda
             1 C cold water
             1 large nail
             water-based acrylic paint and fine brushes
             thin wire or nylon string
Method: 1. Cook the first 3 ingredients over low heat until the mixture bubbles.
                Continue cooking another 2-3 minutes until a dough forms. Remove the
                dough (clay) from the heat and allow to cool slightly.
             2. Form small marble-sized beads with the clay.
             3. Use the nail to poke a hole through each bead. Dry the beads overnight.
             4. Use the nail to hold the bead for painting. Dry the painted bead for
                15 minutes before stringing,

Collar necklace (Central African)

For hundreds of years, many Central African women have been wearing metal collar necklaces. Cloth versions of this collar are still fashionable in Central and Eastern Europe. Let the children make one just to see how it changes their posture and to feel its weight and shape.

Time: 15 minutes
Materials: 1 large paper plate per child
             scissors
             markers
Method: 1. Cut the center out of the paper plate.
             2. Decorate the outer rim of the plate with designs.
             3. Cut a slit through the rim so that it can be worn as a collar.

Silver pendant (South American)

Time: 15 minutes
Materials: 1 cardboard star per child
             glue
             scraps of yarn
             2 matching aluminum-foil stars per child
             hole punch
Method: 1. Spread glue on one side of the cardboard star, and arrange patterns of yarn on
                the glue.
             2. Press 1 foil star over the yarn until it sticks.
             3. Repeat this process on the other side of the cardboard star.
             4. When dry, punch a hole near the top of one point.

Brick making

Children today always seem to be on the move — from the apartment to the day care, from one city to the next, from one family group to another. Through all of this they carry an image of home as a place of refuge, a place of their own. Children help in many practical ways to make this home. They may decorate their rooms, tidy a bookshelf, or sweep the floor. In rural areas they may carry wood and pass nails to a builder.

All children have a responsibility and a role in "home-making". In warmer countries older children may even make blocks. Children can learn to mold a soft substance into a shape, then let the sun harden it. The sides of the brick or block may not be smooth, but they will be solid. To motivate the children, show them pictures of adobe homes and cement block buildings. Read them Terry Cash's book, **Bricks** (A and C Black, 1988) and show them the photographs.

This is a two-day activity: one for making, and one for unmolding. The warmer and drier the weather, the faster the block dries. This activity is best done outdoors in summer with a washtub full of water ready for the clean-up.

Cement block

Materials: 1 C fine gravel
1 bucket full of water
2 C sand/cement mixture
1 disposable plastic container

Method: 1. Soak the gravel in the bucket of water, then add it to the sand/cement mixture.
2. Add water to the dry ingredients until the mixture can be poured into the container.
3. Let the block harden overnight. When it is completely dry, crack off the mold.

Adobe brick

Materials: 2 C outdoor soil (not potting)
1/2 C powdered clay (if necessary)
2 C water
1 handful of broken straw or dry grass
1 disposable plastic container

Method: 1. Check the outdoor soil for clay content. If it sticks together when squeezed, then it has a high clay content; if not, add some powdered clay.
2. Fill the plastic container 3/4 full of the clay/soil mixture. Remove all sticks and stones from it.
3. Add water until the mixture is fluid.
4. Add straw until the mixture is stiff.
5. Press it flat by hand or with a block of wood.
6. Leave the brick to dry in the sun. When it is completely dry, crack off the mold.

4. Discovery

These group or individual activities are usually done in the quiet area of the room. They tend to focus on a single language function and/or perceptual skill, providing the necessary practice that leads to mastery. Puzzles, manipulatives, games, workjobs, tabletop toys — all of these are quiet activities, yet they elicit plenty of language along the way.

Checklist 4: Discovery

1. Do individual puzzles depict children of all backgrounds?

2. If not, is there an overall multicultural balance in the total puzzle collection?

3. Are there large floor puzzles to encourage co-operative play?

4. Do the fine motor activities incorporate traditional crafts such as weaving and sewing?

5. Are the small toy figures multicultural in appearance — facial features, skin color, and dress?

6. Do the counting materials and the game cards represent a wide variety of objects — produce, utensils, dress, and so on?

7. Are there large, complete sets of manipulatives to encourage co-operative play?

The multiculturalist is a collector, an innovator. Use the materials at hand to make new puzzles and games: paste pictures on bristol board, laminate and cut. Children can make their own puzzles but will probably need help cutting the heavy board. Pattern workjobs on traditional ethnic games. Use Russian stacking dolls, gourds, or chopsticks for sequencing, and follow up with a related craft activity. Use mango seeds, cowrie shells, trouble dolls, oware beads, beads on a string, or an abacus for counting games, and play them in more than one language. Children love the simple rhythm of counting songs, and will repeat them in a variety of languages. As with the alphabet songs, the goal is not to teach a second language but to enrich the child's understanding of the global richness of language. Use multicultural counting books such as the following:

Anno, Mitsumasa. **Anno's Counting House**. New York: Philomel, 1983.
Little windows and doors expose a variety of people to be counted in this fun, hands-on book.

Dunham, Meredith. **Numbers: How Do You Say It?** New York: Lothrop, Lee and Shepard, 1987.
This English, French, Spanish, and Italian counting book presents colorful objects to count.

Feelings, Muriel. **Moja Means One**. New York: Dial, 1971.
Traditional African instruments and clothing illustrate this Swahili counting book.

Fisher, Leonard. **Number Art: Thirteen 1, 2, 3s from Around the World.** New York: Four Winds, 1982.
Numbers in many languages are beautifully illustrated and explained.

Haskins, Kim. **Count Your Way Through Japan**. Minneapolis: Caroldhoda, 1987.
This is one of an excellent four-part counting series featuring Arabic, Chinese, Japanese, and Russian numbers.

May, David C. **Byron and his Balloon: an English-Chipewyan counting book**. Edmonton: Tree Frog Press, 1984.
Children's colorful drawings illustrate this Chipewyan/English counting book.

Beads on a string: counting games

Beads on a string are used throughout the world for many different purposes. They are primarily an organizational device to co-ordinate fingers, voice, and ears in praying, counting, or just thinking. For many people they are a simple source of comfort, something to hold.

The religions of nearly two-thirds of the world's population use beads on a string for prayer. The number of beads varies from the Hindu 108, to the Islamic 99, Roman Catholic 50, and Buddhist 30. Each bead is said to correspond to a prayer, and the beads are carried to encourage daily praying.

The Chinese use glass beads on a string much like an abacus for counting. The beads are carried in pockets for easy calculations.

Worry beads are also carried in Greece, Turkey, and the Middle East. There are 33 beads in each string of worry beads, and they are made of a variety of materials from olive pits to semi-precious stones.

Stringing beads

Materials: 3 lengths o f 6-in. string for each child
bobby pin that fits through the bead holes
tape
beads of 3 colors, all the same size (for making beads, see p. 26)

Method: 1. Thread the string through the "eye" of the bobby pin, then tape the prongs closed.
2. String only one color of bead first. When enough beads are strung, tie the ends of string together to make a bracelet.
3. Carry these worry beads in your pocket. Count them.
4. String a sequence of colors now. Make a second bracelet.
5. String favorite colors of beads to make a third bracelet.

Group beading

Materials: one 9-ft string knotted at one end
bobby pin to fit through the bead holes
tape
a wok or wooden bowl full of all colors of beads

Method: 1. Thread the bobby pin with string as described above.
2. Sit together in a circle with the wok in the middle.
3. Start the beading by choosing a bead and threading it onto the string. Then hand the pin to the next person.
4. Continue as long as interest is high, then tie the ends of the string together. The string should form a circle of the same size as the one formed by the children.
5. Let each child grasp the string with both hands, holding it loosely so that the beads can travel easily from child to child.
6. Push the beads in one direction, then the other. If there is only one bead you can play "pass the bead" by pushing it on the string all around the circle.
7. Try doing this with your eyes closed for a sensory group experience.

Matrioshka

The Matrioshka doll originally represented a famous figure in Russian folklore, Baba Yaga. Believed to be a witch, she had only one leg so she rolled around on a peg. Today there is a great variety of Matrioshka, each made in a particular province. A unique provincial motif is hand painted on the dolls. Some depict two parents and two children (family set); some depict a little boy growing old (aging sequence); and the most common set, the Rosi, are of a girl doll in various sizes. This is the set used here.

This activity consists of five parts: a story, a sequencing game, a fine motor activity, a craft, and a film. The five parts can be done in sequence, or only one part used at a time. Substitute names of the children in your group for the italicized names I have suggested. Tell the story using the four doll set to illustrate the actions.

1. Olga's rescue

Once upon a time there was a little girl named *Oksana* who lived in the mountains with her mother and her grandmother. She had a baby sister named *Olga* who was always getting lost. Every morning *Oksana* would get up and rush to her window that overlooked the valley. She would look out and smile at the valley below.

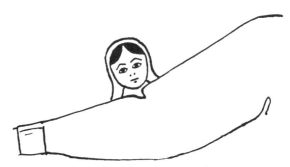

Looking out the window

One morning when she looked out of her window she saw a tiny speck below that seemed vaguely familiar. She looked again. It was *Olga*!

She ran to her mother's room to wake her and tell her the news. Then she ran to her grandmother, crying. What could they do? First grandmother looked out, then mother, then *Oksana*.

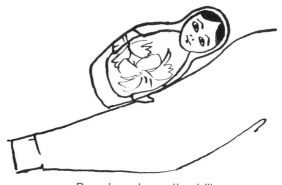

Running down the hill

It was true! Little *Olga* had walked right down into the valley and was all alone. Down ran grandmother. Down ran mother. Down ran *Oksana*.

When they all reached the bottom, *Oksana* said, "*Olga* let me hold you." Then mother said, "*Olga* and *Oksana*, let me hold you both." Then Grandma said, "Oh my darlings, let me hold you all and bring you safely home again."

And that is how the story of *Olga, Oksana*, mother and grandmother ends. They all went back up the mountain and *Olga* never, ever walked down into the valley alone again.

Happy together

2. The sequencing game

Give the child all four dolls to take apart and put together as one. Larger sets of six and seven dolls can also be used, but four dolls is an adequate number for the first attempt.

3. The fine motor activity

Use the pattern provided on the next page to make a fine motor activity that reinforces sequencing skills. The colors are suggestions only; any bright combination can be used.

Materials: two 6-by-3-in. pieces of pink felt
two 6-by-8-in. pieces of orange felt
two 6-by-9-in. pieces of red felt
one 8-by-10-in. piece of yellow felt
one 12-in. square of white blanket cloth
scissors
straight pins
needle and thread

Method: 1. Use the pattern on p. 32 to cut 7 doll shapes out of the felt: 2 tiny pink ones, 2 larger orange ones, 2 larger red ones, and 1 large yellow one.
2. Cut a straight slit from the neck to the bottom of each of the orange, red, and yellow dolls so that they can be opened evenly in half.
3. Pin the yellow doll squarely on the blanket cloth. Stitch all around the outer raw edges of the doll. Do not stitch the slit.
4. Pin the 2 red dolls together. Stitch all around the outer raw edges of the dolls. Do not stitch the slit.
5. Repeat this for the orange and pink dolls. Note that the pink doll has no slit.
6. Tuck the pink doll into the orange, the orange into the red, the red into the yellow. Leave this activity out for the children to discover and use.

4. The craft

For each child use the same pattern as above. Cut out four dolls in four different colors of cardboard or heavy construction paper. Encourage the child to paste them, one on top of the other in sequence.

5. The film

Watch the National Film Board film, **Matrioska** (4:46). In this film the Russian dolls dance to lively folk music. Watching this reinforces the concepts learned in the first four activities.

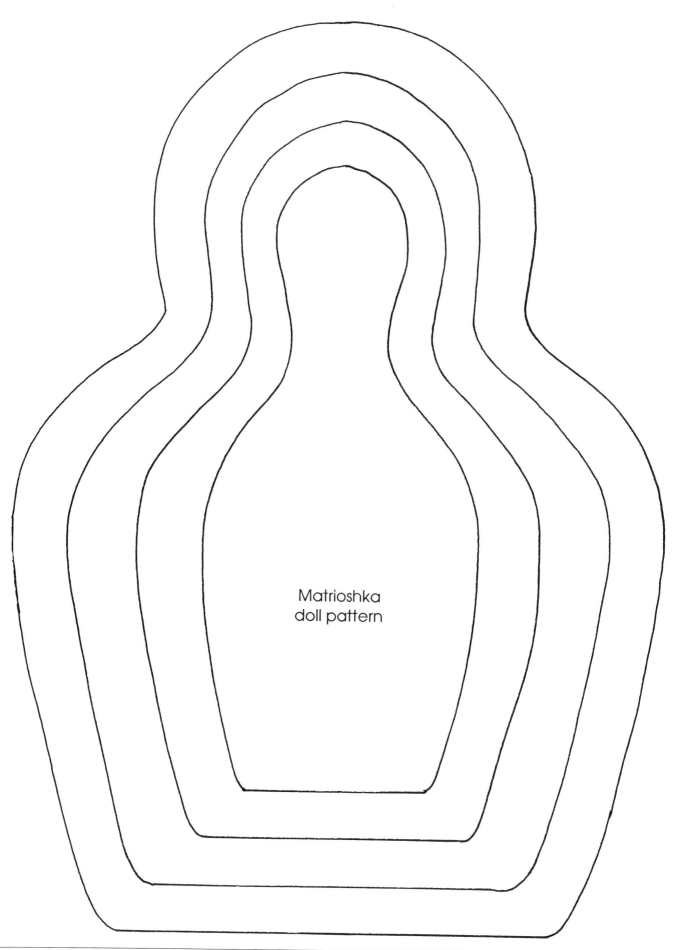

Matrioshka
doll pattern

5. Group time

During group time children learn to co-operate: to share, to wait, and to take turns. They may paint a group mural, sing a song, watch a video, play a game, or discover a new activity together. They may also enjoy having a special experience such as a visitor to the classroom or a field trip outside. The key to group time is togetherness and a warm and supportive mood. Think about your group time with the children and reflect on its format, content, and style. Then ask yourself the following questions.

Checklist 5: Group time

1. Does every child have some cultural link to group time?

2. Are the activities presented in a warm, positive manner, rather than being described as "different" or what "they" do?

3. Is activity rather than information stressed in the presentation?

4. Are the suggested similarities among cultures clear enough for all the children to understand?

5. Are the children encouraged to empathize ("How would you feel if...?") with the characters portrayed?

6. Is there ample time for the children to honestly express their ideas and feelings, their anger and fear?

7. Do the stories that are told reflect the multicultural reality of the United States?

8. Do the visual props balance any shortcomings a story may have or enhance its context?

9. Are languages other than English used occasionally to suit a particular story, game, or fable?

10. Do the visitors represent a good cultural mix and are they drawn from a variety of socio-economic groups?

11. Do field trips reinforce the multicultural reality of the United States by focussing on a wide ethnic, racial, and economic spectrum rather than that of the dominant social group?

Stories, folktales, and poems are a major part of any group time. An annotated list of these is at the end of this section. No single book represents the diversity of the United States or the world. They are rather suggested as a starting point for building a story collection that is multicultural, entertaining, and appropriate for young children.

These are not information books in which the story is less important than the factual information. Nor are these message books in which a moral shouts across the story line. The books chosen here simply offer the multicultural reality through good stories.

They also offer it at a level appropriate to the child. Many bibliographies present books that are just too difficult for preschoolers. There is value to stretching vocabularies but not at the expense of boring or losing listeners.

For those who want a comprehensive checklist to determine the degree of cultural bias present in a story, the Council on Interracial Books for Children (1841 Broadway, New York, NY 10023) publishes a monthly bulletin with book reviews and a **Guideline for Selecting Bias Free Textbooks and Storybooks** (1980). Based on their work, here is my own short checklist for selecting bias free books for the very young:

- Check the book's message. Is the storyline acceptable? Are certain groups criticized and is this fair? Are all individuals portrayed as equal and deserving of respect?

- Check the author's credentials. Is the author qualified to write on this particular subject or about this group? What, if any, is the author's connection to the subject?

- Check the illustrations. Is there a realistic balance of people portrayed? How are lifestyles and customs portrayed? Are these stereotypes or accurate portrayals?

- Check the text. Is the dialogue realistic, or is it racist or stereotypical in intent? Is the language appropriate for young children? Sometimes the words are difficult but the beauty of the language overrides this.

Folktales are also told at group time. They are the oral expressions of a specific culture and often encapsulate a traditional moral or truth. Current cultural norms suggest that many folktales are too complex and too violent for young children, and need considerable adaptation before they can be used. Killing animals, patronizing females, using weapons — these activities are offensive to many. A sample adapted folktale suitable for young children has been included in the group-time section of each chapter.

In American libraries now there are a number of well illustrated and appropriate folktales from a variety of cultures. These are listed on p. 40. Guidelines for using a folktale are simple:

- Keep it short. If the tale is too long, either condense it or read only a portion at a time.

- Keep it friendly. Excitement is great, but not the violence of gouged eyes and torn heads.

- Keep its flavor. Parents may be able to tell the story, or read it with the help of one of the suggested bilingual books. Even if you can use only one word of the original language, the tale becomes very special to children who recognize that word. They may even offer to pronounce it correctly!

- Keep telling it. Repeat. Repeat. Repeat. The tale can be read from a book, then acted out, told again by the children, drawn, then read again. Children love to join in with a story, and frequent repetition of a folktale lets them do this. So the tale becomes a familiar part of the multicultural oral tradition of the classroom.

Props and materials help with this repetition and enhance the enjoyment of the story. They also make new vocabulary and ideas more concrete. Suggested props are wooden puppets, shadow play figures, origami figures, or paper and pencil to draw the story as it emerges.

A sample folktale: trouble dolls

Many gift shops now sell Guatemalan trouble dolls, a set of tiny fabric dolls in a small box similar to a wooden matchbox. Inside each box is a slip of paper saying that these dolls are used by parents to get rid of a child's troubles. In Central America they were used by a healer or curandero to tell a story. The dolls were then put back into the box and buried, the idea being to bury the troubles along with them.

All children love dolls, especially tiny ones, and can readily identify with troubles. A child may want to hold one of the dolls and talk about a trouble or problem, or have an adult hold the doll and embellish the story. Make simple trouble dolls by winding a tiny piece of woven fabric around a wooden matchstick, then tell the following story.

Good-bye troubles!

In a small city in Guatemala lived a family of five: a grandmother, a father, and three small children. The children went to school every day, and after school they helped their grandmother at home before going out to play. One day the youngest boy, Pepe, saw an iguana carrying a delicate coffee blossom in its mouth.

Now an iguana is a big lizard that moves very slowly except when it is very hungry. Pepe watched the lizard move slowly across the dusty path, so slowly that Pepe could see the wrinkles in its legs. Pepe squatted down on the path and the iguana stopped moving altogether. The lizard stared at Pepe, and Pepe stared back.

At the same time his older brother, Carlos, was going to buy food for his grandmother. With his bag full to the brim, Carlos decided to take the short cut on the dusty path rather than going the long way by road.

At the very same time Pepe's older sister Ramona was looking for him to help with the chores. She set out toward the school, for Pepe still had not returned home.

Carlos couldn't see over his big bag of food when he stumbled over the iguana. The iguana let out a hiss, terrified Pepe, and sent the groceries flying onto Ramona who had just caught up with her brother.

Back they ran, broken eggs on Ramona's hair, empty bag in Carlos' hands, and all three shouting at once. Grandma held her hands to her ears. "Silence," she said. When the house was as quiet as the noonday sun, she said, "Now tell me your troubles, one by one."

After hearing the three sad tales, Grandma went to the fireplace and picked up three small pieces of wood. "Now this is you, Ramona, angry and messy through no fault of your own. And this is you, Carlos, trying to help Grandma make the dinner. And this is you Pepe, still crying about such a sight and sound."

Then she carried the three small pieces of wood outside and poked them deep into the sandy patch under the verandah. "Good-bye troubles. Stay in the ground. Don't come back and visit us again."

Multicultural storybooks for children

These storybooks have been chosen because they are both good literature and multicultural. The characters in the stories are individuals from a variety of ethnic and cultural backgrounds who experience life at a level understandable to young children. Toddlers and the very young will simply enjoy the spell of the story and the multicultural world presented. Preschool-aged and school-aged children, however, will develop global awareness through seeing and hearing another culture's understanding of a situation.

This list is the basis for a good multicultural storybook collection. Subsequent chapters will suggest other books specific to that chapter's theme; these can be gradually added to this list. All the books are currently available in American bookstores and libraries.

While folktales may be adapted to suit the group and poetry read selectively, storybooks are best read as a whole unit. They have been age-coded for the very young (2-4-year-olds), the older ones (4-6-year-olds), and both groups (2-6-year-olds). Use this coding as a guide to selecting age-appropriate stories for your group.

Storybooks for the very young (2-4 years)

Benjamin, Floella. **How Do You Eat It?** London: Marilyn Malin, 1988.
A single sentence on each page describes one culture-specific way of eating; equally amusing is Benjamin's **We're Going Out**.

Breinburg, Petronella. **Doctor Sean**. London: Bodley Head, 1974.
This story of little Sean playing doctor is colorfully illustrated by Errol Lloyd; equally good are Breinburg's **My Brother Sean** and **Sean's Red Bike.**

Bryant, Donna. **One Day at the Supermarket**. Nashville: Ideal, 1988.
A young Asian boy finds shopping fun when he decides to explore the shelves.

Dunham, Meredith. **Shapes: How Do You Say It?** New York: Lothrop, Lee and Shepard, 1987.
Colored shapes on contrasting backgrounds are described in Spanish, Italian, French and English.

Gomi, Taro. **First Comes Harry**. New York: William Morrow, 1984.
Harry, a young black boy, just has to be first all day long; equally good are Gomi's **Toot** and **Coco Can't Wait**.

Hayes, Sarah. **Eat up, Gemma.** London: Walker, 1988.
A young black boy is the hero when he finds an amusing way to convince his baby sister to eat.

O'Brien, Anne Sibley. **Don't Say No!** New York: Holt, 1986.
This is one of a series of eight multi-ethnic board books, all bright and colorful.

Oxenbury, Helen. **Say Goodnight**. Vancouver: Douglas and McIntyre, 1987.
Simple vocabulary and large, multi-ethnic pictures make this an ideal board book. Equally good stories are Oxenbury's **Tickle, Tickle, All Fall Down**, and **Clap Hands.**

Pelligrino, Virginia. **Listen to the City**. Los Angeles: Price Stern, 1988.
Simple one-word captions describe Patricia Wong's multi-ethnic urban scenes.

Provensen, Alice and Martin. **El libro de las Estaciones**. New York: Random, 1982.
This Spanish/English book of seasons is full of colorful pictures.

Steptoe, John. **Baby Says**. New York: Lothrop, Lee and Shepard, 1988.
Two black brothers play together, identifying one special word on each page.

Weir, LaVada. **Howdy**. Austin: Steck-Vaughn, 1972.
Luke, a black American boy, makes everyone smile with his infectious "howdy".

Storybooks for older children (4-6 years)

Andrews, Jan. **Very Last First Time**. Vancouver: Douglas and McIntyre, 1985.
Eva, an Inuit girl, realizes her strength in her first hunting trip alone.

Bang, Molly. **The Paper Crane**. New York: Greenwillow, 1985.
A stranger offers an origami crane to pay for his meal, and the crane comes to life in a boy's hands. This simple tale introduces origami and is a good precursor to **Sadako and the Thousand Paper Cranes** by Eleonor Coerr.

Garcia, Maria. **The Adventures of Connie and Diego**. San Francisco: Children's Book Press, 1987.
Twins born with vividly colored faces eventually join other humans in this anti-racist fantasy.

Grifalconi, Ann. **Darkness and the Butterfly**. Boston: Little, Brown, 1987.
Little Osa lives in rural Africa and is terrified of the dark, but overcomes her fear with the help of a wise old woman and a butterfly.

Kurusa. **The Streets are Free**. Scarborough: Firefly Books, 1985.
This is based on the true story of children in Venezuela who inspired their community to build an inner-city park.

Langer, Nola. **Rafiki**. New York: Viking, 1977.
Rafiki breaks down the gender-based workload of the animals in an African jungle by using humour and some Swahili too.

Levinson, Riki. **Our House is the Sea**. New York: Dutton, 1988.
A fun-loving Hong Kong boy goes to school in the city but returns to his houseboat every night.

Singer, Yvonne. **Little-Miss-Yes-Miss**. Toronto: Kids Can, 1976.
Cicely moves from Jamaica to Canada and finds her first day at school painful.

Surat, Michele Maria. **Angel Child, Dragon Child**. Milwaukee: Raintree, 1983.
This story of a Vietnamese girl separated from her mother is poignantly illustrated by Vo-Dinh Mai.

Waterton, Betty. **A Salmon for Simon**. Vancouver: Douglas and McIntyre, 1978.
This affirmation of the right to life told by a Native boy who loves to fish on the shores of British Columbia is vividly recreated by Ann Blades.

Wheeler, Bernelda. **I Can't Have Bannock, but the Beaver Has a Dam**. Winnipeg: Pemmican, 1984.
A Native Canadian mother helps her son to understand why their electricity is out, and how animal and human needs sometimes conflict; equally good is Wheeler's **Where Did You Get Your Moccasins**?

Williams, Vera. **Something Special for Me**. New York: Greenwillow, 1983.
Mother and Grandmother from Europe pool all the savings in the coin jar for Rosa's birthday, but it is Rosa who must choose the gift.

Winter, Jeanette. **Follow the Drinking Gourd**. New York: Alfred A. Knopf, 1988.
This exciting tale of the Underground Railway describes a slave's escape to Canada.

Storybooks for all age groups (2-6 years)

Alexander, Sue. **Nadia the Wilful**. New York: Pantheon, 1983.
When her favorite brother disappears in the desert forever, Nadia, a young Arab girl, refuses to let him be forgotten.

Asch, Frank and Vladimir Vagin. **Here Comes the Cat!** New York: Scholastic, 1989.
This Russian/English cat-and-mouse parable shows how reality can conquer fear and hatred.

Calleja, Gina. **Tobo Hates Purple**. Toronto: Annick, 1983.
This is a simple, amusing tale about racial acceptance and pride.

Cohen, Miriam. **Will I Have a Friend?** New York: Collier, 1967.
This is a touching story of a boy's first day in a multi-ethnic day care.

Daly, Niki. **Not So Fast, Songololo**. London: Victor Gollancz, 1985.
A black South African boy who loves to run learns a lesson in love when he takes his grandmother shopping.

Duchesne, Christiane. **Lazarus Laughs**. Toronto: James Lorimer, 1977.
This is an amusing tale of a sheep who does not speak French but does speak the universal language of laughter.

Eyvindson, Peter. **Kyle's Bath**. Winnipeg: Pemmican, 1984.
Kyle, a Native Canadian, decides to stay clean all day to avoid his nightly bath; equally good are Eyvindson's **The Wish Wind** and **Old Enough**.

Havill, Juanita. **Jamaica Tag-Along.** Boston: Houghton Mifflin, 1989.
Jamaica, a black girl, follows her brother and his friends, and is in turn followed by a toddler.

Keats, Ezra. **Apt. 3**. New York: Macmillan, 1971.
Sam and his brother Ben, two young black boys, find a friend in the blind harmonica player of Apt. 3; equally touching are Keats' **A Letter to Amy**, **Peter's Chair**, and **Goggles**.

Khalsa, Dayal Kaur. **How Pizza Came to our Town.** Montreal: Tundra, 1989.
Mrs. Pelligrino changes lives in the community when she introduces pizza and all the fun that goes with it.

Konner, Alfred. **Pippa and the Oranges**. London: Macdonald, 1986.
This Italian tale of Pippa's ingenuity in saving her father's oranges is feminist in flavor.

Lewin, Hugh. **Jafta's Mother**. London: Evans, 1981.
Jafta, a black South African boy, recalls all the wonderful ways his mother makes him feel; other equally good South African tales are Lewin's **Jafta's Father** and **Jafta and the Wedding**.

Nolan, Madeena Spray. **My Daddy Don't Go to Work**. Don Mills: Dent, 1978.
This short book about a little black girl's reaction to having her dad at home and out of work is both emotional and thought-provoking.

Pellowski, Anne. **The Nine Crying Dolls**. New York: Philomel, 1980.
This Polish story offers a solution to a mother's troubles very similar to the Guatemalan one of making trouble dolls.

Rogers, Jean. **Runaway Mittens**. New York: Greenwillow, 1988.
Pica's Inuit grandmother knits him wonderful red mittens, but he is always misplacing them.

Root, Phyllis and Carol Marron. **Gretchen's Grandma**. Milwaukee: Raintree, 1983.
Gretchen learns to communicate with her German grandma despite the language barrier.

Scott, Ann Herbert. **On Mother's Lap**. New York: McGraw Hill, 1972.
Michael, an Inuit boy, learns that there is always room on his mother's lap for all her children.

Truss, Nancy. **Peter's Moccasins.** Edmonton: Reidmore, 1987.
When he sees his friends' acceptance, Peter dares to wear his own moccasins in class.

Walton, Marilyn Jeffers. **Those Terrible Terwilliger Twins**. Milwaukee: Raintree, 1984.
Trevor, a young black boy, tries to help his older twin sisters with little success.

Poetry books

Adoff, Arnold. **All the Colors of the Race.** New York: Lothrop, Lee and Shepard, 1982.
Melodic verse takes the reader through the lives of a racially mixed family; equally interesting is Adoff's **Black is Brown is Tan**.

Agard, John. **I Din Do Nuttin**. London: Bodley Head, 1983.
These short and amusing poems depict everyday life for young blacks.

Clifton, Lucille. **Some of the Days of Everett Anderson**. New York: Holt, 1970.
This rhythmic and melodic description of a week in the life of a young black boy is amusing; equally humorous is Clifton's **Everett Anderson's Nine Months Long**.

Giovanni, Nikki. **Spin a Soft Black Song**. Toronto: Collins, 1985.
This collection of short poems about black children is actively anti-racist in tone.

Giuseppi, Neville and Undine. **Sugar and Spice.** London: Macmillan Education, 1978.
Short, amusing poems look at subjects from a black child's perspective.

Hughes, Shirley. **All Shapes and Sizes**. Vancouver: Douglas and McIntyre, 1986.
Each drawing of a multiracial group of children is explained in two lines of verse.

Lenski, Lois. **Sing a Song of People.** Toronto: Little, Brown, 1987.
Bright, textured pictures by Gilles Laroche illustrate these short poems.

Maher, Ramona. **Alice Yazzie's Year**. Toronto: Longman, 1977.
By following Alice's year we catch a glimpse of her Navajo world.

Zim, Jacob, ed. **My Shalom, My Peace**. Tel Aviv: Sabra, 1975.
This inspiring collection of poems and drawings by Middle Eastern children offers a realistic picture of life in the war zone.

Folktales

Aardema, Verna. **Who's in Rabbit's House?** New York: Dial, 1977.
This is a Masai (African) tale of a caterpillar who pretends to be a conqueror; equally amusing is Aardema's **Why Mosquitoes Buzz in People's Ears.**

Cameron, Anne. **Orca's Song**. Madeira Park: Harbour, 1987.
This Native legend celebrates the blended offspring of a black killer whale and a white osprey.

Cleaver, Elizabeth. **Loon's Necklace**. London: Oxford Press, 1977.
This Tsimshian legend can be introduced with the film of this legend; equally good is Cleaver's **The Enchanted Caribou,** with its shadow puppet patterns.

Cohen, Barbara. **Yussel's Prayer**. New York: Lothrop, Lee and Shepard, 1981.
This Jewish tale of a small shepherd's prayer winning over the cynical prayers of the rich is warmly told.

De Paolo, Tomie. **The Legend of the Indian Paintbrush**. New York: Putnam, 1988.
Little Gopher dreams about capturing the colors of the sunset on his buckskin canvas.

Mascayana, Ismael. **The Daughter of the Sun**. Toronto: Kids Can, 1978.
This bilingual (English/Spanish) Peruvian love story tells of a girl's sacrifice for a young shepherd boy and his life on earth.

Matsutoni, Myoko. **The Crane's Reward**. London: Adam and Charles Black, 1983.
Large, colorful pictures by Chihiro Iwasaki depict this beautiful Japanese folktale.

Nakamura, Michiko. **Gonbei's Magic Kettle**. Toronto: Kids Can, 1980.
This bilingual (English/Japanese) folktale tells of a raccoon who changes into a tea kettle, bringing magic to the lives of the villagers.

Rohmer, Harriet and Jesus Guerrero Rea. **Atariba and Niguayona**. San Francisco: Children's Book Press, 1988.
Brilliant color drawings by Consuelo Mendez illustrate this bilingual (English/Spanish) tale of love.

Seeger, Pete. **Abiyoyo**. New York: Macmillan, 1986.
This amusing and melodic South African tale is best introduced by Seeger's own record, **Abiyoyo and other Songs for Children.**

Siberell, Anne. **Whale in the Sky.** New York: Dutton, 1982.
The meaning of totem poles gradually unfolds in this tale of Thunderbird and his friends.

Wolkstein, Diane. **The Banza**. New York: Dial, 1981.
Large color drawings by Marc Brown illustrate this Haitian tale of a goat protected by his banza (banjo).

Films and videos

Dozens of films recommended for this age group were previewed. Most of these could be described as sexist, violent, too long, or too informational. Some fit all four descriptions. However, a few offered interesting multicultural material that was non-sexist and non-violent.

Film can be a total learning experience for children, a rich visual image they will remember. Prepare the children for the film by first reading them the story, telling them about the main characters, or showing them related pictures. During the screening, model the quiet attentiveness you want the children to develop, the respectful attitude to film as art. Afterwards, talk about the film, reminding the children about it. Then extend their experience through art or music.

To borrow these films write to the National Film Board (NFB), 1251 Avenue of the Americas, 16th Floor, New York, NY 10020, or call them at (212) 586-5131.

The Little Men of Chromagnon (8:24) NFB
Tolerance and the pleasures of mutual exchange are acted out by amusing, round "Mr. Men" characters who learn to live together.

Summer Legend (8:00) NFB
This version of the familiar Micmac legend is animated with rich and unforgettable images. Glooskap rides a whale across the sea to find Summer dancing with garlands of flowers. He carries her back to the land of snow. This is also available on the Native Indian Folklore video cassette.

The Trout that Stole the Rainbow (8:02) NFB
This visually beautiful animated fable tells the story of the rainbow trout. Some of the images (such as the summer storm) may be frightening for younger children, and some of the language is sophisticated, but the overall message and beauty of the film override this. This is also available on the Fables and Fantasy video cassette.

6. Food to share

Snack time is as important for children as the universal "coffee break" is for adults. It is a time to share ideas and a taste of another culture through broadening food experiences. It is also a special time for sitting next to a friend and feeling part of the group.

Parents work hard to buy, bring home, and carefully prepare that food for their families. They want their children to have enough of the right kind of food to grow and to be healthy. Just as eating the right food is encouraged, playing with food is to be discouraged. That explains why seeing children playing with rice and cornmeal, or painting and stringing pasta is so repellent and hurtful to many parents.

For young children, on the other hand, food is part of their environment and they want to explore it — touching, smelling, and then tasting. While it is important to encourage sensory awareness of food, it is equally important to respect its life-giving quality. Think about the food experiences in your program and consider the following questions.

Checklist 6: Food to share

1. Is there a cultural variety of food presented every day, or is the food chosen a reflection of one person's preferences?

2. Are various ways of eating food modelled and practiced?

3. Do the children help to prepare and serve the food?

4. Are negative comments about food handled sensitively?

5. Is consideration given to allergies, lactose intolerance, and dietary regulations before snack time so that those children are not made to feel different or self-conscious?

6. Is leftover food used either as a future ingredient or as compost?

7. Are alternates considered when an activity suggests food as an art material?

Food preferences and eating habits are cultural norms and should be handled sensitively. Lactose intolerance, for instance, can be the mis-diagnosis of a preference for warm or canned milk. A child may react severely to cold, 2% milk, if unaccustomed to it. Similarly, raw vegetables may not appeal to children used to eating these stir-fried, deep-fried, boiled, or mashed.

Statements such as, "eating bugs is dirty" or "that's a funny way of eating" can be very hurtful to a child. The calcium content of a locust is much higher than in a potato chip, and the former is probably far more nutritious. This is not to suggest adding bugs to the menu, or heating up milk every day, but it is a cautionary note to be more tolerant and open when food is shared.

Consider using all the parts of food: inedible skin for printing, seeds for art, husks for brushes, bones for ornaments. Be frugal and recyle discarded food parts. Try keeping a covered compost bin in your classroom. Empty out the bin every week, then cover the compost with leaves and sand. Wash out the bin and start collecting more discarded produce. As the seasons change, so will the compost. It is a lovely gift for the springtime flowers, and it does not cost a penny!

Bread

Multicultural snacks need not be exotic and expensive food bought at specialty shops. Start with a very basic food such as bread. Avoid the peanut butter and cracker trap and put a variety of breads on your snack plate instead. Slice them, stuff them, spread them, dip them, toast them, or cut them with cookie cutters to make interesting shapes. Some of the breads you may want to use are listed below.

Bagels (Jewish)
Baguette (French)
Bannock bread (early Canadian)
Bran bread
Bread sticks, cheese sticks
Buns
Buttermilk biscuits
Challah (Jewish)
Chapati (Indian)
Christonomo (Italian)
Cornbread
Corn pone (Central American)
Croissants (French)
Datebread
Fry bread (Navajo)
Gingerbread
Injera (Ethiopian)
Irish soda bread
Kamaj (Palestinian)
Klaben (German)
Knackbrod (German)
Laufabrod (Icelandic)
Matzot (Jewish)
Muffins
Nan (Indian)
Pita (Middle Eastern)
Popovers
Potato bread
Pumpernickel
Pumpkin bread
Raisin bread
Roti (Caribbean/East Indian)
Rye bread
Scones
Steamed buns (Chinese)
Taboun (Palestinian)
Wholewheat bread

Bagel

Croissant

Irish soda bread

Muffin

Pita

Steamed bun

Show the children photographs of people baking bread. Use the book **Bread • Bread • Bread** (Lothrop, Lee and Shepard, 1989) to give a photo tour of world cultures and the breads specific to each. Then buy the bread or try your hand at making some. Unleavened bread or bread leavened by an agent other than yeast is best to make with young children because it is so quick. Try these recipes, adjusting quantities to suit the group. Each recipe serves about 20 children.

Bannock (early Canadian, originally Scottish)

Ingredients: 3 C flour
dash of salt
3 T baking powder
2 T water
2 t oil

Method:
1. Use a fork to mix together all the dry ingredients.
2. Make a well in the dry ingredients, then pour in the water.
3. Mix the dough by hand, kneading it then pounding it flat.
4. Fry on an oiled griddle until puffy and golden on both sides.

Chapatis (Indian)

Materials: 2 C wholewheat flour
1/2 t salt
3/4 C water

Method:
1. Mix wholewheat flour, salt, and water to form a stiff dough. Add more water if necessary.
2. Let the dough rest for 1/2 hour, then roll into small balls.
3. Flatten the balls then fry them on a very hot griddle until brown spots appear on the dough.
4. Take them off the griddle and brush with butter or serve plain.

Tortillas (Mexican)

Materials: 2 1/2 C corn flour
1 C water
rolling pin or tortilla press
2 t oil
2 t butter

Method:
1. Mix corn flour with enough water to make a stiff dough.
2. Roll into small balls, then flatten with a rolling pin or tortilla press.
3. Fry in a lightly oiled pan, turning until cooked.
4. Brush with butter and serve.

CHAPTER TWO

Harvest

Harvest: a time to give thanks

The giving of thanks for food is an ancient custom. Native Americans celebrated many thanks-givings before the arrival of the Europeans. Late in the summer when the crops were ripe, they danced in honor of the harvest; when game was killed, they thanked the spirit of the hunt or of the animal. Today the Iroquois still celebrate the harvest in the Green Corn Festival, and other native groups hold similar celebrations.

Harvest thanksgivings are held in most communities around the world. Some mark specific fruit or vegetable seasons: in Europe, the strawberry crop may be celebrated in the spring, peaches in the summer, and grapes in the autumn. In Asia, two crops of rice a year are common, and each one may prompt a celebration of thanks. Some are distinct rural festivals, while others are national celebrations uniting both farmers and city people.

Today most city people buy their food rather than grow it. They do not pick the grapes or drive the combines in the wheat fields. However, the growing popularity of "pick-your-own" farms does suggest that many people want to take part. As urbanites rediscover the labor and rewards of the harvest, they also pause with the farmers to offer thanks to God, a spirit, Mother Nature, or simply to one another.

Harvest is represented by many symbols. The cycles of life and of the seasons are symbolized by the circular wreath, the round harvest loaf, moon cakes, spinning tops, and the harvest moon itself. The spirit of giving is symbolized by the making of special dolls and the sharing and offering of food. The type of doll or food may differ from community to community, but the global message is the same: thanks for this year's harvest, and hope for good crops in the years to come.

This communal thanks is usually formalized at a festival. In the northern hemisphere, many of these festivals are in the September-October-November cycle of the year; in fact, World Food Day (October 16) is right in the middle of this cycle. The United Nations inaugurated this as a day to think about world distribution of food. Young children may not realize the gravity of this subject, but they can learn to share food with others and to respect its life-giving power. The harvest season is an ideal time to encourage this respect.

Mention a few festivals to the children, and talk about the similarities among them. Circle festival dates on the program calendar. Acknowledging and sharing this information will show your interest in the rich cultural traditions of the community, and will encourage parental participation in the multicultural program.

On the next page is a list of harvest festivals and their corresponding dates. Dates marked with an asterisk (*) are movable and depend upon either lunar or religious calendars. If a festival is associated with a particular place or people within a country, this is noted in parentheses. Although many of these festivals are celebrated in the United States, the place of origin of each one is keyed by number to a point on the map.

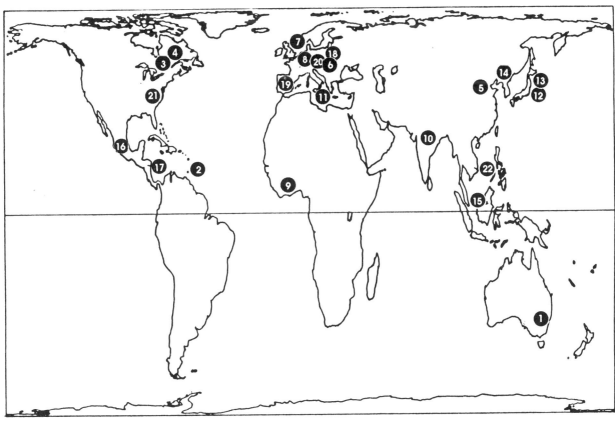

1. Australia	Harvest Time	March
2. Barbados	Crop-over Festival	June
3. Canada	Thanksgiving Day	second Monday in October
4. Canada (Iroquois)	Green Corn Festival	September
5. China	Harvest Moon Festival	* September/October
6. Czechoslovakia	Obzinki	August 15
7. England	Harvest Festival	October
8. Germany	Oktoberfest	October
9. Ghana	Momowo	August
10. India	Pongol	* January/February
11. Italy	San Martino	November 11
12. Japan	New Taste Festival	November 23
13. Japan (Akita)	Kanto Matsuri	mid-August
14. Korea	Ch'usok	* September
15. Malaysia	Gawai Dayak	* June
16. Mexico (Huichol)	Wimakwari	October
17. Nicaragua	El Día del Maiz	May
18. Poland	Dozynki	September
19. Spain (Frontera)	Grape Festival	September
20. Switzerland	Grape Festival	September 23
21. United States	Thanksgiving Day	fourth Thursday in November
22. Vietnam	Têt Trung-thu	* August/September
Hinduism	Divali	* October/November
Judaism	Sukkot	* October

Using the harvest theme

GOAL   To show the universality of harvest celebrations

OBJECTIVES   To familiarize the children with the richness and variety of the global harvest

To demonstrate the interdependence of rural and urban life in the community

To make and use traditional harvest toys and to play harvest games

To introduce and use the basic vocabulary of this theme

Add your own objectives to suit the program. For instance, if the group shares a common, homogeneous diet, concentrate on the first objective. In the context of familiar fruits and vegetables, introduce one that is less familiar to the group (ask a parent for suggestions here). Examine it: smell it, touch it, then taste it. Talk about its versatility and explore its many uses. The objective here is to instill interest in and respect for this particular food rather than just to relate facts about it.

The harvest theme can be explored from September through November. Harvesting and giving thanks (Thanksgiving) are intrinsically linked, and can be celebrated together. Some materials and activities can also be re-introduced in the spring to reinforce the connection between planting and harvesting.

VOCABULARY LIST

Post these words on the bulletin board or write them on a vocabulary card made from one of the harvest symbols. Let each child add drawings or collage materials to the vocabulary card before taking it home. Alternatively, choose just one word from the list and ask bilingual parents to translate it. Then write the word in many languages on the card before giving it to the children. This is another way to encourage family participation in a multicultural program.

harvest	coconut	shelling	rake
thanksgiving	grain	peeling	hoe
sharing	rice	picking	fork
gathering	corn	slicing	shovel
trading	wheat	grinding	wheelbarrow

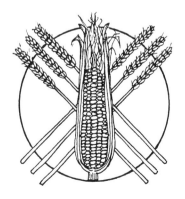

Vocabulary card, front and back faces

1. Setting the mood

Harvest centers around crops; specifically vegetables, fruit, and grains. Encourage the children to use all their senses to experience food. Transform the outdoor play area into a farm, or the indoor play area into a garden. Make the housekeeping center a communal kitchen and dining area. Remember to reflect a global reality rather than only using commercial toy-kitchen sets. Suggestions follow.

Outdoors

- Put out large and small rakes, hoes, forks and shovels. Try to use real garden tools rather than the plastic variety which tend to be both frustrating and inefficient. Young children can learn to manipulate large tools for a specific task. Five- and six-year-olds in many parts of the world pick fruit, lead water buffalo, and harvest rice all day.

- Introduce communal play by giving each child a task dependent upon that of the next child. Suggested tasks for pairs of children are raking leaves and putting them into bags; digging the soil and removing the stones; digging out a hole, putting in compost materials, then covering them with soil. Help the children by giving them small, manageable tasks that last no longer than five minutes. Give the rakers a colorful bag to fill; give the diggers a little metal bucket for the stones to clink. In this way children can have fun while they fill their bags or buckets.

- Put out weighted plastic vegetables and wheelbarrows, wagons, sacks, bins, and bushel baskets. Introduce scales to weigh the produce. Let the children experiment with and compare weights.

- Use thick ropes to join several wagons or to haul bags of produce. Attach rope ladders to a strong tree or play structure. String up a low clothesline to move sacks of produce from one tree or pole in the yard to another.

- Put out woven or burlap mats to display produce for an outdoor market. Some children may want to carry net bags or straw baskets and act out the role of shoppers. Give them each a commodity such as a toy, book, marker, or scarf to trade for the displayed food.

- Use an unlit hibachi or barbecue to pretend to cook kebabs (sponge balls on toothpicks) or vegetables (plastic ones wrapped in foil). Turn the kebabs over with metal tongs or long chopsticks. Wear oven mitts to pick up the foil-wrapped vegetables.

- Put a big soup pot over some wood logs. Mix plastic vegetables with water in the pot and pretend to make soup. Use a wooden ladle or calabash to mix the soup.

- Visit a farmer's market, apple orchard, pumpkin patch, or the garden of one child in the group. That child may be able to show a favorite flower, vegetable, or weed to the group. This flower may be growing in a pot or window box on an apartment balcony. Patio and balcony gardens are fun to visit and are often more appropriate and familiar to city children.

- Make playdough tortillas with white or yellow playdough and a tortilla press. Make interesting spaghetti strands with playdough and a pasta maker or a garlic press.

- Crush real nuts, ginger root, cinnamon sticks, nutmeg, or garlic by hand using a mortar and pestle. Smell, touch, and taste the results.

- Make a produce bowl out of playdough, plasticine, or clay. Make a leaf serving dish by lining a shallow plate with plastic wrap or waxed paper. Mold leaves into the shape of the plate, then add a layer of glue and a second layer of leaves. Let the plate harden overnight. Pop the plastic wrap out of the dish, then peel the wrap off the back of the leaf dish.

Indoors

- Display pictures of large and small farms and gardens, traditional and mechanized harvesting. Older children may have heard the word "organic" at home, and may be ready for a brief explanation and taste of organic food. Go to look at organic food, and buy a small portion to taste.

- Put up a "garden" backdrop in the play area. Tape a large rectangle of laminate to the wall with the sticky side out. Press a brown strip of paper across it to indicate ground level. At the top of the sheet, stick a big yellow paper sun. Beside the sheet put a bushel basket full of paper vegetables. Let the children press on both surface crops such as corn, wheat, beans, and grapes, and root crops such as kohlrabi, turnip, garlic, and potatoes. When the children have finished (this may take a week) fill in the ground area with real sand, then preserve the whole picture with a second large sheet of laminate.

- Set up an indoor co-operative store based on trade rather than money. Let the children trade their harvested crops for other goods in the store.

- Lay a carpet of artificial turf under the climber, and hang pruned tree branches over it. This covered enclosure or sukkah symbolizes the tents used by the Jewish people during their exodus from Egypt. At harvest time (Sukkot) Jewish families traditionally make a sukkah out of branches and leaves, decorating it with fresh fruits. For the five days of Sukkot they eat many meals in the sukkah, occasionally even sleeping in it.

- Hang a hammock from the sides of the climber and fill the hammock with plastic fruit and vegetables. Pull up the sides of the hammock to cover the food, then tie a rope around the hammock to store the food.

- Grow a red pepper or tomato plant in a sunny window. Buy a small orange tree. These plants will not only beautify the room during the long winter, but may also provide an occasional, very fresh snack.

Sharing the harvest

2. Music and movement

Recycling discarded produce extends the growing cycle. Use shells and other inedible parts of harvest foods to make musical instruments, then play harvest music with them. As the seeds and shells age, their sounds change. Keep making these instruments during the theme so they are in many stages of drying. This is also a practical way to learn about moisture and preservation.

The instruments

- Buy a dried ornamental gourd (or dry a gourd for two weeks) and cut a hole in one end. Shake out the seeds, then drop in a handful of small stones. Tape over the hole to make a gourd rattle. Alternatively, leave in the seeds. For added durability, spray the gourd with varnish.

- Using a short tapestry needle and strong thread, string an assortment of inedible seeds and seed husks. Cut off the needle and tie the thread ends together to make a musical bracelet.

- Make rhythm sticks out of unpeeled sugarcane. Cane is hard and makes a hollow sound when two pieces are tapped together. Use the cane for no more than a week, then peel, slice thinly, and eat it for snack. Alternatively, use corncobs after the kernels have been eaten and the cobs dried. These dried cobs make soft, scratchy rhythm sticks.

- Use a hacksaw to cut a coconut in half. Scrape out the pulp to make any one of these three instruments: bells, cymbals, or drums. To make a bell, punch out the eyeholes on one half of the coconut. For the handle, thread a string through two of the holes and tie the ends of the string together on the inside of the coconut. For the clapper, tie a large bead onto a shorter piece of string and insert the string in the third hole. Knot this string on the outside top. To make two cymbals that sound like horse's hooves, simply clap the two halves of the coconut together. To make a drum, stretch leather or rubberized material over the cut side of one half, then secure this material with an elastic band.

Coconut instruments

Vibersko (Yugoslavian)

This fast line dance or kolo from Yugoslavia is called "Crushed Peppers". It mimics the crushing of red, green, and chili peppers to make sauces and condiments, a task done not only in Yugoslavia but also in Asia, Africa, Central and South America, and parts of North America.

The original dance requires eight or more people who link arms in a line. This simpler version involves one or more children who may or may not hold hands. Before the dance, show the children real peppers, fresh and dried, and a picture of a pepper plant. Then talk about the foods that have peppers in them; some are sweet and some are hot. This is a good dance to do just before enjoying a snack with peppers such as pizza, tacos, or stuffed peppers.

Method:
1. Stomp around the room or in a circle singing the chorus line: "Crushing peppers, crushing peppers, I am crushing all the peppers."
2. Stand in one place, stomping and singing, "Crushing peppers, crushing peppers, crushing peppers with my feet."
3. Kneel down. Lift one knee, then lower it while singing, "Crushing peppers, crushing peppers, crushing peppers with my knees."
4. Repeat, using other parts of the body such as the elbow, the forehead, or the shoulder.
5. End the dance with the line, "Crushing peppers, crushing peppers, now my harvest work is done."

 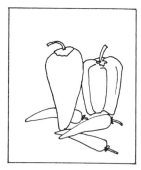 

Vibersko

Harvest games

To play these four games, photocopy the food cards on pp. 59-62. Color, mount, and laminate them. **Musical Vegetables** is played more easily with large cards, so enlarge the pictures when they are photocopied. All of these games are co-operative, so all the players "win".

Feely food

Materials: 1 opaque feely bag
6 food cards
6 corresponding foods (real or plastic)

Method: 1. Put all 6 foods in the feely bag and display the food cards so that everyone can see them.
2. Feel inside the bag. Hold 1 food and try to guess its name. Name it or point to the corresponding food card.
3. Take the food out of the bag to see if the guess is correct. Place the food on its corresponding card.
4. Feel inside the bag again, repeating the game until all the food names have been guessed and the bag is empty.

Pass the food

Materials: 1 food card per child
1 wooden bowl or straw basket

Method: 1. Put 1 card in the bowl and pass it around the circle.
2. Pass it around a second time to the rhythm of a simple chant such as, "We're passing around the food. We're passing around the food. Munch, munch, it's time for lunch. We're passing around the food." Substitute the name of the card for "the food."
3. Put another card in the bowl. Repeat the chant.
4. Repeat until all the cards are in the bowl, then ask one child to take out 1 card; for example, "Rosa, please give me the peanuts." When everyone has had a turn to take out 1 card and give it to the leader, the game is over.

Fill the basket

Materials: 1 beanbag per child, each with a food card sewn or taped to it
1 bushel basket
1 thick rope tied to the bushel basket
1 weigh scale

Method: 1. Toss 1 beanbag food at a time into the basket, naming the food as it is tossed.
2. When all the beanbags are in the basket, weigh the basket, pull it around the room, or load it onto a wagon or boat.

Musical vegetables

Materials: 6 enlarged food cards
masking tape or stones
coconut cymbals or corncob rhythm sticks

Method: 1. Tape the food cards to the floor, leaving plenty of space between each card. If this game is played outdoors, scatter the cards, weighting each one with a stone.
2. Begin playing the cymbals or sticks while the group runs, hops, jumps, or skips.
3. Stop the music and name 1 food. Everyone stops to listen, then runs to that food card.
4. Start the music again, repeating the game until all the cards have been named.

Corncob and ring game (Colombian, Ecuadorian, Native American)

Some Algonquin play this game at harvest time: four corncobs, each pointed at one end and decorated with feathers at the other, are tossed through a cornhusk ring. Similarly the Inuit play iyaga with one ivory pin and several rings made of bone. Ecuadorians and Colombians play bolero with a wooden pin and rings. This eye-hand co-ordination game is fun both to make and to play.

Time: 20 minutes
Materials: 1 dried corncob, without kernels
            1 tapestry needle threaded with a 12-in.
              string
            one 1-in. ring, cut from a toilet roll
            markers
Method: 1. Knot the string at the end. Pull the needle
               through the tip of the corncob, then
               through the ring.
            2. Remove the needle and tie the string
               around the ring, leaving a good length of
               string between the tip and the ring.
            3. Hold the base of the corncob. Flick the
               wrist to toss up the ring and catch it on the
               tip of the corncob.

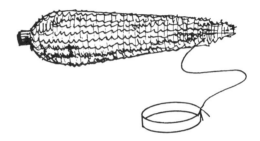

Spinning top

Spinning tops were probably first developed in Asia where conch shells were used as tops; today they are popular everywhere. In the United States the Navajo call their tops nimitchi or dancers, and they flick them with buckskin thongs. Italians play a game called turbo with their tops; and in the Dominican Republic they play moteca. The Maori of New Zealand make humming tops out of small gourds. Ask the parents to name spinning tops in their own languages, then post all the names on the board alongside pictures of the wooden, gourd, plastic, and metal toy tops.

The spin of the tops symbolizes the agricultural cycle of planting and harvesting. As one top spins and stops, another takes its place; as it stops, another replaces it, and so on. In New Guinea and Borneo the tops are charms to ensure a good harvest. In other rural communities top-spinning is part of the harvest festivities. Make simple harvest tops with the children. Note that the sharp pencil makes this toy inappropriate for toddlers and very young children.

Time: 20 minutes
Materials: one 4-in. cardboard circle per child
            markers or food stickers
            hole punch
            tissue-paper scraps
            1 sharpened pencil per child
Method: 1. Draw patterns or stick food stickers on the
               circle.
            2. Punch holes around the rim of the circle.
            3. Push tissue-paper scraps through the holes.
            4. Push the pencil through the center of the
               circle. Spin the circle on the point of the
               pencil.

3. Art

Edible foods, such as apples or potatoes, are inappropriate as play or art media. On a global scale, using food for play is offensive to those who work so hard to grow it and those who die for lack of it. On a daily basis, such misuse disparages all those who buy and prepare food.

Instead, use discarded skin or seeds as part of your recycling program. This material is not only interesting for the children to manipulate but also educational: discards encourage both flexible thinking and a respect for all the parts that make up a whole. Collage materials for harvest time include cornhusks and corn silk, used coffee grounds and tea leaves, raffia and string, dried leaves and flowers, dried grasses, inedible seeds and pods, nut shells, stems, and pinecones.

Gourd designs

Gourds are inedible but are harvested, dried, decorated and used as food containers, utensils, and musical instruments in Africa, Asia, and South America. The loofah gourd may be familiar as a backscratcher, scrubbing brush, or skin massager.

Designs are often carved into the singed or dyed rind of the gourd. To imitate this, dry some real gourds for at least six months, or purchase commercially dried ones. Let the children decorate the gourds, then keep them on the musical instrument shelf or in the housekeeping center. Show pictures and examples of many kinds of gourds either intact or fashioned into spoons, dippers, or bowls.

Time: 20 minutes
Materials: 1 dried gourd per child
     black crayons
     1 blunt, flat-topped nail
     spray varnish (for adult use only)
Method: 1. Crayon all over the gourd until it is completely black.
     2. Scratch a design on the gourd with a blunt nail.
     3. When the design is complete, spray the gourd with varnish.

Gourd designs

Seed creatures

Seeds can be sprouted or planted; some seeds, such as pomegranate or pumpkin, can be eaten too. Seeds in many countries are dried, polished, painted, or waxed and used in murals and mosaics, toys and dolls. To make the following toys, use the seeds of the food eaten at snack time. This makes material collection easier and cheaper, and makes the connection between food and seed more obvious to the children.

Mango monster

Mangoes grow in tropical areas and taste like very sweet, juicy peaches. Unripe and green, they are used for condiments. When ripe, they are peeled and eaten whole. The long, hairy seed of the mango is texturally interesting, and children may enjoy simply stroking the seed and shaking it like a rattle.

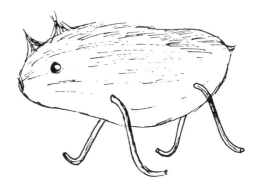

Time: 15 minutes
Materials: 1 mango seed per child
bin or bucket of water
scrubbing brush
1 hammer and a flat-topped nail
2 pipecleaners per child
markers
Method: 1. Holding the seed under water, scrub off some of its hair with the scrubbing brush. Dry thoroughly.
2. Hammer the nail through the seed in 2 places.
3. Insert 1 pipecleaner through each hole, twisting the ends to make legs or arms.
4. Draw eyes or patterns on the monster.

Avocado organizer

Avocadoes grow on large, spreading trees in warm countries. You may have tried sprouting an avocado seed by using toothpicks to suspend it halfway in a jar of water. I have always been unsuccessful at this, and prefer using the seed as an art material instead.

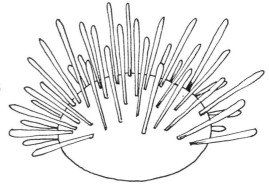

Time: 20 minutes
Materials: 1 washed avocado seed (no older than a week)
toothpicks, colored or plain
Method: 1. Push the toothpicks into the seed until it is covered with toothpicks and looks like a porcupine. Leave the base of the seed uncovered so that it can lie flat.
2. Use the avocado organizer to hold pencils or notes.

Harvest dolls

Harvest dolls are made in many rural communities, and are often sold in the city at harvest time. Ancient customs are associated with these dolls. An Iroquois legend explains one such custom. The Iroquois believed that the Corn Goddess lived underground and moved up the stalk as the corn grew. When the corn was harvested, it was feared that the Goddess would become homeless and leave the field. To keep her, the last stalks of corn were gathered and woven into a doll. In spring this doll was carefully plowed back into the ground. The Scots, Mexicans, and Czechoslovakians tell similar legends about the Corn Goddess.

Harvest dolls are made from a variety of materials. On the Ivory Coast they are made from whole clumps of grass, and in Europe from straw. The Lithuanian straw harvest doll or baba is decorated with ribbons and flowers and kept as a charm for the spring planting, as is the rice harvest doll of Malaysia and Indonesia. In England harvest dolls are woven from wheat, while in Czechoslovakia, North America, Scotland, and Mexico, the dolls are made from corn.

Make your own cornhusk and corncob dolls after a snack of fresh corn (for recipes see p. 75). Use the dolls as harvest symbols on a harvest wreath, or wear them as lucky charms. If fresh husks are not available, use dried ones, dipping them in warm water for 15 minutes to make them pliable.

Cornhusk doll

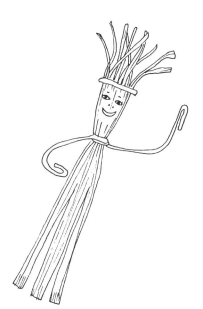

Time: 10 minutes
Materials: 1 cornhusk per child
1 pipecleaner per child
circle stickers or markers
Method:
1. Twist the pipecleaner around the middle of the husk. Use the ends of the pipecleaner as arms, bending them into shape.
2. Flatten out the top part of the husk as the face. Draw or stick on the eyes, and fray the top slightly to look like hair.
3. Fray the bottom of the husk and fluff it out to look like a skirt.

Corncob doll

Time: 20 minutes
Materials: 1 sun-dried corncob per child
2 thumbtacks per child
corn silk
glue
assorted pieces of brightly colored cloth
Method:
1. Push in the thumbtacks as eyes on the top half of the cob.
2. Glue strands of corn silk as hair to the top of the doll.
3. Tie a small piece of cloth for a scarf over the top of the cob.
4. Tie a second piece of cloth for a skirt around the bottom.

4. Discovery

Harvest is an opportunity to use all five senses to experience food. It is also a chance to learn more about the food harvested around the world. Introduce one new vegetable, grain, or fruit each day and let the children explore it: touching, smelling, then tasting it. Tell the children where it is grown and how it is used. Show pictures of the growing vegetable, grain or fruit, and save the seeds and peel whenever possible. Then try the suggested games, using the names of the foods you have introduced.

Food card games

Use the pictures on pp. 59-62 to play card games with the children or to illustrate a story. Photocopy the pages and color the pictures. Glue the picture sheet to one side of a piece of cardboard, and the corresponding name sheet to the opposite side. Laminate, then cut out the cards along the lines. Some games require two sets of cards; in this case, make two photocopies of each page, and proceed as described above. Keep the cards in a sturdy, suitably decorated box. The following are suggested colors:

Beans	green or yellow
Cabbage	green or purple
Corn	yellow kernels and green husks
Eggplant	cream flesh and purple or white skin
Garlic	white
Peanuts	light brown nut and green leaves and stem
Peppers	red, green, purple, or yellow
Potatoes	brown or red
Rice	brown grains and green plant
Soya beans	white bean and green pod
Wheat	light brown
Yam	orange flesh and brown skin
Avocadoes	pale green flesh and dark green skin
Banana	yellow flesh and yellow or red skin
Cherries	red
Coconut	white flesh and brown shell
Dates	golden brown
Figs	green (fresh) or brown (dried)
Grapes	blue, purple, or green
Mango	red or orange
Melons	red flesh and green skin, or orange flesh and grey skin, or green flesh and white skin
Papaya	light orange
Pineapple	light brown skin and green leaves
Sugarcane	green or brown

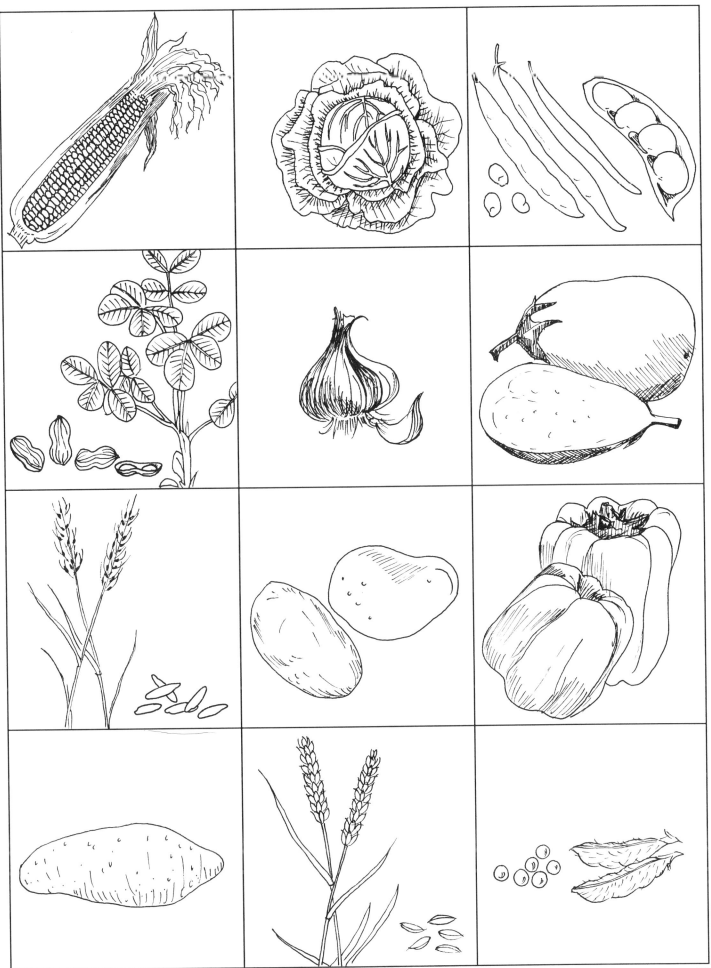

Beans	Cabbage	Corn
Eggplant	Garlic	Peanuts
Peppers	Potatoes	Rice
Soya beans	Wheat	Yam

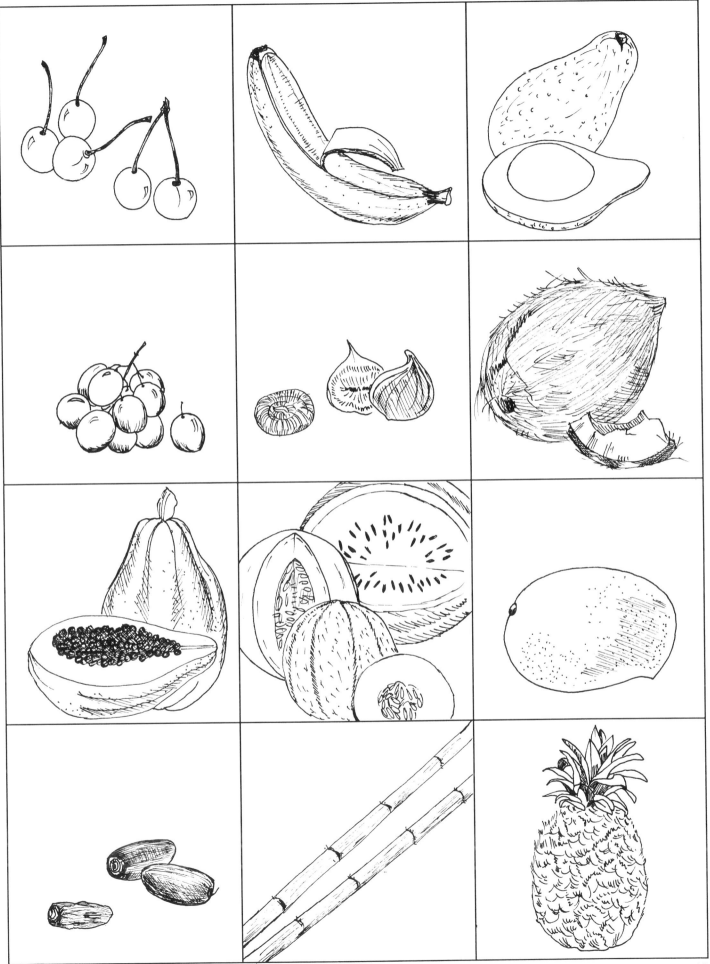

Avocadoes	Banana	Cherries
Coconut	Figs	Grapes
Mango	Melons	Papaya
Pineapple	Sugarcane	Dates

Food card games

- Play a game of memory with two sets of cards. Scatter any five pairs face down on the table. Try to find the pairs by taking turns to pick up any two cards. Name them as they are turned over. Keep playing until all five pairs are found. Repeat the game using six pairs, and so on.

- Collect seeds to correspond with some of the cards. Glue each seed onto a cardboard square. Try to match the seed card with the food card.

- Put all the cards in a wok. Use a pair of metal tongs or chopsticks to take out one card. Name it. Repeat until all of the cards have been taken out of the wok.

- Play store with the cards. Put up a pictorial price list in the store that shows how many cents each card costs. With five cents to spend, go shopping in the store. Name the food that is purchased.

- Use a card, a matching seed, and a matchbox to make a guessing game. Tape a card to the underside of the box. Slide the tray out of the box and put a matching seed into it. Slide the tray back into place. Now slide open the matchbox to look at the seed, then guess its name. The answer (food card) is on the underside of the box.

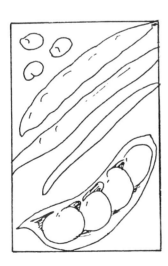 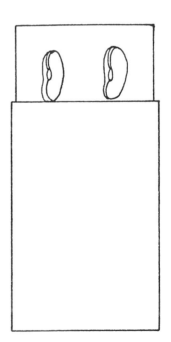

Matchbox bottom showing bean card, and top with tray open

Texture board

A texture board is fun to make. Let the children suggest and collect the raw materials; older children may even want to make their own personal boards. Feeling the different materials stimulates both verbal and non-verbal responses. After using the board as described in Method 5, leave it out for individual, quiet play.

Materials: 1 cardboard yogurt flat with 12 holes (free in supermarkets)
masking tape
12 cardboard circles cut to fit the holes
12 examples of harvest textures (suggestions below)
glue
storage box (pizza box is ideal)
aluminum foil to fit over the flat

Method: 1. Flatten the yogurt flat and tape down all 4 sides.
2. Choose 12 examples of harvest textures, such as coconut hair, cornhusk or corn silk, dried pineapple skin, pumpkin or gourd shell, walnut or peanut shell, hemp, straw, dried grass or wheat, bamboo, dried and waxed leaves, and inedible seeds.
3. Glue half of 1 harvest texture onto a cardboard circle, and glue the other half into a circle on the yogurt flat. Repeat for the remaining 11 textures.
4. Put the completed texture board, 12 circles, and piece of foil into a labelled and suitably decorated box.
5. Use the game in several ways. Talk about the textures, comparing them to each other. Then play a matching game, placing each of the 12 circles onto its counterpart on the board. When the texture board is familiar, let the children press the foil over the whole board to feel the shapes and name the textures.

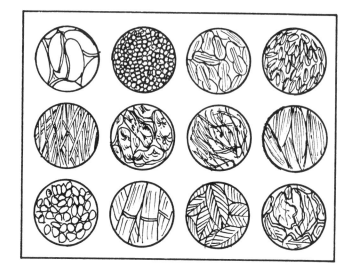

Texture board and cardboard circles

Indoor harvesting

Some food is quick and fun to grow indoors, even in windowless rooms. Planting a seed and seeing what comes up is exciting and encourages questioning. Use this tactile experience to introduce information about what plants need to grow.

Multicolored or Indian corn is often used as a harvest decoration. The colors of the kernels range from yellow to deep purple, and the husks are often purple or brown. Children are fascinated by this corn as it is so different from the yellow corn eaten all year round. The sprouts are multicolored too, and are beautiful to see and eat.

Chinese cress grows well in potting soil. It has a flavour similar to watercress or curled endive lettuce, and can be used as a filling for sandwiches or a topping on peanut butter or cream cheese. Harvest the cress with scissors, leaving some of the plant to go to seed. The seeds will drop, and more cress will appear in a few weeks.

Multicolored corn sprouts

Time: 2-3 days
Materials: 1 cob of Indian corn
            1 shallow tray
            warm water
Method: 1. Put the cob in the tray. Add enough water to cover the lower half of the cob.
            2. Put the tray in a warm place out of direct sunlight. Leave it for a few days.
            3. Watch the sprouts grow, adding warm water if necessary.
               Leave the cob in the sunlight for a day to green the sprouts.

Chinese cress

Time: 2-3 weeks
Materials: 1 potting tray full of potting soil
            Chinese cress seeds
            water
Method: 1. Sprinkle the seeds over the soil, then water well.
            2. Put the tray in a warm, sunny location.
            3. Shoots will appear in a week. When the stem is long and the head
               full of leaves, use scissors to harvest the cress.

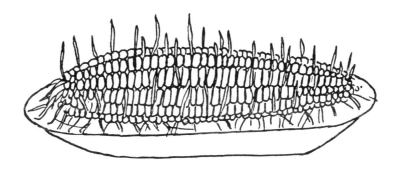

Growing multicolored corn sprouts

5. Group time

Harvest group time centers around food. Choose a food, then use the methods suggested below in the coconut and rice group times to make your chosen food equally memorable. Do the suggested activities for at least a week so the children have time to ask questions and participate. Repeat, using a second chosen food. Then tell the Japanese legend, **The Fox and the Bear** (p. 68), substituting the foods you have chosen for the ones in the story.

Coconut group time

The copra tree (coconut palm) grows in tropical areas, and is a major source of food and goods for more than half the world. Immature, green fruits from the tree can be eaten as spoon coconut, although the solid white pulp of the one-year-old, brown-shelled fruit is preferred by most people. The oil from the pulp is an ingredient in soaps and cosmetics. The leaves of the tree are used to make thatched roofs and mats. The hair on the shell is woven into scrubbing brushes and copra rope. The shell itself is used as a bowl, scoop, bell, or clapper. Let the children use a coconut shell as a shovel for the sandbox or a boat for the water table.

Meeting the coconut

Materials: 1 coconut in an opaque feely bag
1 twist-tie or plastic-coated wire
1 hammer and short nail
1 bowl
1 small, disposable cup per child
1 hacksaw, 1 knife (for adult use only)
one 8-oz package of unsweetened shredded coconut

Method: 1. Pass the feely bag around the circle. Try to guess what it contains.
2. Take out the coconut and pass it around the circle. Let each child pull a hair off the coconut. Tie all the hairs together with a twist-tie, then pass this brush around the circle. Use this later as a paintbrush.
3. Shake the coconut to hear the liquid. Try to guess what is inside, what color it might be and how it might taste. Hammer a nail into the eyes of the coconut — the 3 holes at the end. Pour a small amount of the liquid into each cup. Taste it.
4. Saw the coconut in half, then cut out the pulp with a knife. Cut it into thin slices for the children to taste, reserving the leftovers in the bowl. Compare the taste of this pulp to that of packaged coconut. Use the pulp in the recipes on pp. 72-73.
5. Use the shell as a musical instrument (see p. 51), spoon or dipper in the house-keeping center, boat in the water, or scoop in the sandbox.

Rice group time

Rice grows in warm, wet climates and is a major crop in Asia and the United States. After a four-week sprouting period, each shoot is planted out in the field. In about three months, the grain ripens and flowers. Then it is threshed, dried and hulled.

Although it is labor-intensive to grow, it is simple to prepare as a food. Unlike all the other major grains, it is merely hulled before cooking: no milling, no grinding, no cracking needed. It is eaten daily by over half the people in the world and is so important that in many Asian languages the word for rice is the same as the word for food. Be mindful of this, taking care to wash, cook, and eat all the rice that the children have examined. No colored rice in the sandbox, please!

Meeting rice

1. Wash hands carefully.
2. Put a small bin of uncooked long-grain white rice (1 lb. maximum) in the middle of the circle. Touch it and mold it into various shapes.
3. Put small plastic containers, such as film canisters, into the bin. Half-fill the canisters with rice, close them, and shake them. Listen to the sound. Repeat, using different amounts of rice.
4. Try to hold a single grain of rice, then examine it with a small magnifying glass. Taste the un-cooked grain of rice.
5. Wash the rice in cold water. See some rice float to the top, while most remains at the bottom. Remove any dirt or small stones, then drain off the water. Put half the rice in a saucepan with double the amount of cold water. Bring it to a boil, then reduce the heat and simmer, covered, for ten minutes or until tender.
6. Put the other half of the rice in a saucepan with double the amount of cold water. Add 1 T turmeric or curry powder and mix well. Cook as above.
7. Show the two colors of cooked rice. Smell the rice, then taste it. Use the leftover cooked rice in the recipes on p. 74.

Cheng dwah (Taiwanese)

This traditional outdoor game simulates the action of a farmer growing rice. At the end of the game the farmer turns into a leech and pinches the other players. The version described below offers a happier ending. Let an adult be the farmer first until the children pick up the rhythm of the dialogue.

1. Crouch down in a circle.
2. One player, the farmer, walks around the outside of the circle and taps each child on the back, saying, "I am planting my rice today."
3. The farmer then walks around the outside of the circle a second time and asks each child, "Has the rice sprouted?" Each child replies, "Yes," and stands up.
4. When everyone is standing, the farmer goes around again and asks each child, "Has the rice grown tall?" to which the child replies, "Yes," and stretches.
5. When all the children are stretching up, the farmer says, "Now it is time to gather the rice." Then the farmer runs around the circle trying to catch the other players who run and try to escape.

The fox and the bear

This adaptation of a Japanese folktale illustrates the difference between surface and root crops, and is a good introduction to the wall garden described on p. 50. Use real vegetables, seed packages, or the cards on pp. 59-62 as props. Use the patterns of the fox, the bear, the bee, and the beehive to make puppets or feltboard figures. Let the children improvise costumes to act out the story. When the story is familiar, introduce the Japanese words for fox and bear, and use them in the story. Note that the original folktale, unlike an Aesop fable, offers no moral and lets the listeners alone decide on the hero.

A bear and a fox once decided to farm together: the bear would dig and weed the soil and the fox would plant the seeds and water the plants. The bear worked hard all day long, lifting out heavy rocks and stones, pulling out all the weeds, and turning over the soil.

Along came the fox to see the bear's hard work. "You have done a good job, my friend," said the fox. "Now I will plant the seeds for us."

Carefully the fox dug tiny holes, dropped in the seeds, and covered them. When this was done the fox watered the new seeds well. Then the fox turned to his friend and said generously, "Since you did the hardest work, you can take everything that grows above the ground. I will take only what remains below."

"What a kind friend," thought the bear. "How lucky I am to work with the fox." But what grew? Peanuts! The bear had only the bitter flower stems to eat, while the fox ate all the delicious peanuts from under the ground.

The next year the fox again asked the bear if they could work together. This time the fox offered to take everything above the ground, while the bear could have everything underground. The bear liked that idea, and never thought to ask what they would grow. All the bear could think of were the delicious peanuts of the year before.

But what grew? Corn! The bear only had some thin roots to eat, while the fox ate up all the corn.

The next year the bear refused to work with the fox. From now on the bear would look for food rather than grow it.

This time the fox offered the bear everything they found. The bear liked that idea and, without thinking, agreed to work with the fox again. Off they went together to look for honey. When they found a beehive, the fox generously offered it to the bear.

"Many thanks, dear friend," said the bear, taking the hive. But the hive was heavy, too heavy for the bear. Down it crashed. Out flew the bees, angry and ready to sting. Away ran the bear, screaming in pain.

Meanwhile the happy fox stayed behind with the broken hive, and licked up all the delicious honey!

くま・クマ・熊

Bear / Kuma

きつね・キツネ・

Fox / Kitsune

Bear / Kuma

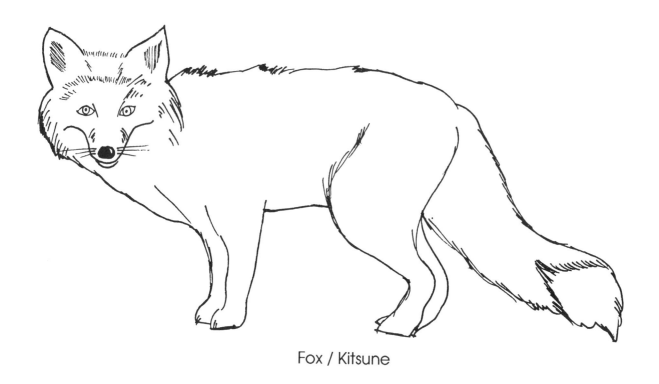

Fox / Kitsune

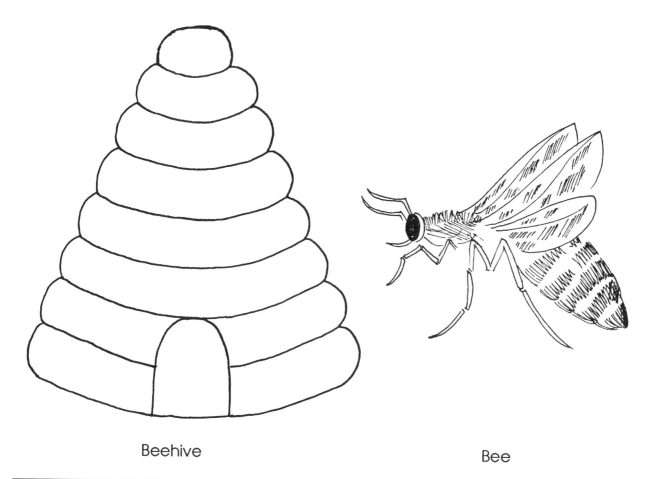

Beehive   Bee

6. Food to share

Food preparation is a valuable learning experience that may last from five minutes to an hour. Talk about each step and let the children take part so they can feel the responsibility for this task. Name each fruit or vegetable and let the children touch and smell it. Talk about the color, then try to guess what color it might be inside. When the children are ready, let them cut the food both horizontally and vertically to expose the seed pattern. Then look at the seeds and peel, and enjoy eating some of them too. Ask families for their recipes of special harvest foods. Suggestions follow.

- Peel and thinly slice fresh sugarcane and arrange the slices on a plate.

- Peel and slice kiwifruit, then peel and cut lychees in half, removing the seed. Arrange alternating slices of green kiwi and white lychee on a plate.

- Cut a papaya or an avocado in half, scoop out the seeds or seed, and slice into wedges. Squeeze lime juice onto the fruit, then sprinkle with sugar to taste.

- Peel and slice red or yellow bananas and mix them with pomegranate and passion fruit seeds.

- Serve a selection of fresh figs, dates, and apricots.

- Arrange many varieties of sliced apples on a plate. Beside each variety put one whole apple of that type. Core the whole apple and fill the hollow with raisins.

- To make dried apples, rub leftover apple slices with lemon and thread them on a long string. Hang them in a warm, dry place for a week and turn them daily. If there is no hanging place, simply put the slices into a brown paper bag for a week, shaking the bag once a day.

- Offer raw pole beans, string beans, and lima beans for tasting.

- Thread string beans on a long string, and hang them in a warm, dry place for a week. These dried beans, called "leather britches" by some American farmers, make a tasty snack.

- Leave grapes out in the sun for a week to dry into raisins.

- Put out an assortment of fresh and dried produce: plums and prunes, grapes and raisins, fresh figs and dried, fresh apricots and dried, bananas and banana chips.

- Grind peanuts, almonds, or walnuts into nut butter to spread on pita bread or rice cakes.

- Arrange squash in a bushel basket: acorn, fuzzy, spaghetti, butternut, and hubbard. Choose one squash and cook it. Spaghetti squash, baked whole in the oven until the outside feels soft, is especially fun for children to eat. Cut it open to reveal the spaghetti-like strands, then top it with spaghetti sauce.

- Make a harvest salad by using only cabbage: green, red, bok choy, napa, and savoy. Use a simple mayonnaise or oil-and-vinegar dressing.

- Lay out a harvest wreath on a plate using green pea pods to make the circle shape, then decorate with red cherries. Eat the wreath. Note that the inner pea is eaten and the shell is discarded. The opposite is true with cherries. The inner seed is discarded, while the outside is eaten.

- Use two round, flat stones to grind kernels of wheat. Boil the ground wheat in water to make cereal. Serve this cereal topped with a spoonful of honey and a portion of cold milk.

Coconut snacks

Enjoy these foods at coconut group time, making and eating them together. Each recipe serves ten.

Coconut milk

Ingredients: 1 coconut
water

Method: 1. Make holes in the eyes of the coconut and drain the liquid. Add enough hot water to this liquid to make 3 cups.
2. Crack the coconut and cut the pulp into small cubes.
3. Place the cubes in a blender, adding the 3 cups hot liquid. Process for 30-40 seconds, then leave for 30 minutes.
4. Pour the liquid into a bowl through a double thickness of cheesecloth. Squeeze the cloth to get about 2 cups coconut milk.

Coconut milk drink

Ingredients: 2 C coconut milk (made as above, or canned)
1/2 C lime juice
1/2 C sugar
2 C pineapple juice
ice

Method: 1. Process the first 4 ingredients in a blender for 10 seconds.
2. Put ice into each glass, and pour the drink over the ice. Alternatively, serve this drink in a hollowed-out coconut shell.

Coconut chips (Hawaiian)

Ingredients: 1 coconut
salt and sugar to taste

Method: 1. Cut open the coconut and scoop out the pulp. Use a vegetable peeler to slice the pulp thinly into strips.
2. Toast the strips in the oven at 400° F for 5 minutes, or until brown and crisp. Sprinkle half with salt and half with sugar.

Banana surprise

Ingredients: 5 bananas
2 C yogurt
3 C unsweetened shredded coconut

Method: 1. Peel the bananas and cut each one in half. Skewer a half on a craft stick.
2. Dip this half into the yogurt and coat well, then roll in coconut.
3. Repeat for the other 9 banana halves.

Rotis (Sri Lankan)

Ingredients: 2 C rice flour
1/2 C unsweetened shredded coconut
1 t salt
1 C water
2 t oil

Method: 1. Mix the first 4 ingredients together. Form into 10 balls, then flatten.
2. Fry on a greased griddle. Turn once to brown both sides.

Akwadu (Ghanaian)

Ingredients: 3 medium bananas
3 t margarine or butter
1/2 C orange juice
3 t lemon juice
1 C unsweetened shredded coconut

Method: 1. Preheat the oven to 350° F.
2. Peel and cut the bananas in half crosswise, then lengthwise in half again.
   Arrange the bananas on a greased pie plate.
3. Dot the bananas with margarine or butter, then drizzle with the juices,
   and sprinkle the coconut on top.
4. Bake for 10-12 minutes, or until the coconut is golden.

Loz-e-nargil (Iranian)

Ingredients: 1 C sugar
3/4 C water
1 C unsweetened grated coconut
4 T chopped pistachio nuts
2 t shortening or margarine

Method: 1. Boil the sugar with the water until the sugar dissolves.
2. Remove the saucepan from the heat and stir in the coconut.
3. Quickly pour the mixture into a greased 8-in. square pan.
4. While the mixture is still warm, sprinkle the nuts over the top,
   then gently press them into the surface.
5. Cool, then cut into traditional diamond shapes.

Ambrosia (American)

Ingredients: 2 C sour cream or yogurt
2 C miniature marshmallows
2 C unsweetened shredded coconut
2 bananas, peeled and sliced
2 C mandarin orange segments

Method: 1. Mix all the ingredients in a bowl and chill.
2. Serve in 10 small bowls or use as a filling in orange cups
   or melon slices.

Rice snacks

In contrast to instant and converted white rice which are virtually tasteless, whole rice is a delicious, aromatic grain. Try brown rice, basmati, long- and short-grain rice, cooked plain or with sauce. Wild rice is also delicious and nutty in flavor, although it is not actually rice but grass harvested by hand from lakeshores. Make these recipes together, and enjoy their texture and taste.

Rice pudding

Ingredients: 2 C cooked brown rice (or other leftover rice)
2 C milk
1/4 C honey
2 T butter
1 cup currants or raisins

Method: 1. Combine everything but the currants in a saucepan and cook over low heat for 20 minutes, stirring often.
2. Add the currants and continue cooking another 10 minutes.
3. When the pudding is slightly thick, take it off the heat and serve.

Sushi rice (Japanese)

Ingredients: 2 C cooked sushi (sticky) rice
1/4 C rice vinegar
1/2 C diced egg, dried shrimp, or raisins

Method: 1. Combine the rice and rice vinegar in a bowl. Divide equally into 10 portions.
2. Divide the third ingredient into 10 equal parts, and add each one by hand to a rice portion. Form the portions into balls.

Rice cake fiesta

Ingredients: 10 commercially packaged rice cakes
one 14-oz can refried beans (or homemade beans)
1 large avocado, peeled and mashed
2 C sour cream
2 C grated Cheddar cheese

Method: 1. Spread a layer of beans, then avocado, then sour cream, on each cake.
2. Top with the grated cheese.

Corn snacks

Corn or maize is indigenous to America and was a food staple for early Native People. They told legends that explained its power and associated it with the sun and the beginning of life itself. A Corn Goddess was said to live in each stalk of corn, and a demon inside each kernel of popcorn. When the kernel was heated the demon became angry and blew up, becoming popcorn.

There are three main types of corn: popcorn for popping, sweet corn which we eat as corn-on-the-cob, and field or cattle corn. The last one is the basis of animal feed, cornstarch, cornmeal, cornflakes, corn oil, corn syrup, and corn chips. Kernels of corn may be hard or soft, large or small, yellow or multicolored. They may be creamed, pickled as a relish, cooked as a soup, or used to make tamales, tortillas, cornbread, corn fritters, or corn pudding. Other recipes are suggested below.

Succotash (Native American)

Ingredients: one 10-oz can corn niblets
one 10-oz can kidney beans
one 10-oz can chickpeas
2 C cooked wild rice
1/4 C oil-and-vinegar dressing

Method: 1. Drain the cans of corn, beans, and chickpeas. Mix them with the rice.
2. Coat well with the salad dressing and serve in small bowls.
This is also delicious as a filling for pita bread.

Corn pone (Central American)

Ingredients: 1 1/2 C cornmeal
3/4 C flour
3 t baking powder
2 eggs, well beaten
1/4 C margarine, melted
1 C milk

Method: 1. Mix the dry ingredients and the liquid ones separately.
2. Combine the two, stirring just until moistened.
3. Pour into an 8-in. square greased pan and bake at 350° F for 20 minutes.

Popcorn balls (American)

Ingredients: 1 C miniature marshmallows
2 T butter
10 C popped corn

Method: 1. In a saucepan over low heat, melt the marshmallows and butter.
2. Place the popped corn in a large bowl and pour the marshmallow mixture over it. Stir to coat.
3. With greased hands, form spoonfuls of the mixture into balls.

Round harvest snacks

The circle symbolizes the harvest moon and the agricultural cycle. This symbol is echoed in many special foods eaten at this time of year. Some of the foods may be quite complicated for young children to prepare, but they can enjoy substitutes that taste equally good.

Harvest moon cakes (Chinese)

Ingredients: 2 packages sweetmilk biscuit dough
1/4 C filling (see Method 2)
1 egg
1/4 C sugar
2 t water

Method: 1. Divide each package of dough into 10 biscuits.
Put the first 10 onto a cookie sheet.
2. Put a spoonful of filling in the center of each biscuit.
The filling may be dousha or red bean paste, douyung
or yellow bean paste, or lienyung or lotus seed paste.
3. Top each biscuit with a second one and press the edges together.
4. Beat the egg, adding the sugar gradually with the water.
Brush this mixture on the top and sides of each biscuit.
5. Bake the biscuits according to the directions on the package.

Mystery balls

Ingredients: 2 C peanut butter
2 C powdered milk
1 C honey
1/2 C wheat germ
filling: chocolate chips, pitted cherries, almonds

Method: 1. Mix together the peanut butter, milk powder, honey,
and wheat germ.
2. Put a spoonful of batter on a board and press it flat.
Add a filling, then fold up the sides around it to make a ball.
3. Eat the balls right away or store them in the refrigerator.

Harvest wreaths

Ingredients: 10 rice cakes, bagels, wholewheat rounds, or English muffins
1/2 C honey, peanut butter, or cream cheese
raisins, coconut, sliced dried apricots

Method: 1. Spread each rice cake with honey, peanut butter, or cream cheese.
2. Decorate the cake with the fruit, putting it around the rim to
resemble a wreath.

Soup

Introduce children to making soup. Tell them the story of **Stone Soup** or **Chicken Soup with Rice** (see p. 80). Make Harvest soup or other simple soups using vegetables sent in by the parents or purchased on a field trip to a local farmer's market.

Harvest soup

Invite the children's families to share soup and bread (see p. 43), using the sample invitation below. Cut out two invitations from construction paper. Use one as the back, and cut the other one in half as the front. Glue the edges of the front bowl to the back, and attach the front lid to the back with a paper fastener so that the lid can open. Let the children draw or color on the bowl and lid. Use the insert to list the date, time, and place of the harvest meal, then slip the insert into the bowl.

Ask each child to bring in one vegetable. Send a pictogram home with the child as a reminder. A sample selection of vegetables might be: onion, tomato, eggplant, zucchini, green pepper, beans, cabbage. Children may also want to bring in tofu which can be drained and cut into strips, then added to the soup during the last few minutes of cooking.

When all the vegetables are collected, name them and sort them. Wash hands carefully, then clean, peel, and cut the vegetables. Simmer them in water or tomato juice. Add herbs and some rice.

Invitation card, closed and opened to reveal the insert

Gazpacho (Italian)

Ingredients: 2 cucumbers, peeled, seeded, and chopped
1 small onion, peeled and chopped
1 green pepper, seeded and chopped
2 cloves garlic, peeled and chopped
1/3 C olive oil
one 10-oz can tomato juice
1/2 C vegetable juice
one 28-oz can plum tomatoes
dash of paprika, salt and pepper, Worcestershire sauce

Method: 1. Put all the ingredients in a blender and process.

Borscht (Polish, Russian)

Ingredients: two 10-oz cans beets
2 beef/vegetable bouillon cubes mixed with 2 C boiling water
2 T lemon juice
1 C yogurt

Method: 1. Process the beets, bouillon, juice, and half of the yogurt
in a blender or food processor.
2. Cool, then pour into 10 small bowls. Top each serving with a
spoonful of the remaining yogurt.

Fruit soup (Swedish)

Ingredients: one 1-lb can dark sweet cherries in syrup
one 1-lb can sliced peaches, drained
3 T lemon juice
2 C plain yogurt

Method: 1. Process the cherries with syrup, peaches, and lemon juice in a blender or
food processor.
2. Stir in yogurt, then pour into 10 small bowls.

Resources for educators

Beveridge, Mary and Tony Pugh. **What's for Breakfast?** Hove, East Sussex: Wayland, 1984.
This clear and well illustrated book introduces breakfast foods as part of the **Food Around the World Series** which also includes **What's for Lunch?** and **What's for Dinner?**

Birch, Beverley. **Food from Many Lands.** London: Macdonald Educational, 1984.
Simple text and color photographs illustrate the global variety of foods, how they are produced, and how they are eaten.

Garner, Betty. **A Matter of Thanksgiving.** Hamilton: Image, 1986.
Harvest celebrations of many communities are described and their backgrounds discussed.

Johnson, Sylvia A. **Rice**. Minneapolis: Lerner, 1985.
Clear text and color photographs describe the growing and harvesting of rice.

Kalman, Bobbie. **We Celebrate the Harvest**. Toronto: Crabtree, 1986.
This well illustrated book draws similarities between harvest festivals in many parts of the world.

Wexler, Jerome and Millicent Selsam. **Eat the Fruit, Plant the Seed**. New York: William Morrow, 1980.
This book describes how to grow indoors six different fruits — avocado, papaya, citrus, mango, pomegranate, and kiwi.

Whitlock, Ralph. **Harvest and Thanksgiving**. Hove, East Sussex: Wayland, 1984.
Good color photographs and simple text focus on the history and celebration of harvest.

Storybooks for all age groups (2-6 years)

Adams, Edward, ed. **Two Brothers and Their Magic Gourds**. Seoul: Seoul Publishing, 1983.
This bilingual (English/Korean) folktale of the rivalry between two brothers is beautifully illustrated by Dong Ho Choi.

Aliki. **Corn is Maize: the Gift of the Indians**. New York: Harper and Row, 1976.
This simple history of corn describes its first cultivation and its many uses.

De Paolo, Tomie. **Watch Out for the Chicken Feet in Your Soup**. New York: Simon and Schuster, 1974.
Joey, embarrassed by having an Italian grandmother, gains a new appreciation and love for her when he sees how much she is admired by his friend.

Dobrin, Arnold. **Josephine's Imagination**. New York: Four Winds, 1973.
A little Mexican girl makes her own corn dolls to sell at the local market.

Health and Welfare Canada. **The Hole in the Fence**. Hull, Quebec: Ministry of Supply and Services, 1985.
Vegetables come alive in this garden; they solve problems, form friendships, and confront racism in 19 related stories. A Teacher's Guide accompanies this book.

Maiorano, Robert. **Francisco**. New York: Macmillan, 1978.
This story of a little boy's ingenuity in earning money to help his family takes place in the Dominican Republic, and is a good companion story for **Josephine's Imagination** by Arnold Dobrin.

Pasternak, Carol. **Stone Soup**. Toronto: Kids Can, 1973.
In this adaptation of the popular folktale, a janitor helps a frustrated teacher communicate with her multi-ethnic class through food.

Politi, Leo. **Mr. Fong's Toy Shop**. New York: Charles Scribner's Sons, 1978.
A toymaker and his young friends create a shadow puppet play about Cheng-O, the Moon Goddess, for the Harvest Moon Festival in Chinatown.

Politi, Leo. **Three Stalks of Corn**. New York: Charles Scribner's Sons, 1976.
Angelica's Mexican grandmother tells her the many legends of corn, then shows her and her Californian school friends its many uses.

Rohmer, Harriet. **The Legend of Food Mountain**. San Francisco: Children's Book Press, 1982.
This bilingual (English/Spanish) Mexican legend of how corn came to the people is vividly illustrated by Graciela Carrillo.

Sadu, Itah. **How the Coconut Got Its Face**. Toronto: Carib-Can, 1988.
This Caribbean legend of the coconut is illustrated by Rasheeda Haneef.

Spalding, Andrea. **A World of Stories**. Red Deer, Alberta: Red Deer College,1989.
This collection of short stories with the younger reader in mind combines English and non-English words in just the right mix; its Chilean version of Stone Soup, "Sopa de Piedra," demonstrates this.

Wallace, Ian and Angela Wood. **The Sandwich**. Toronto: Kids Can,1985.
Vincenzo Ferrante learns to deal with the jibes of his Grade Two classmates in coming to terms with his own ethnic identity.

Williams, Vera. **Cherries and Cherry Pits**. New York: Greenwillow, 1986.
Bidemmi, a young black girl, loves to draw and eat cherries, and wants to share them with children around the world.

Yoda, Junichi. **The Rolling Rice Ball**. New York: Parents Magazine, 1969.
This Japanese folktale tells of one man's compassion and love and another man's greed, and how each one is rewarded.

Films

Zea (5:17) NFB
This wordless film shows corn popping in slow motion. Only in the last minute does the viewer realize that this is actually popcorn.

Chicken Soup with Rice (3:00) Weston Woods
This rocking, multi-ethnic film tells the story by Maurice Sendak.

CHAPTER THREE

Masquerade

Masquerade: a celebration of imaginative play

Children and adults often feel the desire to pretend to be someone or something else. This need is practical for the actor, whimsical for the prankster. It may also be spiritual for those who hold Christian beliefs in resurrection (Easter), wandering souls (All Souls' Day), and a spirit world. It may, in fact, have a social purpose: a time to escape daily demands by acting out new roles. This time can be described as "masquerade," a celebration of imaginative play.

Whether the name be Hallowe'en, Mardi Gras, or Vappu, masquerade comes from a secular response to Christian beliefs. To suit this spiritual world, masquerade is often celebrated at night with bonfires, lit pumpkins, and fireworks. Masks combine with the darkness to hide the identities of the celebrants and to protect them from the evil spirits.

Hallowe'en originated 2000 years ago as a Celtic summer's end festival called Samhain. Over the centuries Samhain blended with Roman and Christian ceremonies and became a day to play tricks and make mischief. In the Middle Ages, the Catholic Church created All Hallows' (Saints') Day in the belief that this religious holiday would end the pranks. Instead, All Hallows' Eve became a night for wearing costumes to fool the roaming souls. Gradually, the secular holiday of Hallowe'en gained more popularity than All Hallows' Day.

The Latin origin of the word Carnival is "good-bye to meat." Carnival marked the beginning of Lent, the 40 days of fasting before Easter. The last day of Carnival was a time to eat and drink in excess, and it became known as Mardi Gras from the French for "Fat Tuesday." As with Hallowe'en and All Hallows' Day, the festivals of Carnival and Mardi Gras eventually overshadowed the fasting of Lent. Once again, the excitement of a secular holiday eclipsed the solemnity of the religious one.

Today, masquerade festivals have many names but the common threads are disguise, magic, and fire. Masquerade explores the world of imaginative play through masks and costumes that the children can create and wear themselves. It is a time to discover the spiritual meanings of totems and masks and the masked celebrations that bring people together.

On the next page is a list of masquerade festivals and their corresponding dates. Dates marked with an asterisk (*) are movable and depend upon either lunar or religious calendars. If a festival is associated with a particular place or people within a country, this is noted in parentheses. Although many of these festivals are celebrated in the United States, the place of origin of each one is keyed by number to a point on the map. Unlike spring or harvest celebrations, many masquerade festivals share the same name; in particular, the names of Mardi Gras and Carnival. These festivals also share very similar customs.

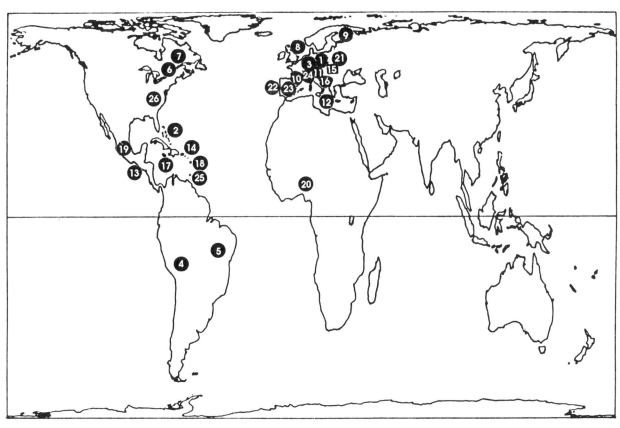

1. Austria	Fasching	* before Lent (March)
2. Bahamas	Junkanoo	December 26-January 1
3. Belgium	Carnival	* before Lent (March)
4. Bolivia (Oruro)	Mardi Gras	* before Lent (March)
5. Brazil	Carnival	* before Lent (March)
6. Canada, United States	Hallowe'en	October 31
7. Canada (Quebec)	Carnaval	February
8. England (Somerset)	Punky Night	October 31
9. Finland	Vappu	May 1
10. France	Mardi Gras	* Tuesday before Lent (March)
11. Germany	Fasching	* before Lent (March)
12. Greece	Apokreis	February
13. Guatemala	All Souls' Day	November 2
14. Haiti	Carnival	* before Lent (March)
15. Hungary	Farsang	* before Lent (March)
16. Italy	Carnival	* before Lent (March)
17. Jamaica	Junkanoo	December 31
18. Martinique	Vaval	* Wednesday before Lent (March)
19. Mexico	Carnival	February 25-March 5
20. Nigeria	Eyo Masquerade	* August
21. Poland	Zapusty	* before Lent (March)
22. Portugal	Mardi Gras	* Tuesday before Lent (March)
23. Spain	Mardi Gras	* Tuesday before Lent (March)
24. Switzerland	Fasnacht	February
25. Trinidad	Calypso Carnival	* before Lent (March)
26. United States	Mardi Gras	* before Lent (March)
27. Vietnam	Trung-Thu	August 15

Using the masquerade theme

GOAL To show the universality of masquerade

OBJECTIVES To experience with the children the global similarities of masquerade music and dance

To familiarize the children with the special meaning of certain masks and clothing

To distinguish between special clothing and everyday wear

To create masks and disguises that can be used throughout the year

To introduce and use the basic vocabulary of this theme

You may also add your own objectives. For instance, if the children are fascinated by music, use this theme to further develop a diverse collection of musical instruments or folk dances.

This theme is an appropriate multicultural alternative to celebrating Hallowe'en. Remember that the cats, owls, witches, and ghosts of Hallowe'en are repeated endlessly during October in North American schools, stores, and communities. There is no need to duplicate that effort; instead, present Hallowe'en as only one part of the broader context of masquerade. At the same time reassure new Americans that the trick-or-treating their children may want to do on Hallowe'en is a customary part of the holiday. Advise them to expect young visitors on Hallowe'en night, and suggest that, if they want to take part, they have some small treats ready. Discuss basic safety rules for Hallowe'en night.

You could use parts of the masquerade theme to brighten the grey days of February and March, or to celebrate the summer sun. It is easier to put on and take off costumes when the weather is fine and the children wear fewer layers. It also lets the children experience lightweight costumes outdoors, play that is often impossible in an American October.

VOCABULARY LIST

totem	dress-ups	traditional	hiding
jack-o'-lantern	costume	special	covering
pumpkin	disguise	fancy	chanting
yam	mask	plain	dreaming
shadow puppet	veil	everyday	pretending

Vocabulary card, front and back faces

1. Setting the mood

Fun is the key to the masquerade theme. Display pictures of smiling and laughing children, dancers, and party-goers. Remember the spirit of Hallowe'en tricks, too! Challenge the children's imagination by showing them images with more than one message, optical illusions, doors that open to other doors, pictures hidden in pictures, and other visual games. Suggestions follow.

- Hang parasols, kites, balloons, crepe-paper streamers, curly ribbons, paper masks, and costumed puppets from the ceiling to create a party effect.

- Put small masks or veils on the dolls and soft toys in the room.

- Tape photographs or self-portraits of the children on the wall. Suspend masks or veils from the ceiling to dangle in front of the faces. Use both half-face and full-face masks to create different effects and to elicit vocabulary by asking, "What's missing?"

- Put stickers on the children's backs and ask them to identify their particular sticker. To help them, point out the mirror(s) in the room. The children can look in the mirror to try to see what the sticker depicts. They can also apply the stickers to one another. This game helps them learn to visually transfer from right to left and vice versa. To extend the game, give matching stickers to pairs of children and let them find each other.

- Show pictures of animals that adapt to their surroundings; for instance, the chameleon, the tree frog, or the Arctic hare.

- Introduce the children to flip books, kaleidoscopes, and periscopes that let them see stages and parts of movement.

- Show the children prints by the artists Magritte, Dali, and Escher to stretch their visual flexibility. Introduce books such as **Anno's Counting House** (Anno, 1982) and **Take Another Look** (Hoban, 1981). Use the pattern below to make a masquerade optical illusion.

Do you see a vase or two people?

Masks

Masks may be worn as a disguise or for protection. The umpire's mask, the hockey player's mask, and the fencer's mask protect the wearer from injury. In a hospital, masks worn by the staff protect the patient from germs. The mask can also protect identity: thieves and carnival-goers share a common desire not to be recognized.

Masks can also depict character. Actors in the Noh theatre of Japan wear large character masks, the designs of which are generations old. Other theatrical groups use masks to cover more than one actor, or no actor at all; in the latter case, the mask becomes a character itself. Masks may also represent spiritual beings or forces. Many West Africans, Canadian Inuit, and Mexican Hopi believe that when dancers put on their masks, they also put on the spirit of the mask.

Confronted by the unfamiliar, we sometimes laugh out of nervousness and fear. The mask as a spiritual totem is unfamiliar to some children and may make them laugh. Other children may be used to seeing such masks at ceremonies and in their homes. When their friends laugh at these masks, they may feel self-conscious and embarrassed.

Adults can help both the nervousness of one group and the hurt feelings of the other by familiarizing all the children with masks as symbols and making the mask part of a familiar setting. Some parents may also distrust the mask, seeing it as a pagan custom. They may not want their children to dress up or wear a mask. By being sensitive to their concerns, the teacher can model respect and sharing to these parents as well.

Animal totem mask

Time: 15 minutes
Materials: 1 large brown paper bag per child
            scissors
            glue
            raffia, wool, string, crepe-paper streamers
            markers or crayons
Method: 1. Choose an animal to be the totem for this mask.
            2. Cut out most of one wide side of the bag, leaving a small border along the top and sides.
            3. Glue any of the trim materials onto this border.
            4. Complete the mask by coloring it to resemble the chosen animal.

Totem mask

Time: 15 minutes
Materials: 1 large paper plate per child
scissors
markers or crayons
1 craft stick per child
masking tape
8 construction-paper strips (1-by-3-in.) per child
assortment of sticker symbols (sun, moon, birds)
glue
Method: 1. Cut 2 eye-holes out of the plate. Outline the eye-holes with a marker or crayon.
2. Tape the craft stick to the bottom of the plate as a handle.
3. Choose 8 symbols, sticking one on the end of each paper strip.
4. Glue the other end of each strip to the back rim of the plate so that the strips are evenly spaced, radiating out around the plate.

Foil mask

Time: 10 minutes
Materials: 1 square of aluminum foil per child
Method: 1. Hold the foil against the face so that the diagonal corners meet the ears.
2. Press the foil onto the face to imprint facial features onto the foil.
3. Take off the foil and poke out the eye-holes.
4. Foil edges may be sharp, so turn under the edges around the eyes to make sure they are smooth. Turn under and smooth the outside edge of the mask to make it stronger.
5. Wear the mask by simply pressing it onto the face.
6. Play a correspondence game with the mask. Arrange all the foil masks on the table, then ask the children to match each mask to its owner.

Head mask

Time: 15 minutes
Materials: 1 sheet of construction paper per child
scissors
markers or crayons
feathers, sequins, glitter
glue
1 paper fastener per child
Method: 1. Use the pattern indicated to cut out a construction-paper mask.
2. Color the mask with markers or crayons.
3. Decorate with feathers, sequins, glitter, or other collage materials.
4. Push a paper fastener through the middle of the 3 ends and tighten it to hold them together.

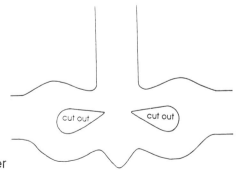

Veils

In North America the veil is most often associated with weddings. Globally, it may also signify mourning, beauty, or the humility, modesty and holiness of a religious order. It has been worn for centuries to keep men from looking at women's faces. The veil may cover the whole face or only half; it may be detachable or it may be part of an entire body covering; it may be sheer and alluring or heavy and opaque. But the result is the same: the concealment of women.

Among the Tuareg of the Sahara this practice is reversed. Women go without veils while men cover their faces. They wear their veils outside even when they eat and drink, believing that non-Tuaregs should not see their faces.

Some veils such as the yashmak are quite sheer. This translucent face cover worn by women in the Middle East is usually made of fine muslin. It consists of two pieces: one covering the nose to the breasts, and the other covering the hair to the eyebrows, leaving the eyes uncovered.

This veil does not obscure the woman's body to the same extent as the chadar, chuddar, chadri, carsaf, burko'o, or haik. All of these words refer to a similar-looking garment: an all-enveloping mantle or cloak worn in public by many Moslem women. Draped over the body to cover everyday clothes, this mantle leaves only the face visible. It is often black and sometimes hooded. Held in place by a belt, sash, or just the hands, it is both warm and modest.

Many children initially find both veils and masks claustrophobic and frightening. Let them experience the feeling of veils and get used to seeing themselves and their friends in them. Let them see the veil change their appearance and that of their friends. Let them also learn that they can remove the veil to look at the faces underneath. In all these experiences, take care to comment positively on the use of the veil. Suggestions follow.

- Provide large black blankets or cloaks for the children to use as wraps.

- Use a stretch headband to hang a mesh or gauze face veil over the child's face.

- Tie a chiffon scarf at the back of the head so that it falls over the child's nose and lower face.

- Put out long and short sheer scarves to be draped over heads and shoulders. Include scarves edged with tassels or sequins.

- Bend a wire hanger into a diamond shape. Stretch a nylon stocking over the hanger until it is taut. Wind tape around the hook to make a handle, and let the child play with this hand-held veil.

- Use a variety of colored stockings to make hand-held veils. They can be held over the face or hung over photographs in the room.

Make-up

Make-up is used by many women and some men to embellish or to hide certain facial features. Actors and actresses also wear stage make-up to reveal their characters. In the Kathakali theatre of India, the patterns and colors on the dancers' faces denote their roles. In Chinese opera, make-up designs are called lien p'u or "the face that shows a record." The male heroes, villains, gods, and demons of Japanese Kabuki theatre wear kumadori make-up; each pattern on the white base make-up represents the flowing blood of a particular emotion.

The stylistic use of make-up is also common outside the theater. In Sudan, Nuba men paint their faces every day. In Mexico, the Huichol sometimes paint their faces with detailed yellow designs. In India, Yemen, and the Middle East women paint intricate, lacy designs on their hands for weddings and other special celebrations. In North America, children enjoy face-painting at shopping malls, fairs, and parties. Give the children an experience in many styles of make-up with readily accessible materials rather than expensive, commercial face paints. Make sure that all materials are gentle to the skin and non-allergenic, and use an individual swab to apply make-up on each child.

- Actors, dancers, and geisha in Japan wear oshiroi, a white powder applied to the face, neck, arms, and hands. During Carnival, Argentinians use a starch and water paste to create the same effect. Let the children rub cornstarch or talcum powder on their faces, arms, and legs to simulate this theatrical quality and to experience another skin color.

- Imitate mendhi hand-painting. Use a fine brush and henna to paint on color curlicues. Alternatively, use a washable felt-tipped red marker.

- Children of many cultures often have their fingernails painted. Let the children choose from a wide variety of fingernail polish. Let them count the number of nails painted, and name each color as it is used.

- In some areas of India and Pakistan a red bindie, tika, or tipa on the forehead is a sign of beauty, marital status, class, or religious affiliation. Hindu men often wear a tika, while women may wear any of the three. Buy a package of bindies, ready to stick on, at an Indian store or use small red circle, star, or flower stickers.

- With yellow chalk draw circular patterns of yellow dots on the children's cheeks as the Huichol of Mexico do for festivals. Yellow circle stickers can also be used to create the same effect.

- Use charcoal on the children's cheeks to draw straight black lines representing the cut marks of the Kenyan Masai.

- Buy some inexpensive tubes of facial mask cream and give the children a facial. Let the cream dry, then let the children wash it off themselves for a tingling facial sensation. Do the same with ordinary soap. Leave it on the face for five minutes until the skin feels tight, then wash it off.

- With individual cotton swabs apply lipstick to children's lips. Then let them make kiss prints by kissing colored paper.

Wearing a bindie

2. Music and movement

Masks, costumes, and music are so intermingled during masquerade that it is difficult to separate them. The children can literally dance their way through this theme using their own instruments, costumes, and masks.

Calypso is the traditional music of Carnival. It originated in Trinidad, and was modified in other parts of the Caribbean. In Cuba and Puerto Rico, calypso became salsa, and in Jamaica, reggae. Play this kind of music for the children and you will find them moving spontaneously to the powerful new rhythms. See p. 120 for suggested records and tapes.

They may also want to use their own instruments to make dance music. While this may sound noisy and discordant at first, over time a natural rhythm will evolve. Be patient and let the children play their music inside and outside. If the instruments are accessible, there is plenty of space, and the mood is accepting and open, the children will feel free in their musical creations. The only guideline is to support one another in making good masquerade rhythms.

Making the instruments

- Drums are often the only instruments used at a Native pow wow or potlatch. Made of hide and wood, their steady, strong beat is meant to echo the pulse of the universe. Let the children imitate this sound by beating on overturned cardboard ice-cream tubs, wooden barrels, watermelon shells, basketballs, or boxes. Let them try chanting or singing with the beat.

- During World War II in Trinidad, Carnival was banned. Afterwards local musicians looked around for a cheap source of instruments. From oil drums left behind by the American Navy they made the first steel drums or pans. When the panman pounds these drums from below, they make higher sounds than when pounded from above. Each panman usually plays a set of at least six drums. Turn over a variety of metal cans, pots, or pans and let the children make their own steel drum band.

- In Bali and Java bands are often based on the gamelan (gong). Imitate this by hanging up a row of pot lids, metal disks, or foil pie plates. Let the children use a metal spoon, fork, chopsticks, or their hands to strike these in succession, creating varying rhythms.

- African dancers often shake one or two shawaro, artistically decorated tin rattles. Imitate a shawaro by dropping small stones or beads into a hole in the top of an empty tin can. Push a dowel through this hole. Tape around the hole so that no stones fall out. Let the children hold the dowel and shake this shawaro. A simpler shawaro can be made by putting a few stones in a foil pie plate. Put over another foil plate as a lid, and tape the two plates together.

- In Mexico matracas or noisemakers are used instead of bells to call people to church during the Christian Holy Week before Easter Sunday. On the Jewish festival of Purim, similar noisemakers or greggers are also used. Make your own noisemaker by pushing a dowel through the sides of a stone-filled tin can, using the method described above. Let the children hold the end of the dowel and twirl it, spinning the can on the other end.

- To set the pace or to indicate a rhythm change, dancers in many African countries use a tlukere. Originally fashioned out of a horse's tail, a tlukere makes a swishing sound when whisked across the floor. Palm branches and dried corn husks make a similar sound, as does a brush on a steel drum. Let the children make a tlukere by using a twist-tie to wrap together the bases of three or four cornhusks (or five or six crepe-paper streamers). They can then wave and whirl this tlukere during the dancing.

- A favorite Carnival instrument in Haiti is the vaccine, a hollow tube of bamboo. Big vaccines make a low note while little vaccines make a high note like flutes or Bolivian panpipes. Long paper-towel tubes contrast with short toilet-paper tubes in a similar way. Experiment by humming through different lengths of tubes or by taping together several long tubes to make a very long vaccine.

- Similar to this is the Australian aboriginal instrument, the didgeridoo. This hollow tube of bamboo is played like a vaccine and makes a sound like the moan of the wind. Let the children imitate this by humming through one end of a length of rubber hosepipe to make a low, eerie sound. They can also cover one end of the hose with waxed paper, secure it with an elastic band, and poke a hole near the band. Humming through this with the hole open or covered produces a moaning sound.

Making music

The dances

The traditional Carnival dance is the samba, but the tango, flamenco, and watusi are also danced during this festival. Young children can improvise these dances.

Tinikling dance (Filipino, Indonesian, Polynesian)

This dance imitates the long-legged tinikling bird as it picks its way between grass stems and fallen trees. Two long poles on the floor are held at either end, then are clapped rhythmically together. The dancer hops between and on either side of these two poles. As the tempo increases, the poles move faster and the dancer does too. Do this dance with the children. Use broom handles or bamboo poles and let the children co-operate, making sure no feet are caught between the poles. Improvise a song, while dancing.

Let's all dance like the bird tinikling,
Jump in and out, out and in,
Hop over poles as they move,
The song is sweet and the dance is smooth.

Long thick dowels or broom handles can also
be used for limbo dancing (Filipino, Hawaiian)
and pole jumping (Inuit, Jamaican).

Dancing masks (Argentinian)

This imitates the Argentinian round dance or Carnavalita which is danced at Carnival time. Do this dance in a circle with the children while they are wearing their masks. Beat steadily on either a steel or wooden drum and improvise a simple tune. Let each child play a particular instrument as it is named in the song.

The masks are coming, the dancing masks.
Listen to the music of their dance.
Listen to their feet stamp.
Listen to their drums beat.
Let me hear the vaccine blow.
Let me hear the shawaro.
Let me twirl my matracas.
Let me ring my gamelan.
Let me swish my tlukere.
On our own Carnival day!

Flamenco dance (Spanish)

Dance the flamenco to Spanish music such as "El Vito" (**B.L.U.M.A.**). Stand in a circle to dance and follow the actions suggested by the English version of the song. Rather than snapping their fingers, younger children may want to clap their hands together or to use castanets. These can be made by taping the back of a flattened bottle cap to the thumb and another to the index finger. The two caps are then clicked together during the song.

Con el vito, vito, vito. Con el vito, vito, va. (repeat twice)
El amor de las mujeres
Lo comparo a la cazuela.
Que arde mucho dura poco
Y no alumbra pero quema.
Con el vito, vito, vito. Con el vito, vito, va. (repeat twice)

And you snap your fingers this way,
And you snap your fingers that way,
And you snap your fingers slowly,
And you snap your fingers quickly.

Adapt the words to suit the vocabulary of the child; for example,

You can click your fingers up high,
You can click your fingers down low,
You can click your fingers fast,
You can click your fingers slow.

Goosh va damagh (Korean)

Quiet times during masquerade give the body a chance to slow down. They also give the group a time to remember and reflect on the games, songs, and dances they have played. This Korean mime game called Cover Your Ears is much like the Inuit game of silence called Guk. One player begins by covering both ears. The player to the left covers the right ear with the right hand. The next player does the opposite, and so on, alternating around the circle. The pace is fast and any player who hesitates is out.

An easy co-operative version for younger children is described below. Lead the game yourself, then let a child lead. If the pace is slow and quiet, the children can relax and gradually wind down. This game can conclude with some deep-breathing exercises or yoga (see p. 23).

Method: 1. Sit in a circle and wait until there is silence.
               2. Cover both ears, then turn to the person on the left who copies the action. The next person copies it, and so on until everyone around the circle has their ears covered.
               3. Mime another action (cover the face, bow the head, or shut both eyes) and proceed as above.

3. Art

An important part of masquerade is costume and disguise. With sufficient materials and motivation, children can create their own disguises out of dress-ups and art materials. This is an opportunity to look more closely at costuming and clothing, and for children to experiment with the medium of cloth rather than paper.

In weaving co-operatives attached to schools in North Africa and India, children weave exciting, colorful tapestries, demonstrating their dexterity and imagination. In North America children adapt their own clothing by painting on designs or adding buttons, stickers, and patches. Functional artwork is a great motivator for children.

- Give the children cotton balls or balls of raw wool. Pull the ball apart repeatedly until it becomes threads. Hand-spin the threads by pulling out several and twisting them together.

- Lean a "loom" against the wall or put it on the floor. The loom may be a sturdy picture frame, an open cardboard box, or a wooden fruit crate. Wrap a continuous length of string or yarn tightly and closely around the loom about 30 times to make a warp (lengthwise threads on a loom). For the weft (crosswise threads) use materials such as colored paper strips, sparkly pipecleaners, chenille strips, or cloth scraps. Let the children weave these weft materials over, under, over, and under the warp.

- Put out plastic berry baskets and colorful strips cut from plastic bags. Let the children weave these strips over and under the plastic to make solid berry boxes.

- Stretch an old onion bag or a square of chicken wire over a frame of cardboard and staple it into place. Thread tapestry needles with colourful yarn for the children to weave through the holes.

- Button blankets are still made by the Haida on the west coast of Canada. The buttons are sewn in symbolic patterns on the blankets to make ceremonial clothes for pow wows and potlatches. The finished product resembles the button-covered outfits worn by the Pearlies in England. Put a blanket on the floor with an assortment of large buttons. Let each child choose a button and a special place on the blanket. Then help the child to sew on the button. Very young children can use fabric glue to attach their buttons to the blanket. Afterwards, cut a hole in the middle of the blanket so that it can be worn as a poncho.

- In Panama the Cuna people weave headbands with red, yellow, and black designs. Japanese and Korean students wear white headbands, often with political messages written on them in black. Some Native Americans wear headbands made of leather decorated with symbolic beadwork. Give the children long narrow strips of unbleached cotton. Let them use toothpicks and tempera paint to print designs all along the band. When the band is dry, tie it around the child's head.

Junkanoo costume (Bahamian)

In the Bahamas on Junkanoo, scraps of crepe and tissue-paper on empty boxes become colorful costumes for the parade.

Time: 30 minutes
Materials: 1 cardboard box
             scissors
             tissue-paper scraps
             two 2-by-24-in. straps
Method: 1. Cut the top and bottom flaps off the box.
             2. Decorate all 4 sides with tissue-paper scraps.
             3. Cut 4 holes at the top of the box.
             4. Tie one end of each strap to the box, adjusting
                the straps at the other end to fit the child.

Adire eleko cloth (Nigerian)

The Yoruba people of southwest Nigeria make adire eleko cloth, a blue fabric with intricate white designs on it. It is made by spreading a cassava and alum paste on white cotton, then dyeing the cotton blue. After the cotton has dried, the paste is scraped off to reveal the white pattern.

Children can make their own adire eleko cloth by using sticks of paraffin wax as the paste, and ink on ink ball rollers as the dye. The wax resists the ink and lets the original designs magically emerge through the blue. Making the cloth is not only a multicultural activity, but also a tactile experience of negative space.

Time: 15 minutes (without drying time)
Materials: 1 square of unbleached cotton per child
             thick pad of newspapers
             masking tape
             sticks of paraffin wax or white crayons
             blue ink ball rollers
Method: 1. Put the cloth on the newspapers, taping the sides down so the cloth is stretched flat.
             2. Use the wax or crayon to draw a design on the cloth.
             3. Roll the ink heavily back and forth over the cloth. Watch the design emerge.

Adinkra cloth (Ghanaian)

Adinkra means good-bye in Ashanti and the adinkra cloth of Ghana and other West African countries was originally worn at the departure of guests or at a funeral ceremony. Today, special clothing is made of adinkra cloth printed by hand using a calabash printer. The printing ink is made from the roots of plants, and the dyed cloth must dry for a year before it can be washed without the colors running.

Children can make their own adinkra cloth. Use a utility knife to cut adinkra symbols out of squares of sponge. Show the children a sample or picture of adinkra cloth and the prepared stamps. Then dip each stamp into black acrylic paint. Press the stamp onto paper to print out a sample symbol before printing on the cloth.

Traditionally, each strip of cloth is printed with a single symbol. This strip is then sewn with bright thread to another strip, and so on, to make a big square similar to a quilt. Try this with the children, and make an adinkra wall hanging for the room. The children will enjoy telling their families which strip they printed and what their own symbol means.

Time: 20 minutes (without drying time)
Materials: sheets of paper for printing samples
             one 6-by-24-in. strip of unbleached cotton per child
             thick pads of newspaper
             black acrylic paint
             1 sponge adinkra stamp per child
             fabric glue, tape, stapler, or a needle and bright thread
Method: 1. Put the strip of cloth on a thick pad of newspaper. Choose a stamp.
             2. Print the chosen symbol on the strip many times.
             3. Hang up the strip to dry.
             4. When all the strips are completely dry, use glue, tape, stapler or a needle and thread to join them together.
             5. Hang the cloth from a curtain rod by folding over the edge and stapling it into place. The light shining through the window will illuminate the symbols. Alternatively, hang it on the wall or the bulletin board as a backdrop for the masquerade theme.

From left to right, adinkra symbols of royalty, safety, and forgiveness

Mola (Central American)

Mola means blouse in the Cuna language of Panama, but it has come to mean the decorative panel in a blouse. When making this panel the sewer first bastes together several layers of brightly colored cotton cloth. Then the sewer cuts away parts of the cloth to expose the layers underneath. The edges of the cut are turned over and appliquéd, and other colors are embroidered in the cutaway spaces. A single multi-colored mola may take weeks to complete.

This is an opportunity for children to experiment with colored tissue paper, layering it to create new colors, then cutting away again to expose hidden colors. Paper art replaces fabric art as cutting tissue is much easier than cutting cloth. Rather than using scissors, younger children can tear away sections of the tissue paper. Show the children pictures of molas made in Central America, and let them imitate the exuberant colors. When their molas are complete, hang them in a window as suncatchers.

Time: 15 minutes
Materials: 1 construction-paper frame per child
            different sizes and colors of tissue paper
            glue stick
            scissors
Method: 1. Glue a sheet of tissue paper to the frame.
            2. Glue on a second sheet and so on, until there are several layers of tissue paper.
            3. Cut or tear off some of the layers from both sides to expose the other colors.

Tapa cloth (Polynesian)

Tapa cloth is made from the bark of the white mulberry tree, and is used as a ceremonial cloth. The largest tapa cloth ever made was over a mile in length. It was made as a carpet for Queen Elizabeth II's Rolls Royce when she visited Polynesia. Make an imitation tapa cloth with the children, then use it as a ceremonial wall hanging or banner.

Time: 30 minutes
Materials: 1 square of craft paper per child
            black, brown, and red crayons
            sheets of waxed paper
            iron
            newspaper pad
            masking tape
Method: 1. Draw a design on the craft paper, coloring it in heavily.
            2. Crumple the paper into a tight ball.
            3. Open the paper out and flatten it.
            4. Put it on the newspaper pad, cover it with waxed paper (waxy side down), then iron it flat. The lines left on the paper resemble the bark patterns of the mulberry tree.
            5. When everyone has made a tapa cloth, tape all the squares together. Put the tape on the back side so that the front of the tapa cloth looks like one large sheet.

4. Discovery

Playing with dolls is a global pastime. The shape, size, and fabric of the dolls may differ, but the urge to dress and care for them is universal. The paper dolls on the following pages offer a two-dimensional manipulative experience in dressing dolls, an opportunity to develop fine motor skills, co-ordination, and creativity. Let the children make up interesting combinations from the fancy and everyday clothes, familiarizing themselves with this clothing on a daily basis.

Several ways to use the set are given below. Choose the method most appropriate to the age group and improvise variations. You may also want to add clothes that are suggested by the families in the program. Remember to read the notes that follow the dress-ups for background information on the names, uses, and suggested colors for each outfit. Take care to name each outfit correctly when identifying it for the children. Remind them that many of these dress-ups are only worn for special parties and dances, and are not worn every day.

- Photocopy and color the dolls so that there are at least four pairs corresponding to the following flesh tones: dark brown, tan, peach, and black. Glue the dolls to a bristol board or cardboard backing and laminate. Cut out the dolls. Photocopy the dress-ups and color them as suggested. Put them on a backing and laminate. Use masking tape to attach the dress-ups to the dolls.

- Photocopy the pages of dolls and dress-ups, making a copy for each child in the program. Glue the pages onto construction paper, then cut them out. Give each child a pair of dolls to color. Give them a few dress-ups each day to color and use with these dolls.

- Photocopy and glue as described immediately above. When cutting out the dress-ups, add two top tabs to each one so that the dolls can be dressed up, then moved around the table or floor area. Make doll houses and tents out of blocks and scarves and use these dolls for dramatic play.

- Photocopy, color, and laminate as described in the first suggestion. Tape each doll to a craft stick and use it as a puppet in your puppet theatre. Alternatively, glue a felt backing onto the back of the doll and use it as a feltboard figure. For this activity, make sure the dress-ups have tabs.

- Photocopy, color, and laminate as in the first suggestion. Using a needle and thread, sew a thread through the top of each doll so that it can be hung up in the room. Alternatively, glue the doll to a clothespeg and hang it up on a clothesline. Let the children choose what each doll should wear that day, then use masking tape to attach the dress-up to the doll.

- Make enlarged copies of all the dolls and dress-ups, with extra copies of the dolls. On one wall tape a long sheet of construction paper at child height. Let the children draw or paint a mural on the paper. Then glue the dolls onto the mural. Let the children color the dolls and stick scraps of fabric onto the dress-ups. Dress these dolls every day to make an ever-changing masquerade wall mural.

Masquerade dolls

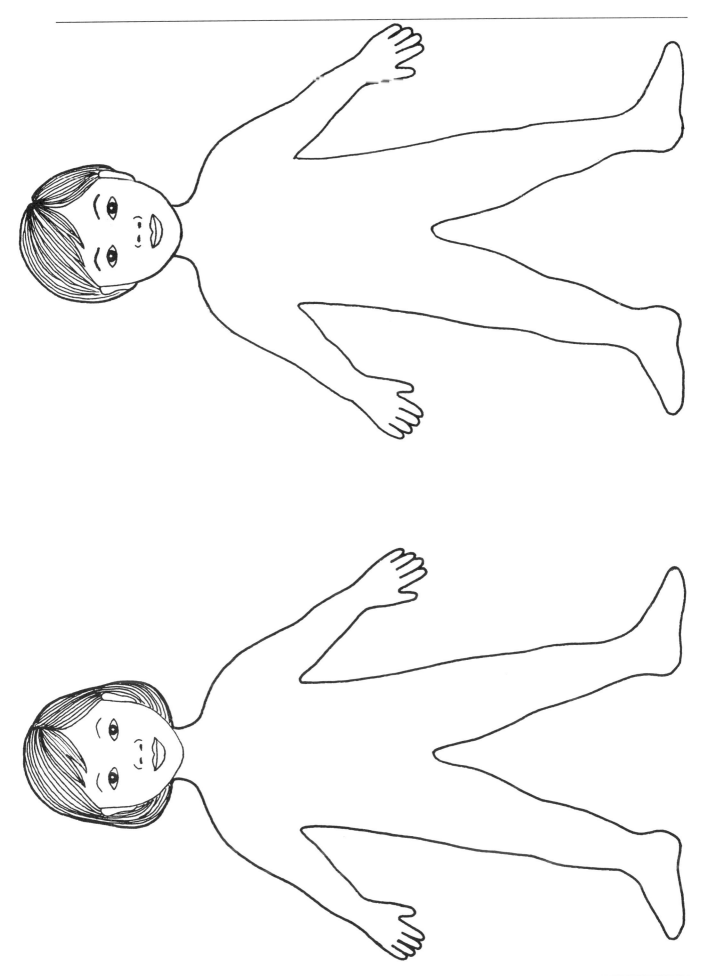

1

2

cut out

3

4

5

6

8

7

9

10

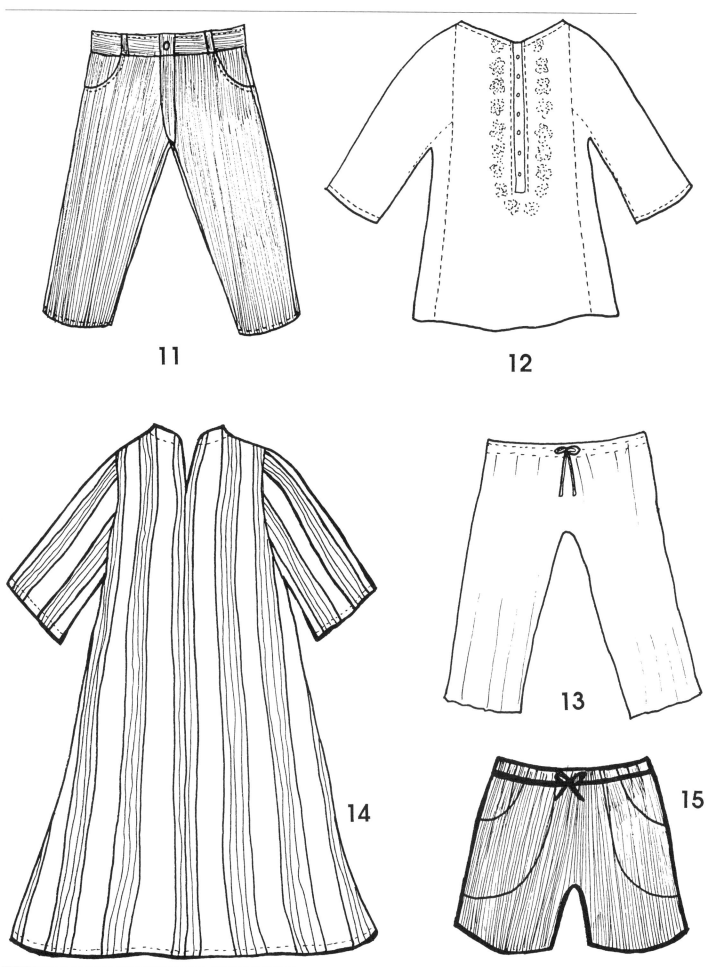

11

12

13

14

15

16

17

18

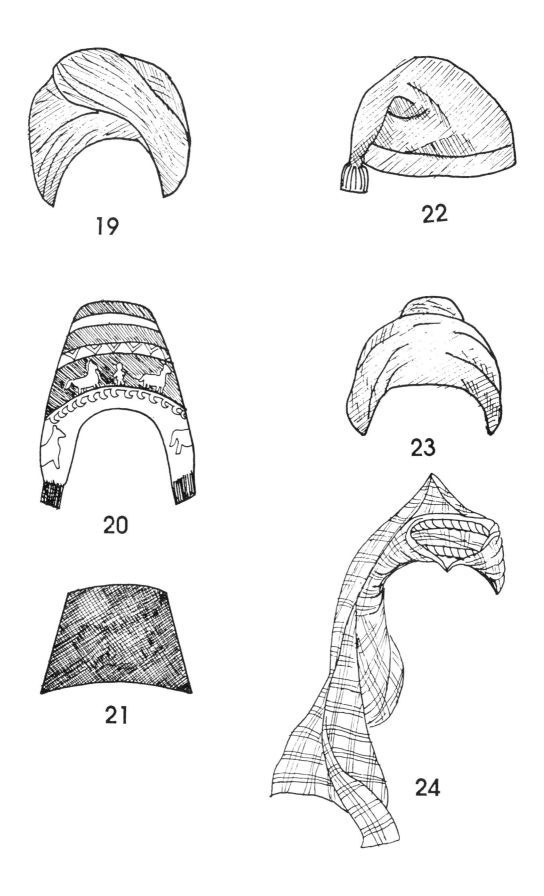

19

20

21

22

23

24

Dress-up information

1. Tea-picking Dance kimono

This kimono is worn with obi (sash), obijime (sash cord), and apron by girls in the Tea-picking Dance of Japan. The outfit represents the stylized clothes of a female field-worker. On the feet are white cotton ankle socks (tabi), and sandals (zori); the latter are also depicted at the bottom of the page. The headpiece decorated with flowers and tassels is a kansaki.

Suggested colors: blue or yellow kimono, pink obi and obijime, white apron, white trim on the kimono, black zori, white tabi

2. Doeskin fancy dress

This dress is worn by Algonquin and Haida girls for special dances, pow wows, and potlatches. It is shown with kamik, soft Inuit boots worn for special occasions. The hair is decorated with hair-ties (see p. 203).

Suggested colors: white or tan dress with multi-colored beadwork

3. Fantasia Dance dress

This dress is worn by girls in the Fantasia Dance of Sudan. It has decorative padding on the shoulders and is worn with coin jewelry and a yashmak (see p. 88 for more information about the yashmak).

Suggested colors: purple or pink dress, blue shawl, gold jewelry

4. Flower Dance dress

This dress is worn by girls in the Flower Dance of Central America. Several layers of skirts may be worn to give added bounce. The dancer's hair is woven with ribbons and flowers, and she may even balance a basket of flowers on her head during the dance.

Suggested colors: white blouse, blue, pink, and white skirt

5. Kente

The kente is a wrap tied in a knot at one shoulder. It is worn by many people in Africa and is the national dress of Ghana. It is sometimes worn with a headscarf.

Suggested colors: bright, multi-colored

6. Chogori and chima

Korean traditional dress consists of the chogori, a short bolero-type blouse or jacket, worn over the chima, a long high-waisted wrap-around skirt. The chogori is tied at the center front in a flat bow, the long ends always falling on the right side. This dress for girls and women has been fashionable for centuries and is traditionally worn on the first and the sixtieth birthdays.

Suggested colors: yellow chogori, pink chima, red flowers, green bow and cuffs

7. Vest

The vest is usually worn over a shirt or blouse by both boys and girls around the world. Vests are often padded for extra warmth.

Suggested colors: bright, multi-colored

8. Poncho

This woollen blanket has a slit in the middle for the head. Like the vest, it is worn everywhere, particularly in Mexico and Central America.

Suggested colors: yellow, red, or bright blue

9. Lenga and kameez

This outfit is worn by girls in India and Pakistan. It consists of the lenga (skirt), the kameez (blouse) and the dupatta (scarf). The dupatta is worn loosely around the neck, and is sometimes pulled gently over the head.

Suggested colors: red or blue with a lighter colored scarf

10. Shan and trousers

These are worn by both male and female Chinese Ribbon Dancers. The shan or jacket is often silk.

Suggested colors: pink or peach with green trim and design

11. Jeans

Denim pants are worn with or without a belt by boys and girls everywhere.
Suggested colors: blue

12 and 13. Kurta and shalwar

The kurta is a light, loose shirt worn with the shalwar or pyjama (drawstring pants). Both are worn as daywear by children in Pakistan and India.
Suggested colors: white, peach, or saffron with darker shades of embroidery

14. Bashiki

This cotton caftan is worn by both boys and girls in the Caribbean.
Suggested colors: multi-colored

15. Shorts

These are worn by children almost everywhere. Teamed with a shirt, shorts serve as a boy's school uniform in many parts of the world.

Suggested colors: khaki, beige, grey

16. Kente

See number 5 for description. This kente is shown with a tarboosh or kufi, a pillbox hat worn by Moslem males either by itself or under a turban.

Suggested kufi colors: white, saffron, orange, khaki, black

17. Gi

This suit consists of a hakama (shirt) and pants. Originating in Japan, it is worn everywhere today as a karate suit.

Suggested colors: white, belt color indicates level of mastery (yellow, brown, and so on)

18. Cepken and zivka

This outfit is worn by Turkish boys for special occasions. A cepken (vest) and zivka (pants) are accented with a colorful sash similar to the Métis or French Canadian flechée.

Suggested colors: white shirt, green or red pantaloons, multi-colored sash, black or red boots

19. Turban

A turban is a long piece of cloth that is wound around a person's head. Wrapping a turban is like tying a huge knot with the head at the centre. The ends of the turban are passed over and under each other, around and around, then tucked under the folds. Sometimes, for special events, turbans are fastened with a jewelled pin. Turbans are worn by some males in the Middle East, India, and parts of Asia and Africa. In Botswana and Senegal some females wear turbans, too. In the United States turbans are often associated with Sikhs because Sikh men and boys wear turbans every day. The Sikhs call the turban a keski and consider it a symbol of their religion. Sikh males do not cut their hair, but comb it into a bun which is held in place by a patka (see number 23). The turban is then wound over all.

Suggested colors: white or saffron

20. Chullo

This knitted or woven, tight-fitting helmet originates in Peru where it is usually made of llama wool. It commonly has an animal or people motif knitted along the band.

Suggested colors: bright blue with white motif

21. Fez

This cap in the shape of a truncated cone is worn by men and women in the Balkans and North Africa. It sometimes has a tassel.

Suggested colors: red or black

22. Berritta

This long, knitted hat for winter weather originated in Italy.

Suggested colors: black or navy with red trim and tassel

23. Patka

This cloth holds the hair in place under the turban. It is tied with a band called a fifti.

Suggested colors: black, brown, or navy

24. Kaffiyeh

This is a square headcloth worn by some Arabian males. The square is folded into a triangle and is placed over the head with the two points falling over the shoulders to provide an optional tie. The last point hangs in the back to protect the neck. A skullcap is often worn underneath and an agal, or decorative cord, holds the scarf on the head. It is especially popular amongst Palestinian males.

Suggested colors: red-and-white checked or black-and-white checked

5. Group time

Much masquerade group time revolves around role-playing and acting out stories of the pumpkin and jack-o'-lantern. Combine the two ideas and dress up your pumpkins for a multicultural masquerade!

Pumpkins are like people: they come in many shapes and colors. On the inside, however, they are all alike: yellow-orange pulp with edible seeds. Here is a sample of pumpkins to look for:

Chinese — yellow, red, or white, round
East, South African — white, flat-topped
Jamaican — dark green, long-necked
Middle Eastern — yellow or orange (white ones are considered lucky)
North American — orange, round
South American — yellow or orange
Spanish — green or grey, flat-topped

Go to specialty grocery stores and buy a variety of pumpkins from around the world. If there are enough, let each child choose one. Then photocopy and enlarge the hats from the Discovery section (p. 106). Color, laminate, and cut them out for dressing up the "pumpkin faces" below.

Pumpkin faces

Time: 10 minutes
Materials: variety of pumpkins
              markers
              masking tape
              hats from the Discovery section (p. 106)
Method: 1. Draw faces on the pumpkins with markers.
              2. Stick a hat on each pumpkin with masking tape. Real hats, veils, and scarves
                 can also be used.

Pumpkin faces

Pumpkin shadow play

Shadow plays or wayang kulit originated in Java over a thousand years ago. They are performed by one person, the dhalang, who manipulates the puppets and speaks all the voices as well.

The wayang or puppet is brightly colored on both sides. Its color is often symbolic. Black signifies calmness and maturity; gold, goodness; and pink, crudeness and violence. These stylized puppets are not meant to look like ordinary people but represent personality types. Make wayangs with the children using the pumpkin pattern below. Play with them in a shadow theater, and let the children be the voices for the wayangs. Put on a show using the pumpkin shapes, as well as fingers or objects such as leaves, feathers, or masks.

Time: 20 minutes
Materials: construction paper
               scissors
               crayons or markers
               one 12-in. dowel for each shape
               masking tape
               white sheet
               flashlight
Method: 1. Use the pattern below to cut several pumpkin shapes out of construction paper. Change the facial expressions to suit the puppet you want to create.
               2. Tape one end of the dowel to the back of each shape and use the other end as a handle.
               3. Hang the sheet over a table like a tablecloth. Sit under the table.
               4. Hold a shape in one hand and shine the flashlight at the back of the shape so that its shadow appears on the sheet.

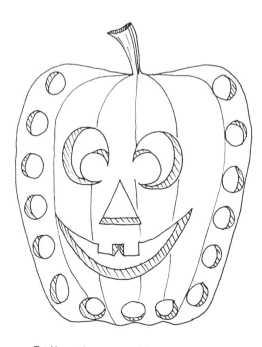

Pattern for pumpkin wayang

Pumpkin recycle

Recycling materials should be a regular part of all programs. In a multicultural program it is particularly important as a way of fostering global consciousness. Use the pumpkin to demonstrate the advantages of recycling, showing how all the parts of this food can be used.

Materials: 1 pumpkin
1 sharp knife (for adult use only)
liquid tempera paint
sheets of light brown paper

Method:
1. Cut the top off the pumpkin. This is mostly inedible but can be used as a stamp.
2. Hold the top by the stem and dip the top in the paint. Press the top onto paper to make a printed pattern of many colors of circles.
3. Scoop the seeds and pulp out of the shell. Use the seeds to make snacks (see p. 116), and serve them in the empty shell.
4. When the shell has been used and is soft, break it up and put it into the compost bin. Pumpkins grow best in ground rich with compost.

Cinderella

There are over 700 versions of this story told around the world: the tale of a girl magically transformed into a princess obviously has universal appeal. In many versions a pumpkin is changed into a magical coach that carries the girl off to the ball. Use any of the props suggested below to tell this favorite tale to the group. Then act it out with the children. You might also like to read one of the less familiar versions of the story to the children (see pp. 119-120).

- Use the doll patterns on p. 99 to make the characters: three ugly sisters, one Cinderella, one fairy, and one prince. Color each doll to suit the character, then dress them appropriately. Save a selection of fancy clothes for Cinderella's transformation. Glue backing on the dolls and laminate them.

- Put a small plastic bag inside the hollowed-out pumpkin to keep Cinderella clean in her coach.

- Carry the pumpkin coach by hand or in a sling or stretcher around the circle to bring Cinderella to the ball.

- Cut out a magic slipper using the zori sandals pattern on p. 100.

6. Food to share

Because masquerade festivals often precede a period of fasting, drinking, eating, and enjoying interesting flavors and textures are important at this time. Encourage each child to try a small portion of the delicious drinks and snacks suggested below. Each recipe serves ten.

Ginger beer (African)

Ingredients:
1 lb ginger root, peeled and grated
1 C sugar
8 C water
4 C soda water
ice

Method:
1. Put the grated ginger and sugar into a pan with the water. Boil for 1 minute, then simmer gently for 1 hour.
2. Drain the liquid into a pitcher. Discard the ginger and let cool.
3. When completely cool, add the soda water and ice and enjoy.

Tamarind juice (Caribbean)

Ingredients:
1 lb dried tamarind (available in Caribbean groceries)
1 C sugar
8 C water
ice

Method:
1. Put the tamarind and sugar in a pan with the water. Boil for 1 minute, then simmer gently for 1 hour.
2. Drain the liquid into a pitcher. Discard the tamarind seeds and let cool.
3. When completely cool, add ice and an equal amount of water.
Make this juice at the same time as the ginger beer, then compare tastes!

Banana shake (North American)

Ingredients:
3 bananas, cut into pieces
3 C milk
4 C ice cream
2 t cinnamon
ice

Method:
1. Process the bananas, milk, and ice cream in the blender until smooth. This may have to be done in 2 batches.
2. Add ice, and top each shake with a dash of cinnamon.

Yam recipes

Yams in North America are small orange vegetables with a thin peel like a potato. They are often called sweet potatoes. Chinese yams are club-shaped and grey or black. West African yams, on the other hand, are white and much larger than the North American or Chinese ones. A single one can satisfy the hunger of an entire family for a day.

The white yam has been called the potato of Africa because it is a staple daily food. Traditionally, it is boiled, then peeled and sliced. It is then pounded into a paste called fufu which is eaten with gravy or savory sauce. Other African and Caribbean yam recipes are suggested below. Buy a white yam (or smaller orange one) and try these recipes with the children.

Orange yam cups (Jamaican)

Ingredients: 8 oz yam , peeled and cut into chunks
5 oranges
2 T butter or margarine

Method: 1. Boil the yam until it is soft.
2. While the yam is cooking, cut the oranges in half and scrape out the pulp. Save the pulp and the juice in a bowl.
3. Drain the yam and mash it with the butter and 1/4 C of the saved orange juice. Mix thoroughly.
4. Stuff the yam mixture into the orange cups. Top each with a small scoop of orange pulp. Serve while still warm.

Fried yam chips (Haitian)

Ingredients: 1 lb yam
salt to taste
4 C cooking oil

Method: 1. Peel the yam, then slice it into paper-thin slices.
2. Drop the slices into very hot oil. This should only be done by an adult.
3. When the slices start to curl, take them out and drain them on paper towels. Sprinkle them with salt while still hot.

Baked yam chips (Ghanaian)

Ingredients: 1 lb yam
salt to taste

Method: 1. Peel the yam, then slice it into paper-thin slices.
2. Arrange the slices on an oiled cookie sheet and sprinkle with salt.
3. Bake in a hot oven (400° F) until crispy.

Pumpkin recipes

The pumpkin is a versatile vegetable. The flower that blooms before the fruit appears can be stuffed with meat and rice, then baked. The pulp can be boiled, roasted, or fried as a main course or used as a base for soup, pies, or jam. The seeds can be dried and salted, then eaten whole or shelled. The shelled seeds or pepitas are a popular snack food. The pumpkin shell can also be used as a serving dish for soups or stews. All the parts of the pumpkin are rich in protein, which is perhaps why the pulp is universally favored as a baby food.

Toasted pumpkin seeds

Ingredients: seeds from the pumpkin
pan of salt water (4 C water and 4 T salt)
pan of sugar water (4 C water and 4 T sugar)

Method: 1. Wash the seeds carefully, removing all the pulp.
2. Put half the seeds in the pan of salt water, half in the pan of sugar water. Let them soak in the water overnight.
3. Put both sets of seeds in a colander and drain well. Pat dry with paper towels.
4. Spread out the seeds on a cookie sheet. Dry in a hot oven (400° F) or put into a dehydrator for the prescribed time.
5. Cool, then compare tastes.

Pumpkin soup

Ingredients: 1 small onion, chopped
3 C peeled, cubed pumpkin
3 T margarine or butter
1/2 C orange juice
1 C light cream
salt and pepper to taste

Method: 1. Sauté the onion and cubed pumpkin in the margarine until the onion is transparent.
2. Add the orange juice and simmer 20 minutes or until the pumpkin is soft.
3. Whirl the mixture in a blender until smooth.
4. Add the cream and heat gently until warm. Season with salt and pepper if necessary.

Pumpkin custard

Ingredients: 1 medium-sized pumpkin, hollowed-out
4 eggs
1 C sugar
4 C milk, scalded
1 t ground nutmeg

Method: 1. Beat the eggs in a large bowl until frothy. Slowly add the sugar and scalded milk.
2. Mix well, then pour into the pumpkin shell. Top with the nutmeg.
3. Set the shell in a shallow pan of cold water. Bake for 1 hour at 350° F or until an inserted knife comes out clean.

Coffee time

In countries with abundant year-round rainfall and constant temperatures of around 68° F, the coffee tree grows. This slender evergreen tree produces tiny white blossoms and coffee berries. The unripe berries are green, turning red as they ripen. In the center of each berry is a pair of coffee beans. It is these beans that are roasted, ground, then boiled to make a drink enjoyed around the world.

There are a variety of methods of grinding and making coffee, each reflecting a particular culture. In many countries children drink coffee every morning, while in the United States many children are accustomed to adults drinking coffee. They are usually quite curious about this adult drink. Use this curiosity to introduce children to the aromatic beauty of the coffee berry.

- Show the children a variety of coffee berries or beans from a local coffee shop. Put each kind in a plastic bottle with the flag of its homeland taped to the outside. Examples are: Santa Domingas (Dominican Republic), Harrar (Ethiopia), Antigua (Guatemala), Kona (Hawaii), Blue Mountain (Jamaica), or Mocha (Yemen).

- Tell the story of coffee as recounted in the Turkish legend of Kaldi.

Kaldi

Kaldi the goatherd loved to sleep while his goats ate their grass. One day he awoke with a start to see his goats bleating with joy and dancing. Kaldi could not believe his eyes!

He ran to them and found they were nibbling not on grass but on red berries. He scooped them up and tasted them. His eyes grew bigger and bigger. He felt so awake, not tired or sleepy like before. Excited and full of energy, he ran home to tell his wife and family.

"What nonsense!" they said, as they threw the berries into the fire. But the berries split and filled the room with a most delicious smell. Quickly the family scooped out the roasted berries and dropped them into cold water. The water turned brown and smelled wonderful. Cautiously, they tasted it.

How delicious! They, too, felt awake and alive! Excited, they ran back to the hillside to look for more berries. Kaldi's gift of coffee was much enjoyed and shared for many years. But, I am sorry to say, it was never shared with the goats again!

Invite the families in for a coffee party. Serve the adults several varieties of coffee and compare tastes. Children could have a version of chocolate caliente with very little or no coffee. Most masquerade celebrations feature bonfires, candles, or fireworks as symbols of the burning of a devil or a witch. For the coffee party, put candles in safe containers on the table and light them, or use sparklers to create a festive mood. Some children may be frightened by the whizzing and banging of real fireworks. Holding a sparkler with an adult nearby is a gentler way to enjoy this. Each recipe serves ten.

Boiled coffee (Palestinian)

Ingredients: 4 oz coffee beans
12 C water
1/4 C sugar

Method: 1. Grind the beans to a fine powder using a mortar and pestle or a grinder.
2. Boil together the water and sugar, then add the powder and stir.
3. When the mixture froths pour some of the froth into each cup.
   This froth symbolizes good fortune, so spread the wealth around.
4. Bring the coffee to the boil again, then fill up the cups.

Café au lait (French) or Café con leche (Spanish)

Ingredients: 1/4 C instant decaffeinated coffee
1/4 C brown sugar
10 C milk
1 t cinnamon

Method: 1. Put the coffee, sugar, and milk in a pot and mix slowly over low heat.
2. When the mixture is very warm, pour into cups.
3. Top each cup of café au lait with a sprinkle of cinnamon.

Chocolate caliente (Mexican)

Ingredients: 2 t instant decaffeinated coffee
4 oz unsweetened grated chocolate
1/4 C white sugar
10 C milk

Method: 1. Combine the coffee, chocolate, sugar, and milk and cook over hot water
   until the chocolate melts.
2. When very warm, twirl a molinillo (wooden chocolate stirrer) between your palms
   to whirl the mixture until foamy. Alternatively, whip with a rotary beater.
   Pour into cups and serve.

Resources for educators

Cosner, Sharon. **Masks around the World and How to Make Them**. New York: David McKay, 1979.
Step-by-step drawings show how to make masks of various cultures.

Dundes, Alan, ed. **Cinderella: a Casebook**. New York: Wildman, 1983.
Some of the 700 versions of Cinderella are simply told in this book.

Haldane, Suzanne. **Painting Faces**. New York: Dutton, 1988.
Colour photographs and simple text depict face-painting in many cultures and in many theatres.

Harrold, Robert and Phyllida Legg. **Folk Costumes of the World**. London: Blandford, 1986.
Folk dance costumes are explained and illustrated.

May, Robin. **Festivals: Hallowe'en**. Hove, East Sussex: Wayland, 1984.
The background and stories surrounding Hallowe'en are clearly told and illustrated.

Mayled, Jon. **Festivals: Carnival**. Hove, East Sussex: Wayland, 1987.
Color photographs and simple text document Carnival the world over.

Steitzer, Ulli. **A Haida Potlatch**. Vancouver: Douglas and McIntyre, 1984.
The spiritual meaning of the potlatch is illustrated with photographs of one family's experience.

Tutiah, Marvis, ed. **Folk Costumes: a Colouring Adventure in Canadian Themes**. Winnipeg: Hyperion, 1980.
Coloring books are not generally favored for creativity, but this one offers full-page, detailed drawings of authentic folk costumes.

Storybooks for all age groups (2-6 years)

Aardema, Verna. **Bimwili and the Zimwi**. New York: Dial, 1985.
Fast action and an All-Devouring Pumpkin called Zimwi make this Tanzanian folktale compelling.

Adams, Dawn. **Potlatch**. Vancouver: Wedge, 1985.
Colorful drawings and simple text tell the story of a Haida girl's special potlatch.

Anno, Mitsumasa. **Anno's Counting House**. New York: Philomel, 1982.
This book stretches the child's visual perception skills and can also be read from back to front.

Asch, Rochelle Lisa. **The Longest Hallowe'en**. New York: Scholastic, 1987.
Rebecca, a diabetic, shares Hallowe'en candy with friends in hospital.

Bang, Betsy. **The Old Woman and the Red Pumpkin: a Bengali Folk Tale**. New York: Macmillan, 1975.
A clever grandmother outwits a succession of animals by climbing inside her big pumpkin.

Bannerji, Himanji. **The Two Sisters**. Toronto: Kids Can, 1978.
This Bengali/English Cinderella story rewards one sister with a prince, and one with a python.

Belknap, Jodi Parry. **Felissa and the Magic Tikling Bird**. Honolulu: Island Heritage, 1973.
This is a sensitive story of a crippled Filipino girl who dares to dance at Carnival.

Buchanan, Joan. **Nothing Else But Yams for Supper!** Windsor, Ontario: Black Moss, 1988.
A girl who eats only yams discovers the new tastes of guacamole, bean curd, and burritos.

Czernecki, Stefan and Timothy Rhodes. **The Time Before Dreams**. Winnipeg: Hyperion, 1989.
A Central American Shaman unlocks dreams for some and a nightmare for himself.

Demi. **Liang and the Magic Paintbrush**. New York: Holt, Rhinehart and Winston, 1980.
This fantasy set in ancient China combines magic and illusion to depict a poor boy's dream come true.

Garrison, Christian. **The Dream Eater**. New York: Aladdin, 1986.
Yukio, a Japanese boy, solves the problem of the villagers tormented by bad dreams. Introduce this with the film, **The Man who Stole Dreams**.

Grace, Patricia. **Watercress Tuna and the Children of Champion Street**. New York: Puffin, 1985.
A tuna with a magic throat leads young New Zealanders on a wildly exuberant dance, colorfully depicted by Robyn Kahukiwa.

Hoban, Tana. **Take Another Look**. New York: Greenwillow, 1981.
This wordless book of photographs invites children to look again at everyday objects; equally stimulating is Hoban's **Look! Look! Look!**

Louie, Ai-Ling. **Yeh-Shen: a Cinderella Story from China**. New York: Philomel, 1982.
This Chinese fable, surprisingly similar to the European fairytale, is poetically told and illustrated.

Pachano. **Changing Clothes**. James Bay, Quebec: Cree Cultural Centre, 1985.
Color photographs and simple text contrast Cree clothing worn in the past with that of today.

Price, Christine. **Dancing Masks of Africa**. New York: Charles Scribner's Sons, 1975.
Melodic prose and powerful linocuts depict masks in action in West Africa, with background information for the teacher; equally exciting is Price's **Talking Drums of Africa**.

Steptoe. John. **Mufaro's Beautiful Daughters**. New York: Lothrop, Lee and Shepard, 1987.
There is no pumpkin coach in this Zimbabwean Cinderella, but the beautiful daughter does outwit the cruel one to marry her prince.

Williams, Vera. **Music, Music for Everyone**. New York: Greenwillow, 1984.
When Rosa's European grandmother becomes ill, Rosa and her friends start the Oak Street Band in her honor, and soon they have young and old dancing to their songs.

Records and tapes

April and Susan, **Dinosaur Tango** (Join In Music, 1988).

Brodey, Jerry, **Carnival** (Tapestry, 1982).

Dario Domingues, **Tupac Amaru: Awakening in Rhythms** (AMOK, 1987).

Messenjah, **Session** (WEA, 1984). Especially good is "Reggae Party."

Schneider, Bob. **Having a Good Time** (Capitol, 1983).

Schonbrun, **B.L.U.M.A.** (Bluma, 1977). Available from B.L..U.M.A, 100 Spadina Road, #203, Toronto, Ontario M5R 2I7.

Films

The Man Who Stole Dreams (12:00) NFB
In this animated film a little girl rescues dreams and returns them to their rightful owners.

Masquerade (27:56) NFB
Different ways of making masks and costumes are explored by animated puppets.

The Tender Tale of Cinderella Penguin (9:57) NFB
This animated film without words follows a penguin named Cinderella through the traditional tale.

CHAPTER FOUR

Festivals of light

Festivals of light: celebrations of the human spirit

Light is a universal symbol of the human spirit and its connection with the divine. Candles, fireworks, multi-colored electric lights, and stars are common to many spiritual festivals. In Japan on Obon, candles are placed in small boats on the river just as they are in Thailand on Loy Krathong. In Luxembourg at Candlemas, children carry candles from door to door like Greek carollers and Swedish Star Boys. In the Ukraine, carollers carry a big star as they go from house to house. During the Jewish holiday of Chanukkah, the African-American celebration of Kwanzaa, and the Christian observance of Advent, candles are lit in sequence to mark the days.

Light is especially significant at festivals associated with a nativity; for example, Christmas and the birth of Jesus, and Milad-an-Nabi and the birth of Mohammed. Nativity stories of Buddha, Mohammed, Jesus, and Sikh Guru Nanok show light heralding birth in an extraordinary way. From this association of birth and light has evolved today's custom of candles on a birthday cake. Begin with the children's own birthday experiences when introducing these religious nativity stories.

These important spiritual occasions for the community are also very joyous. There is feasting and gift-giving; family members congregate; holiday treats are prepared; and children anticipate gifts and surprises. At the heart of the celebration is the glow of light.

Acknowledge these festivals and share in their spirit. Many are lengthy: Divali lasts from three to ten days; Chanukkah, eight; and Christmas, twelve. In the Philippines, Christmas is celebrated for almost a month, from December 16 to January 6. Take time yourself to lead into these festivals, setting the mood, then slowly introducing their many similarities.

Following is a list of festivals of light and their corresponding dates. Dates marked with an asterisk (*) are movable and depend upon either lunar or religious calendars. If a festival is associated with a particular place or people within a country, this is noted in parentheses. Although many of these festivals are celebrated in the United States, the place of origin of each one is keyed by number to a point on the map.

1. Armenia	Gaghant	January 1
2. Canada (Quebec)	Le Réveillon	December 24
3. China	Winter Festival	December 21
4. Colombia	El Día de Los Reyes	January 6
5. Dominican Republic	El Día de Los Reyes	January 6
6. France	Le Réveillon	December 24
7. Germany	Lampen Laufen	August
8. Italy	St Nicholas Day	December 6
9. Italy (Sicily)	St Lucia Day	December 13
10. Japan	Obon	July 13,14,15
	Tanabata	July 7
11. Luxembourg	Candlemas	February 2
12. Mexico	Los Posados	December 16
13. Nicaragua	El Día de Los Reyes	January 6
14. Philippines	Christmas	December 16-January 6
15. Poland	Wigilia	December 24
16. Puerto Rico	El Día de Los Reyes	January 6

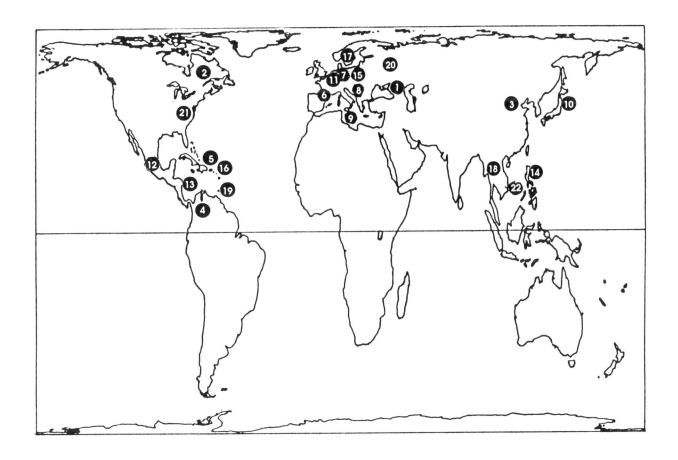

17. Sweden	St Lucia Day	December 13
18. Thailand	Loy Krathong	* November 17
19. Trinidad, Tobago	Deeyah Dewali	* October
20. Ukraine	Sviaty Vechir	January 6
21. United States (African-American)	Kwanzaa	December 26-January 1
22. Vietnam	Gíang Sinh	December 25
Buddhism	Wesak	* May
Christianity	Christmas Day	December 25
Greek Orthodox	Christmas Day	January 6
Hinduism	Divali	* October/November
	Ramnavmi	* March/April
	Janmashtemi	* August/September
Islam	Milad-an-Nabi	* October
Judaism	Chanukkah	* December
Sikhism	Sikh Guru Nanok's Birthday	* November

Using the festivals of light theme

GOAL   To show the universality of celebrations of light and birth

OBJECTIVES   To present similarities among the gift-giving traditions of many cultures and religions

To make and use decorations associated with these traditions

To celebrate some special religious birthdays

To identify and explore sources of light and shadow

To introduce and use the basic vocabulary of this theme

You may also want to add your own objectives. If Christmas is already familiar to all the children, this is an opportunity to introduce other festivals of light. Show the similarities between the traditions of Christmas and those of Chanukkah, Kwanzaa, Tanabata, and so on. Begin with the familiar and gradually introduce the less familiar. This theme is a wonderful balance to Christmas commercialism. By focusing on the more supernatural elements — candles that bring wishes, stars that tell stories — children can enjoy another aspect of the season. When the gift-giving begins, introduce the children to Befana, Babushka, St Nicholas, and other traditional gift-givers. Focus on sharing and giving to others, rather than on making lists for Santa.

As this is often a holiday time for parents, they may have more time to participate in the program. Help them by offering concrete tasks; for example, send home the directions and materials for some of the decorations. Encourage parents to make them with their children in the evening and bring them back to the program in the morning. Such an activity may prompt recollections of similar festivals, memories that parents may be willing to share with all of the children in the program.

This theme can be explored in December with Chanukkah and Christmas, in July with Tanabata and Obon, or October with Divali as the central focus. It can also replace the individual birthday parties of your program. Some Jehovah's Witness or Seventh Day Adventist families may celebrate religious nativities rather than personal birthdays, and may not want their children participating in other children's birthday parties. Be sensitive to this. If there are children who are regularly left out of these occasions, plan a more inclusive nativity celebration.

VOCABULARY LIST

flame	stable	poinsettia	visiting
lantern	crib	star	carolling
lamp	birthday	tree	greeting
candle	nativity	ornament	giving
twinkle	family	bell	decorating

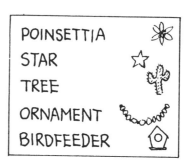

Vocabulary card, front and back faces

1. Setting the mood

The Tree symbolizes hope, unity, and strength. The Chinese call it the Tree of Life; the Hindus, the Tree of Knowledge; the Christians, the Christmas Tree. Make this visual prop the focus of your theme. Rather than the traditional conifer, use the program tree, a tree branch, potted orange or palm tree, or papier mâché cactus. Make decorations from the suggestions that follow, personalize them with special touches, then hang them on the tree. Ask parents to make decorations that incorporate their own cultural symbols.

Decorating or trimming the tree may last several weeks. Tell the story of each decoration at group time, explaining its origin and special meaning. At each stage of decoration photograph both the tree and the decorators (parents and children). The photographs will remind the children throughout the year of the tree and its meanings.

Newspaper tree

Young children may want to take home a small tree. Recycle old newspapers and scraps to make this simple individualized tree.

Time: 30 minutes
Materials: 1 sheet of newspaper per child
masking tape
1 empty juice can per child
spray bottles of liquid tempera paint
glue
tissue paper and fabric scraps
glitter
Method: 1. Fold the sheet of newspaper along the middle fold-line to make a rectangle. Beginning from a short edge, roll it into a tight tube. Tape the tube in place.
2. Tear strips of newspaper from the top to midway to form the branches of the tree. Put the tree in the juice can.
3. Spray the tree with paint so that all the branches are covered.
4. When the paint is dry, dip the scraps into glue, then press them onto the branches.
5. Complete the tree by dabbing glitter on any bare branches.

Blandfordia or Christmas bell (Australian)

Christmas falls during Australia's summer and the red and yellow pendulous blossoms of the Christmas bell hang in bunches everywhere. Show the children pictures of these blossoms, then let them make these weightier imitations to hang around the room.

Time: 10 minutes
Materials: red and yellow balloons
             green raffia or crepe paper
Method: 1. Fill each balloon half-full with water, then knot it at the top.
          2. Tie 2 or 3 balloons together with 24-in, green raffia or crepe paper.
          3. Stretch out the raffia or crepe to resemble leaves.

Poinsettia (Mexican)

A Mexican legend tells of a little girl who had no flowers for the nativity scene. An angel told her to take a bouquet of weeds instead. As she approached the scene, the leaves on the weeds changed to bright red and became poinsettias or "Fire Flowers of the Holy Night".

Time: 15 minutes
Materials: red construction-paper leaf shapes
             red felt leaf shapes to match paper ones
             glue
             hole punch
             paper fasteners
Method: 1. Glue the felt leaf shapes to the paper ones.
          2. Stack 5 or 6 leaf shapes, then punch a hole through 1 end of the stack. Push the paper fastener through the hole.
          3. Fan out the leaves to resemble a flower. Tighten the paper fastener to hold the leaves in place.

Mirror star (Indian, Scandinavian)

On Christmas Scandinavians often put an interlocking star on top of their trees. This shiny paper star resembles shishadur, the mirrored cloth originating in Saurashtra, India.

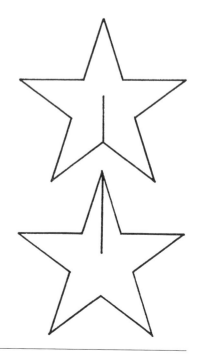

Time: 10 minutes
Materials: 2 construction-paper stars per child
             aluminum foil or silver origami paper scraps
             glue
             scissors
Method: 1. Glue the shiny paper scraps to both sides of both stars.
          2. Cut a slit halfway through both stars as shown.
          3. Fit the 2 stars together.

Straw star (Caribbean, Swedish)

In many European countries, straw is laid under the Christmas tablecloth and is used for tree decorations as a reminder of the straw in the stable of Bethlehem. Recycle straw from old placemats, brooms, or harvest decorations to make these stars, then hang them on the tree and make a wish.

Time: 10 minutes
Materials: four 3-in. lengths of straw per child
             1 twist-tie per child
Method: 1. Scrape the paper off the twist-tie.
             2. Make an X-shape with 2 lengths of straw,
                then bind them together with a twist-tie.
             3. Make a second X-shape, then use the same
                twist-tie to bind the second shape to the first.

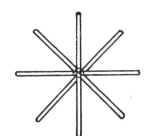

Akuaba doll (Ghanaian)

Large families are considered desirable in many cultures. Much of a woman's status may depend on her fertility. Many children mean many hands to help in the family business, field, or kitchen. Large families also allow parents to look forward to security and care in their old age. It is only recently in Europe and North America that aging parents are often not cared for by their children, and that children are regarded as economic liabilites rather than as assets.

The desire for many children is shown in the fertility charms carried by some women in Asia and Africa. In Ghana, akuaba dolls are carried on the woman's back, or worn around her neck. The head shape of each doll corresponds to the mother's wish for the child: round for wisdom, oval for a girl, square for a boy. Today wooden akuaba dolls are made commercially throughout West Africa. Use your choice of head shape to make the akuaba doll, improvising scrap materials for earrings and necklaces. The doll can be placed in or under the tree or hung from a branch by taping a hook to the back of the doll's head. It can also be used as a nativity figure (see p. 139), particularly since it is a traditional birth charm.

Time: 20 minutes
Materials: 2 craft sticks per child
             glue or masking tape
             4 in. of plastic-coated wire per child
             small clay, plastic, or wooden beads
             one 3-in. cardboard circle, oval, or square per child
             markers or crayons
             2 large safety pins per child
Method: 1. Glue or tape the 2 craft sticks together in
                a t-shape.
             2. String a few beads on the wire, then twist the
                ends together to make a necklace.
             3. Slip the necklace over 1 craft stick.
             4. Glue or tape the circle over this same stick.
                Draw facial features on the circle.
             5. For earrings, push a safety pin through either
                side of the circle, then close each pin.

Choinka (Polish)

The choinka are paper chains that are wound around the tree or used as decorations for windows or doors at Christmas time.

Time: 10-30 minutes
Materials: tapestry needle and thread
             2-in. squares of tissue-paper
             2-in. lengths of drinking straws
Method: 1. Thread the tapestry needle, knotting one end.
             2. Sew through the middle of a paper square, gathering it like a bow.
             3. Push the needle through a straw.
             4. Repeat, alternating bow and straw until the thread is full. Then remove the needle and knot the end of the thread.

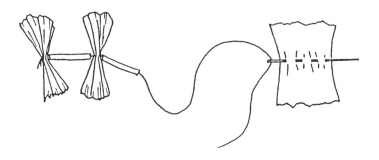

Peace chain

This easy, decorative chain requires no gluing. Precut the shapes from paper scraps (variety adds to the visual appeal), then ask each parent to write a message of peace on a shape. Children can draw or print their own messages on the shape. Link each shape to the next, making a long chain of peace.

Time: 5-15 minutes
Materials: precut circle shapes (see pattern)
             pens, markers, crayons
Method: 1. Draw, print or write a message of peace on the circle shape.
             2. Loop one circle through another, and continue looping each new circle through the preceding one until all the circles are used.

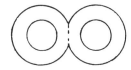

Pattern

Linked circle shapes making a peace chain

Birdfeeder ornaments

Winter is a lean season for the birds as their usual diet of seeds and insects is covered with snow. In most northern countries people put out bread crumbs and other tidbits to help the birds survive the cold winter. In Norway and Denmark during December, sheaves of rye or wheat are tied on posts and high buildings to feed the birds. Hang the following decorations on the tree as reminders of our feathered friends. When the tree is put away, hang the birdfeeders outside on a branch or post and watch them gradually disappear.

Birdfeeder wreath (Swedish)

Time:	15 minutes
Materials:	2 T flour
	1 T water
	craft stick
	waxed paper
	4 T birdseed
	ornament hook
Method:	1. Mix the flour and water together with the craft stick to make a thick paste.
	2. Use the paste to draw a circle on the waxed paper.
	3. Press birdseed onto the paste.
	4. Allow the paste to dry thoroughly.
	5. Carefully remove the birdseed design from the waxed paper, and use a hook to hang it on the tree.

Birdfeeder pinecone (Canadian)

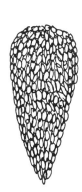

Time:	15 minutes
Materials:	2 T flour
	1 T water
	craft stick
	pinecone
	4 T birdseed
	one 6-in. pipecleaner
Method	1. Mix the flour and water together with the craft stick to make a thick paste. Dab the paste on the tips of the pinecone.
	2. Press birdseed onto the paste.
	3. Place the pinecone on one of the branches. of the tree, or use the pipecleaner to tie it to the underside of a branch.

2. Music and movement

Festivals of light are often times for visiting. People go from house to house with songs and music, nativity scenes, or simply good wishes. During Los Posados, Central and South American communities re-enact the story of Mary and Joseph. The actors representing the couple carry candles through the streets, asking for shelter. At each house they are told there is no room. Their search continues every night until Christmas Eve when they finally find a house that has room. Then everyone kneels before an altar or nativity scene to pray.

Candelita (Dominican)

In Puerto Rico groups of trullas or carol singers walk or drive across the countryside, singing traditional carols. In Greece groups sing out Christmas cheer, going from house to house just as the Ukrainian koliadnyky or carollers do. All of these carollers carry candles, lanterns, or flashlights. Imitate them by playing this game, either outside in the snow or inside in a large space.

Time: 15-30 minutes
Materials: 1 paper or real candle per child (unlit)
Method: 1. Spread out in the yard so that everyone has plenty of space. Put a candle on the ground beside each child.
             2. The leader, who does not have a candle, goes to the first child and asks for a candelita. The child replies, "Ve a la otra esquinita" ("Go to the other corner").
             3. The leader then says, "Okay", and everyone changes places, leaving the candles behind. The leader tries to find an empty place with a candle. The child without a candle is the new leader.
             4. Repeat the game until all the children have a chance to be the leader.

My candles (Jewish)

The chanukiyah or nine-branch candlestick is used just on Chanukkah, whereas the menorah may be used every Sabbath. Use a chanukiyah with one candle in it to play this game. Put it in the middle of the circle with eight children walking or skipping around it. Each child carries a candle with a number on it from 1 to 8, placing the candle in the chanukiyah when that number is called. Sing a song to keep the rhythm.

In the circle I can see the glow
From my chanukiyah way down low,
Who has the first little candle,
On this the first night of Chanukkah?

Continue, changing the numbers each time, until all eight candles have been placed in the chanukiyah.

Piñata (Spanish)

A piñata is a gaily decorated container, often shaped to resemble an animal, that is full of treats or coins. It is hung high at a party. Each person is blindfolded, handed a stick, twirled around, and given a turn to try to break the piñata. The attempts are usually quite hilarious and, when the piñata is finally broken, there is a mad scramble for treats. Although this custom has Spanish origins, piñata parties are held all over America today.

Breaking the piñata is often the climax of Los Posados. It certainly is a moment children anticipate with excitement and longing. Making the piñata can be just as much fun. Fill it with small treats such as candy canes, tissue-paper flowers, tiny toys, or paper horns. Hang it up for at least a week so that everyone can see it and dream about its contents. A simple piñata can also be made by filling a decorated paper bag, and hanging it up for the children to break.

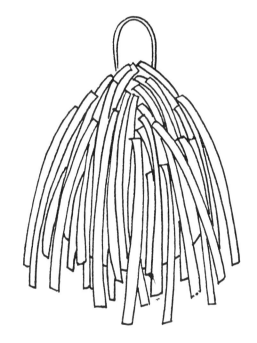

Time: two 30-minute sessions: making and filling

Materials: 1 balloon
newspapers
thin flour-and-water paste
tissue-paper strips
1 sharp knife (for adult use only)
8 in. of plastic-coated wire
filling materials (suggestions below)

Method: 1. Blow up the balloon and knot the top. Place the balloon on a thick pad of newspapers.
2. Tear sheets of newspaper into small strips.
3. Dip each strip into the thin paste, then smooth it over the surface of the balloon. Continue applying strips until the whole surface of the balloon is covered with newspaper. Smooth out all the wrinkles and bumps in the newspaper.
4. Hang the piñata until dry.
5. Paste strips of tissue paper over the newspaper until it is completely covered. Let some strips dangle down loosely.
6. Cut a small hole in the piñata and save the piece. Put in the filling (candy, flowers, blowers, toys). Paste the saved piece back over the hole to seal it.
7. Fasten the wire to opposite sides of the hole to make a handle.
8. Hang up the piñata by the handle so that it is just above head height.

Carolling

Visitors are usually welcome at Christmas time, so share the multicultural spirit of the program with the community by drawing up a list and making visits. Bring the children to see a real nativity scene in a church or a carolling concert. Teach the older children a few lines of songs associated with this time of year, then sing them to local senior citizens. Suggestions follow. Ask a parent to help with pronunciation, or use one of the tapes listed on p. 160 as a guide.

Il est né le divin Enfant (French)

Il est né le divin Enfant,
Jouez hautbois, résonnez musettes,
Il est né le divin Enfant,
Chantons tous son avènement!
Nous voici dans cet heureux temps,
Annoncé par tous les prophètes.
Nous voici dans cet heureux temps,
Appelé de nos voeux ardents!

He is born now the Child divine,
Play the oboes and bagpipes,
He is born now the Child divine,
Let us sing his nativity!
Here are we in this happy time,
Announced by all the prophets,
Here are we in this happy time,
Called by all our dearest wishes!

Feliz Navidad (Spanish)

Feliz Navidad, Feliz Navidad.
Feliz Navidad, Prospero año y Felicidad.
Feliz Navidad, Feliz Navidad.
Feliz Navidad, Prospero año y Felicidad.
I want to wish you a Merry Christmas,
I want to wish you a Merry Christmas,
I want to wish you a Merry Christmas from the bottom of my heart.

Jesous Ahatonhia (Huron)

'Twas in the moon of winter time when all the birds had fled,
That mighty Gitchi Manitou sent angel choirs instead.
Before their light the stars grew dim,
And wandering hunters heard the hymn:
Jesus your son is born. Jesus is born. Jesous Ahatonhia!

On Christmas Day (English)
sung to the tune of, "I saw three ships come sailing in"

There was a pig went out to dig on Christmas day, on Christmas day.
There was a pig went out to dig on Christmas day in the morning.

There was a crow went out to mow on Christmas day, on Christmas day.
There was a crow went out to mow on Christmas day in the morning.

There was a cow went out to plow on Christmas day, on Christmas day.
There was a cow went out to plow on Christmas day in the morning.

There was a sheep went out to reap on Christmas day, on Christmas day.
There was a sheep went out to reap on Christmas day in the morning.

Birthday songs

Many festivals of light celebrate the birth of a religious leader. The circumstances surrounding their births are similar: Buddha, Jesus, and Mohammed were all born in humble surroundings. Krishna was born as a prince but was spirited away to live safely with a humble cowherd. Angels appeared to announce the births of Mohammed, Buddha, and Jesus.

Celebrate these wonderful births and the joy all new babies bring by having a "birth-day" party that includes everyone. This is particularly meaningful for children who do not celebrate individual birthdays, and is another way to let all the children in the program feel special. Sing the following songs to the tune of "Happy birthday to you."

French:

Bonne fête à toi,
Bonne fête à toi,
Bonne fête à _____,
Bonne fête à toi.

Italian:

Buon compleano a tè,
Buon compleano a tè,
Buon compleano a _____,
Buon compleano a tè.

Spanish:

Feliz compleaños a tú,
Feliz compleaños a tú,
Feliz compleaños a _____,
Feliz compleaños a tú.

Hora (Jewish)

The hora is a traditional Jewish group dance. It begins with only a few dancers and ends with everyone in a swirling dance line. Match the complexity of the dance steps to the developmental level of the group. Dance the hora to a traditional song such as "Hava Negillah."

Time: 15-30 minutes
Method:
1. Hold hands with a partner, raising both hands above head-height. Hop and kick once in one direction, then once in the other, in time to the rhythm of the music.
2. Continue, adding a third child to the line, then a fourth, and so on. When all the children are in the line, close it to form a circle.
3. Dance the hora faster and faster and skip in time to the music.

3. Art

Lanterns and candles are used around the world to brighten the darkness of winter. Their flickering light casts more interesting shadows than the electric light bulb. Let the children work in pairs to color in their silhouettes on paper hung on the wall. Make shadow pictures with black and white paper. Capture the brightness of the lights with collage materials such as gold and silver tinsel, aluminum foil, shiny wrapping paper, glitter, sequins, and metallic fabric.

Paper lantern

Before making a real lantern, children may want to experiment with a paper one, learning to carry it and shine light through it. This paper lantern can also be used as a tree decoration or a light for the housekeeping center.

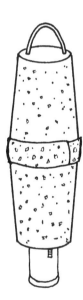

Time: 20 minutes
Materials: 2 paper cups per child
            scissors
            tapestry needle threaded with red yarn
            masking tape
            red liquid tempera paint
            wide brushes
            glue
            glitter
            flashlight
Method: 1. Cut the bottom out of 1 cup.
            2. Sew through the bottom of the other cup to make
               a loop of yarn on the outside for a handle.
               Remove the needle and tie the ends of the yarn
               together on the inside.
            3. Tape the large ends of the cups together.
            4. Use a wide brush to paint over the outside surface
               of the 2 cups and the tape.
            5. When the paint is dry, spread glue over the painted
               surface and sprinkle glitter on the glue.
            6. Shine the flashlight through the bottom of the lantern
               to make it glow.

Tin lantern (German, Mexican, Nicaraguan, Spanish)

Pierced tin lanterns are used in many countries. Spanish children in rural areas may use them for outdoor lighting. Mexican children may carry them in Los Posados. German children often carry them in Lampen Laufen. Like the Indonesian wayang puppets (see p. 112), they cast interesting shadows in the dark.

Prepare for this activity by filling one tin can per child with water, then freezing the cans overnight. An ice-filled can is much easier for young children to punch. Make the lanterns outdoors or indoors on a plastic sheet. Have a bucket and sponge ready to soak up the water as the ice melts.

Time: 15 minutes
Materials: 1 ice-filled tin can per child
               hammers and short nails
               1 bucket and sponge
               1 short, fat candle per child
               one 8-in. plastic-coated wire per child
               long wooden matches
Method: 1. Use a hammer and nail to punch a hole on either side of the
                  can's open end.
               2. Punch more holes all over the sides of the can.
               3. When there are enough holes, empty the ice into the bucket
                  and turn the can upside down to dry.
               4. When it is completely dry, turn it over and place the candle
                  inside.
               5. To make a handle, push the wire through the first 2 holes
                  made on the can. Twist the wire together at each hole to
                  keep it in place.
               6. Hang up the lantern, then light the candle. To carry the lit
                  lantern safely, cover the top of the can.

Ice light (Finnish)

Ice lights are lined up on Finnish window ledges during December just as dipa lamps are placed on ledges and along driveways of Hindu homes during Divali. Both are lit to attract gift-givers — Father Christmas or Lakshmi — and to brighten a holiday time. Make various colours and shapes of ice lights with the children, and use them indoors or outdoors. Used indoors, they also demonstrate melting, so have a bucket and sponge ready.

Time: 5 minutes
Materials: 1 tin can per child
               1 short, fat candle per child
               water
               matches
               food coloring (optional)
Method: 1. Fill the tin can with (colored) water.
               2. Float the candle in the water and freeze the can overnight.
               3. Splash hot water on the outside surface of the can to loosen the ice. Gently ease
                  the ice out of the can. Place it upright and light the candle.

Candlestick (Afro-American, Christian, Jewish)

During Chanukkah a chanukiyah, or nine-branch candlestick, is lit, one candle on the first evening, two on the second, and so on, until all the candles are lit. On Kwanzaa a kinara, or seven-branch candlestick, is lit, beginning with the black candle in the center and alternating from a green one on the left to a red one on the right until all seven candles are lit. During Advent four candles on an Advent wreath are lit in turn, one on each Sunday preceding Christmas. In all three ceremonies, prayers are said as each candle is lit. Ask a parent to bring in a chanukiyah, kinara, or Advent wreath from home, or show the children pictures of them. Then make a simple facsimile and use it when singing the song on p. 130.

Time: 30 minutes
Materials: 7-9 toilet-paper tubes per child
             scissors
             one 4-by-18-in. cardboard per child
             masking tape
             liquid tempera paint
             paint brushes
             yellow and orange tissue-paper scraps
Method: 1. Cut the toilet-paper tubes so that they are graduated in size: cut two 3-in. lengths; two 2-in. lengths; two 1-in. lengths; and, for the chanukiyah only, two 1/2-in. lengths. Leave 1 tube uncut.
             2. Line up the tubes in sequence, putting the uncut tube in the center, and the smallest ones at either end. Tape the base of each tube to the cardboard.
             3. Paint the tubes. The chanukiyah may be any color, but the colors of the kinara are specific: 1 black candle in the middle, 3 green ones on the left, and 3 red ones on the right.
             4. When the paint is dry, stuff the tissue-paper scraps in the top of each candle to represent the flames.

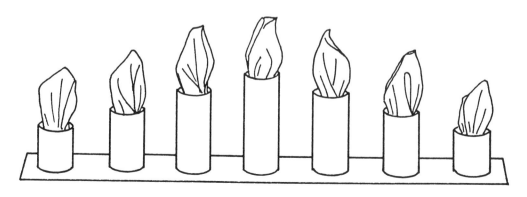

Kinara

4. Discovery

During this theme, experiment with light and darkness, creating shadows and exploring shades of color. If lit candles are not allowed indoors, use them outside, or simulate candles with flashlights. If candles are used, let the children blow out the candles, use a candle snuffer, or hold the hand of the person lighting the candles. While safety considerations are paramount, direct participation can make the safety lessons more relevant. Firsthand experience of campfires, home fireplaces, birthday candles or candlelit dinners will help children to appreciate both the beauty and the danger of fire.

Festivals of light introduce materials such as dreidels, stars and nativity figures that can be used to reinforce classification, sorting, and counting skills. These materials not only interest and excite young children, but also stimulate them to develop a global consciousness. Ask parents for help in making and collecting these materials.

Nativity scene

In the 14th century St Francis of Assisi created the first nativity scene using villagers and real animals to act out the birth of Jesus. Today's nativity play and nativity scene are direct descendants of this first re-enactment.

Christians all over the world make nativity scenes depicting Jesus' birth. In France the scene is called a crèche; in Italy, a presepio; in Haiti, a fanal; in Czechoslovakia, a jeslicky. The scene may be as large as a room, or small enough to hold in your hand. It can be made of many materials: in the Philippines, cloths of pink, green, blue, and white are used; in India, streamers, flowers, and rich tapestries surround the scene. Each scene may present any number of figures, although there is always a mother, a father, and a baby.

Remember other special birthdays at this time:

- Janmashtemi celebrates the birth of Lord Krishna

- Ramnavmi celebrates the birth of Lord Rama

- Milad-an-Nabi celebrates the birth of Prophet Mohammed

Make a nativity scene and use it to talk about birthing and family. By manipulating a nativity scene and by seeing pictures of similar ones, children slowly lose any fear of the larger nativity scenes adorning churches at Christmas time. Parents may help by bringing in a nativity scene from home, or by making and painting the program figures. The simple story of Jesus' nativity is a rich cross-cultural tale told in many languages (see pp. 158-159 for storybook ideas); the religious significance of the nativity need not be stressed.

Making the scene

Time: three 20-minute sessions
Materials: 1 shoebox
             glue
             5-6 sheets of old newspaper
             grey, blue, and brown tempera paint
             wide brushes
             straw, raffia, or dried grass
             clay shaped into 2 large balls and 1 small ball
             acrylic paint and fine brushes
             sections of toilet-paper tubes
             markers
             scraps of fabric
Method: 1. Lay the box on 1 long side and place it inside the lid, which acts as a base.
             2. Glue a sheet of newspaper over the back and the other 3 sides of the box.
             3. Crumple the remaining sheets into loose balls. Glue them onto the covered sides so that the shoebox resembles a stable or cave.
             4. Paint the inside and outside of the shoebox, covering it completely.
             5. Scatter the straw, raffia, or grass inside the box before the paint dries.
             6. Model the 2 large balls of clay into 2 adult shapes. Form the small one into a baby shape. When dry, paint them to resemble a mother, father, and baby.
             7. Draw faces on the toilet-paper tubes. Glue fabric scraps on the tubes for clothes. Place the tubes near or in the stable to represent the baby's visitors.

Nativity scene

Using the scene

The nativity scene can be used for many weeks both by the group during group time and by individual children during quiet play. Try the following suggestions.

- Add more figures to the scene and paint them a variety of flesh tones. Put out fabric scraps with elastic bands so that the fabric can be placed over the top of the tube and secured with a band to represent a turban, bandana, headband, or veil. Act out dialogue, using these figures to draw out language. Add animal figures, wooden blocks, and scarves as tents.

- The horns of domestic animals are sometimes painted and their necks hung with flower collars and garlands during festivals of light. Imitate this by putting small tissue-paper wreaths around the necks of the animal figures in the stable.

- Mohammed, Sikh Guru Nanok, Buddha, and Jesus were born in warm countries. Make tiny palm trees by gluing green crepe-paper scraps to one end of a toothpick. Plant the trees in a playdough oasis. Alternatively, place the nativity scene directly in the sandbox and plant the trees in the sand.

- Do a sandpaper transfer and use it as a flag or banner. Color heavily with crayons on a piece of sandpaper. Cover the drawing with a piece of white paper, then iron on the back of the sandpaper. The heat will transfer the design onto the white paper. Tape this paper to a craft stick to make a flag for the scene.

- Hang up a large, black sheet as the sky behind the scene. Make stars out of crumpled foil balls or glitter on cardboard star shapes. Hang each star from the ceiling so that it dangles freely in front of the black sheet. Make a Milky Way by joining two stars with thin strands of tinsel.

- In the United States, most babies are still born in a hospital. However, more and more families are choosing to have home births. Ask a new mom and her baby or a midwife to talk to the children about birthing and babies. Ask the children to bring in their own baby pictures. Try to match the baby picture to the child.

- Use the animal and people figures to reinforce sorting, classifying, and counting skills. Sort the figures into groups according to clothes, sex, or shape. Count the figures in each group. Count the number of groups. Put all the figures together and count them again. Show one-to-one correspondence by letting each child hold a figure. Now count the children. Compare numbers.

- Use toilet-paper tubes of varying heights. Sequence the figures according to height. Sequence the animal figures according to size.

- Put out scales to weigh the clay "baby" figure. Weigh the other clay figures too, then compare weights.

Dreidel (Jewish)

The dreidel is a four-sided spinning top with a Hebrew letter on each side. The letters — nun, gimmel, hey, shin — are the first letters of the words, "a great miracle happened there". The miracle was the first Chanukkah when a tiny portion of menorah oil burned for eight days. The dreidel game is a form of gambling. Each player in turn spins the dreidel around a pot of gelt or coins. If the dreidel lands on nun, the player gets nothing; on gimmel, the player gets all the gelt; on hey, the player gets half; on shin, the player must put gelt into the pot. Counters or pennies can be used for gelt. Make the game simpler by putting a "happy face" sticker under each Hebrew letter as a reminder of the meaning of that letter (see below).

In an even simpler game the players match Hebrew letters on circles to the ones on the dreidel. This not only familiarizes the players with the Hebrew alphabet but also reinforces the concept of one-to-one correspondence. To play either dreidel game, buy a wood, plastic, metal, or clay dreidel through a local synogogue, or make the simple one described below.

Time: 20 minutes
Materials: 1 empty wooden spool
            markers
            four 2-in.cardboard circles per child
            1 unsharpened pencil
            modelling clay
Method: 1. Draw the 4 dreidel symbols around the spool.
            2. Draw corresponding symbols on each of the 4 circles.
            3. Slide the spool half-way up the length of the pencil.
               Hold up the spool by fashioning a clay ledge under it.
            4. Take turns spinning the dreidel. If it lands on gimmel, put the gimmel circle into the middle of the table, and so on, until all the circles are in the middle of the table.
            5. Sing a dreidel song before each person takes a turn:

I have a little dreidel, I made it just today,
And when my friends are ready, then dreidel I will play,
Oh dreidel, dreidel, dreidel, I made you today,
Oh dreidel, dreidel, dreidel, now it's time to play.

GIMMEL

NUN

HEY

SHIN

Dreidel symbols and corresponding "happy faces"

5. Group time

Figures associated with festivals of light around the world share a surprisingly similar spirit. Sometimes they are morality figures with assistants who punish naughty children. But most often they are kind and jolly, bearing goodies of the season to the children of the world. Descriptions and illustrations of these figures follow. Gradually introduce one or two of the figures, drawing similarities and emphasizing their shared characteristics. Tell a story or do an activity based on the figure. Ask parents for advice and help. They are usually very pleased to recognize familiar cultural or religious figures being described, and may want to bring in additional pictures, puppets, and ornaments. Remember, however, that their own children may know only Santa Claus and may not recognize other traditional figures.

Use the illustrations that follow as patterns for puppets or feltboard figures to accompany the stories. Hang the puppets on the tree to remind the children of these stories. Alternatively, let them make their own puppets by coloring each illustration and taping it to a craft stick or dowel.

Father Christmas

Father Christmas was suggested by Dickens' **A Christmas Carol** as a figure of joy and fun. He wears red and carries a bowl of Christmas punch and a flaming yule log. In Norway he is called Julenissen; in France, Père Noël; and in China either Lan Khoong (nice old father) or Dun Che Lao Ren (Christmas old man). The North American version is Santa Claus, a Christmas figure familiar to children around the world. He fills the stockings of children with presents on Christmas Eve.

St Nicholas

St Nicholas was a bishop in Turkey in the fourth century who saved a poor man's daughters by throwing three sacks of gold down the chimney of the man's home. Legend holds that one sack fell into a sock hanging to dry by the fireplace. Since then, children have hung up stockings by the chimney in hopes that the kindly bishop will leave them presents too. In Holland St Nicholas is called Sinterklaas and is helped by an assistant called Black Peter. In Czechoslovakia and Hungary he is helped by Black Peter; in Austria, Klaubauf; and in Yugoslavia, Djavao.

Father Christmas

St Nicholas

Babushka and Befana

The stories

Babushka was a Russian grandmother who refused shelter to Joseph and Mary, and mis-directed the Magi on their way to Bethlehem. She was just too busy to listen to the travellers. Realizing her mistake, she is said to wander the world on the eve of the Epiphany, looking for the Magi and dropping off presents for children.

Befana was an old Italian woman who was too busy sweeping her floor to accompany the Magi on their journey to Bethlehem. Towards dawn she realized her mistake and ran outside to find them, but they had already left. Today Befana rides around the world on her broom on the eve of the Epiphany, looking for the Magi and dropping presents in children's shoes.

Baba game

Time: 20 minutes
Materials: 1 broom
Method: 1. One child sweeps the floor in the middle of the circle while the other children skip around, singing: "Babushka (Befana), Babushka, come with us. Babushka, Babushka, come with us. Babushka, babushka, come with us. Stop your sweeping now."
               2. On the word "now" all the children sit down and close their eyes. Then the player in the middle rides on the broom around the outside of the circle and taps the shoulder of the next child to be the sweeper.
               3. The next child then takes the broom and sweeps the floor in the middle of the circle, and the game is repeated until all the children have a chance to be Babushka.

Baba doll (Ukrainian)

Time: 15 minutes
Materials: 1 pinecone per child
               1 facial tissue per child
               elastic bands
               fabric scraps
               glue (optional)
Method: 1. Fold the facial tissue in half, then in half again. Put it on one end of the cone, and hold it in place with an elastic band. Fluff it out to resemble a headscarf.
               2. Tie fabric scraps to the bottom of the cone to resemble an apron. Younger children may prefer using glue to attach the fabric scraps.

Babushka/Befana

St Lucia

The story

St Lucia was a young Sicilian girl who had her eyes put out because she would not renounce Christianity. She is usually pictured in white robes with a halo of light over her head. She comes to children in Sweden, Finland, Italy, and the Caribbean on December 13 to break winter's spell and to bring light to the world. An old rhyme describes this mid-winter day: "Lucia-light, Lucia-light, shortest day and longest night."

St Lucia crowns were originally made with pine branches and real candles. To keep the branches from catching fire, a damp cloth was placed between them. Today, battery-operated crowns are often used. In many families the eldest daughter traditionally wears the St Lucia crown on the morning of December 13 when she brings coffee and St Lucia buns to her parents. The eldest son wears a star cap on that day.

The crown

Time: 15 minutes
Materials: 1 large paper plate per child with 4 holes punched at regular intervals
               around the rim
            scissors
            four 4-in. squares of yellow tissue paper per child
            one 24-in. strip of green crepe paper per child
Method: 1. Cut the middle out of the paper plate, leaving the rim intact.
            2. Fold a tissue-paper square into a triangle, then fold again to make a smaller triangle.
               Roll the triangle into a tube (birthday-candle-size), then push the tube into a hole on the rim.
            3. Repeat with the other 3 squares.
            4. Wind the crepe-paper length around the rim to resemble leaves.

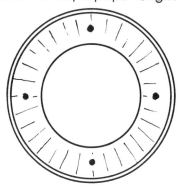 

The star cap

Time: 10 minutes
Materials: one 20-in. square of construction paper per child
            scissors
            clear adhesive tape
            markers or star stickers
Method: 1. Cut on a curved line from one corner of the square to the one diagonally opposite.
            2. Roll the paper into a cone shape so that the straight edges overlap slightly.
               Tape the edges closed.
            3. Decorate the cone hat by drawing on stars or pressing on star stickers.

St Lucia

Lakshmi

The story

Lakshmi is the Hindu goddess of prosperity and the wife of Vishnu, the god of joy. On Divali she is guided to homes by the light of the dipa lamps which are put on window ledges, driveways, and paths. She enters the house and receives her offering (usually food); in return, she leaves prosperity in the form of sweets and presents.

The dipa (dias) lamp

In India on Divali, a dipa lamp is lit, a wish made, then the dipa is put in the river. If it stays lit until it reaches the other side, the wish is granted. In Pakistan a dias lamp is used in the same way. Make a dipa (Indian) or dias (Pakistani) lamp, light it, then float it in a plastic wading pool. Watch the reflection of the light on the water. Count together to see how long the lamp stays lit. Alternatively, place the lamp in a bin of snow, light the wick, then watch the effect on the snow. Keep the lamp to use as a centrepiece at the snack table, an alternative to birthday candles, or a light for other celebrations.

Time: 5 minutes
Materials: 1 small ball of clay per child
           pencil or dowel
           1 t (mustard) oil
           2 cotton balls per child
           matches
Method: 1. Press the thumb into the middle of the ball to shape it into a bowl.
           2. Pull one end of the bowl into a lip shape to hold the wick.
              Press the lip with the pencil to flatten it.
           3. Let the bowl harden overnight, then put the oil into the bowl.
           4. Stretch each cotton ball into a long thread by drawing out and twisting the fibers.
              Twist together 2 threads to make a wick. Put one end of the wick in the oil,
              and the other end onto the lip.
           5. Float the lamp in a plastic wading pool or water bin, or set it in a mound of snow.
              Light the wick.

Dipa lamp

Lakshmi

Tanabata

The story

Tanabata is a Japanese word meaning weaving loom. It celebrates the story of two lovers, Shokujo and Kenju. Shokujo was a princess who was asked by her father to weave a wonderful cloth. Instead of completing the task, she fell in love with a humble shepherd named Kenju. When the king discovered that the cloth was not woven and that his daughter had fallen in love with a commoner, he became angry and he banished his daughter and her lover to the sky. He said that they could meet only once a year on Tanabata. When the two star-crossed lovers tried to meet, however, they could not cross the sky. The lovebirds took pity on them and spread their wings between the two stars to make the Milky Way. That is why once a year Shokujo and Kenju are able to meet again.

The star

On Tanabata beautiful paper decorations symbolizing the Milky Way are hung on long bamboo poles in gardens and streets. Poems or wishes written on long strips of rice paper are hung on the poles. Some of these decorations are over five yards long.

Time: 15 minutes
Materials: 1 construction-paper star per child
            hole punch
            1 facial tissue per child
            glue
            6 tissue-paper strips per child
Method: 1. Punch a hole near the end of one of the points of the star. Pull the tissue half way through the hole, then fluff it out and tear the ends to look like flower petals.
            2. Spread glue on the back of the opposite end of the star. Press one end of each tissue-paper strip onto this glue. Let the other ends of the strips dangle loosely.

Stars

The star of Bethlehem and the stars of Obon were guiding lights, as are the star-shaped lanterns carried by the Star Boys on St Lucia Day. The Ojibway legend of the star who became a water lily, the Plains legend of the star-husband, and the Japanese legend of Tanabata are popular personifications of stars. Our names for constellations also personify stars and come from times when the sky was seen as a magical picture drawn with points of light. We reaffirm this magic when we talk about "wishing on a star" or "catching a falling star".

Young children spontaneously name the stars and seem to feel very close to them. They may see the sky as a blanket, and the stars as their nighttime friends. As one child observed, "The sun is there in the day when it is light anyway, but the stars come out at night to light up the dark sky." Children love to use star stickers, to paint stars on their foreheads, or to stamp them on their work. They can imagine foil balls hanging on strings from the ceiling as stars in the sky. They also enjoy making the simple star picture described below.

Time: 10 minutes
Materials: 1 piece of black construction paper per child
             1 "poker" (thumbtack, golf peg, or blunt pencil) per child
             1 piece of yellow construction paper per child
             clear adhesive tape
Method: 1. Poke many holes through the black construction paper.
             2. Put the black paper over the yellow and tape the sides together.

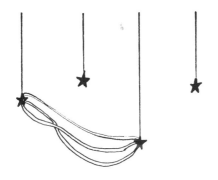

Making the Milky Way

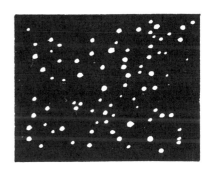

Star picture

Krathong

In Thailand on Loy Krathong, children make krathong by shaping lotus flowers, banana leaves, or paper into cups, animals, or temples. Then they put a candle or incense cone inside the krathong. They take it down to the river, light it, make a wish, and put it in the water. If the candle or incense stays lit until the krathong disappears, the wish is said to come true. In Japan on Obon, children place little ships carrying lanterns and a printed message into the river for the same reason. Make these simple krathong and float them in the water bin. Remember to make a wish before launching the krathong.

Time: 5 minutes
Materials: 1 square of origami paper per child
             1 incense cone per child
             matches
Method: 1. Follow the directions below to make a simple origami boat.
             2. Place the boat in the water. Rest an incense cone inside the boat then light it. The design and the paper finish make this boat relatively watertight.

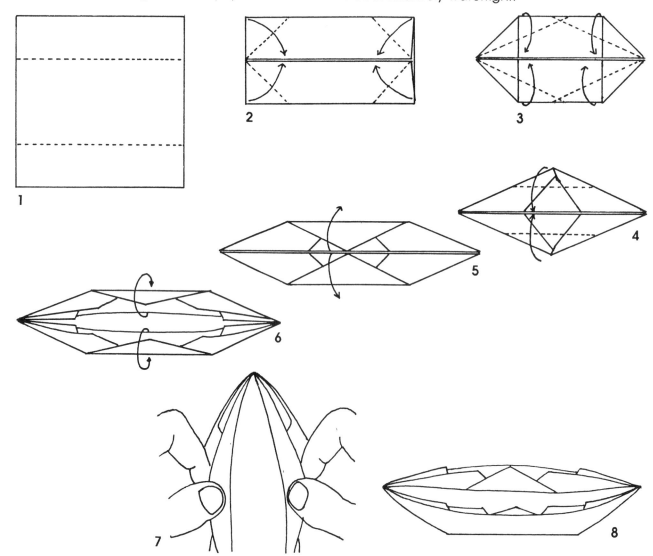

6. Food to share

Food enjoyed at festival time is often sweet but not necessarily lacking in nutritional value. Barfi, for example, is rich in milk and nuts, and eggnog is primarily milk and eggs. Try to balance the high sugar content of some festival foods with fresh fruits and vegetables. Also, only serve small portions of a very sweet food.

Many of the foods are highly decorative and are meant as treats both for the eye and for the palate. Involve the children in creating some of these beautiful dishes so that they can learn to appreciate the color and arrangement of food. Invite families to see and enjoy these creations, and perhaps share their own family favorites too. This is an ideal time to visit a bakery or pastry shop to watch special cakes being iced and decorated by master bakers.

The simple recipes that follow can be complemented by the specialties of the season. Drinks can include cranberry cocktail or white grape juice. Fruits such as pomegranates and mandarin oranges are also seasonal. Scottish shortbread, Middle Eastern marzipan, Italian Christonomo, English plum pudding, German stollen, and Japanese mochi are all festive delights.

Each recipe serves ten except for the bûche de Noël and barfi which serve twenty.

Eggnog (American, English)

Ingredients: 4 C milk
4 T sugar
1 t vanilla
6 eggs
ground cinnamon or nutmeg

Method: 1. Stir the milk and sugar together over low heat until the sugar dissolves. Let cool. Add vanilla.
2. Process the milk mixture with the eggs in a blender and blend until smooth.
3. Pour the eggnog into 10 cups and sprinkle each with a dash of cinnamon or nutmeg.

Solstice punch (Scandinavian)

Ingredients: 4 C apple cider
10 cinnamon sticks
10 thin lemon slices

Method: 1. Heat the cider in a pot until very warm.
2. Remove from the heat and pour into 10 cups. Add a lemon slice to each cup, and a cinnamon stick to stir the punch.

Latkes (Jewish)

Ingredients: 2 C grated potato
2 t grated onion
1 egg
6 T flour
4 T oil
2 C applesauce or yogurt (optional)

Method:
1. Pat the grated potato with a paper towel to remove excess moisture.
2. Mix together the potato, onion, egg, and flour.
3. Heat the oil in a frying pan. Drop tablespoonfuls of the potato mixture into the oil and cook until brown on each side, flipping once.
4. Serve the latkes while still warm or set them aside to be re-heated later for serving. Traditional toppings are yogurt and applesauce.

Fruit candles (Canadian)

Ingredients: 10 canned pineapple rings
5 medium bananas
2 C cottage cheese
5 fresh strawberries

Method:
1. Place a pineapple ring on each plate.
2. Peel the bananas and cut in half crosswise. Place 1 banana piece, flat end down, in the hole in the center of each ring.
3. Spoon some cottage cheese around the base of the banana.
4. Hull the strawberries, then cut them into slices from hull end to tip to expose the flame pattern of the berry. Cut a notch in the top of each banana and insert a strawberry slice.

Fruit candle

Barfi balls (East Indian)

Ingredients: 1/2 C butter
3/4 C sugar
3/4 C milk
2 C powdered milk
1 C ground almonds
1/4 C unsweetened shredded coconut

Method: 1. Melt the butter in a large saucepan over low heat.
2. Stir in sugar and the liquid milk. Bring to a boil and boil hard for 5 minutes, stirring constantly.
3. Remove from the heat and add the powdered milk. Stir in the almonds and coconut.
4. When cool, form into balls.

St Lucia buns (Finnish, Italian, Swedish)

Ingredients: 1 package sweetmilk biscuit dough
20 currants
1/2 C icing sugar
2 t cream

Method: 1. Divide the package into 10 biscuits.
2. Roll each biscuit into a 10-in. strip of dough. Curl the strip into an S-shape, then curl each end into a spiral. Put a currant in the middle of each spiral. The currants symbolize St Lucia's watchful eyes.
3. Cook the biscuits as directed.
4. While the biscuits are still warm, brush the tops with icing made with the icing sugar and cream.

St Lucia buns

Bûche de Noël (French)

This traditional favorite of Le Réveillon is modelled on the flaming yule log. Although it is fussier to make than the usual snack, the result is a marvel for young children. Make this with them as the morning activity so that they can see the transformation of a simple cake into a very delicious and beautiful log.

Ingredients: 1 box angel-food cake mix
2 C chocolate frosting
1/4 C icing sugar
decorations such as marzipan mushrooms

Method:
1. Line 2 cookie sheets, the type with edges all around, with waxed paper. Grease and flour the paper well.
2. Prepare the cake mix as directed. Pour half of the batter into each pan. Bake at 350° F for 20-25 minutes.
3. Immediately turn out each cake, top down, onto a piece of waxed paper that is liberally sprinkled with icing sugar. Remove the lining paper and trim off any crusty edges. While the cakes are still hot, roll up each one from the short end with the waxed paper. Place each cake, seam side down, on a rack to cool.
4. When the cakes are completely cool, unroll them. Take one third of the frosting and divide it into two portions. Spread one portion evenly and thinly on one cake. Spread the other portion on the other cake.
5. Roll up each cake without the waxed paper. To make one long log, place the cakes end to end and seam side down on a tray. Cover with the remaining frosting. Use the blade of a knife or the tines of a fork to make a bark pattern in the icing.
6. Sprinkle icing sugar "snow" on top. Decorate with marzipan mushrooms. Cut into slices, each one having a ring pattern similar to that of a real log.

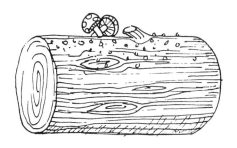

Bûche de Noël

Pepparkakors (Swedish) or Lebkuchens (German)

This cookie dough can be used to make gingerbread houses. Shape the dough into six square slabs and two triangles. Cut a door in one of the slabs; cut small windows in three slabs; and leave the last two slabs and triangles uncut. When the slabs are cooked and cool, stick them together with icing, and decorate with tiny candies or candied fruit. The dough can also be rolled into balls, then shaped into figures for a nativity scene. Making edible art is a very enjoyable experience for the children that draws from them a variety of verbal responses.

Ingredients:
1 C sugar
2 C molasses
1 C shortening
4 t ground ginger
2 t baking soda
6 C white flour

Method:
1. Stir the first 4 ingredients together in a large saucepan over low heat until the shortening is melted. Remove the pan from the heat.
2. Stir in the soda, then gradually add the flour. The dough should be soft but not too sticky. Add more flour if necessary. Wrap the dough in waxed paper and refrigerate 1 hour.
3. Divide the dough into 10 equal balls, one for each child. Sprinkle flour on the work space so that the dough does not stick. Give each child a sheet of aluminum foil for the shaped cookies. Put out an assortment of cookie cutters and small rolling pins. Remember to use a drinking straw to poke a hole in each shape if the shapes are to be hung on the tree.
4. When the cookie shapes are ready, put the foil trays on cookie sheets and bake at 350° F. Bake balls, figures or other rounded shapes 10-20 minutes, depending on size. Bake flat, rolled-and-cut shapes 5-10 minutes, depending on thickness.
5. When done, immediately remove the cookies from the foil and cool on a wire rack.

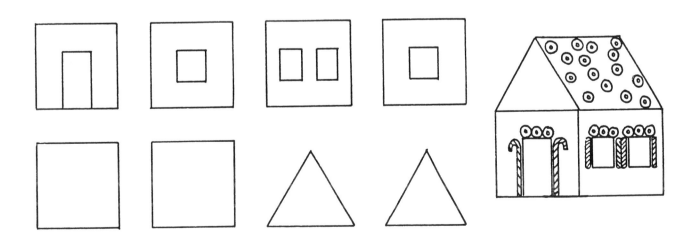

Gingerbread house, in pieces and assembled

Resources for educators

Bennett, Olivia. **Festival: Diwali**. London: Macmillan Education, 1986.
Color photographs and simple text depict a child's experience of Divali.

Bragdon, Allen D. **Joy Through the World**. New York: Dodd Mead, 1976.
The focus of this UNICEF-sponsored exploration of holidays around the world is the season of winter solstice.

Hildebrandt, Greg. **Treasures of Chanukah**. Parsippony, New Jersey: Unicorn, 1987.
The history, music, and significance of this religious holiday are described and illustrated.

Kalman, Bobbie. **We Celebrate Christmas**. Toronto: Crabtree, 1986.
Various ways of celebrating Christmas are described and illustrated.

Quildon, Louis, ed. **A Canadian Christmas**. Hamilton, Ontario: Southern Ontario Social and Cultural Club, 1979.
This book highlights some of the different ways Christmas is celebrated in Canada.

Wikler, Madeline and Judith Groner. **Miracle Meals: Eight Nights of Fun and Food for Chanukah**. Rockville, Maryland: Kar-Ben Copies, 1987.
Recipes and game ideas for Chanukkah are described in this book.

Storybooks for all age groups (2-6 years)

Bierhorst, John. **Spirit Child: A Story of the Nativity**. New York: William Morrow, 1984.
This Mexican nativity tale combines stories from the Bible, medieval legends, and Aztec lore.

Brown, Margaret Wise. **Christmas in the Barn**. New York: Harper and Row, 1985.
This poem re-creates in an old barn the mood of the nativity of Jesus.

Cole, Joanna. **A Gift from Saint Francis: the First Crèche**. Toronto: Kids Can, 1989.
Michèle Lemieux's paintings re-create the wonder of the first crèche.

De Paola, Tomie. **The Legend of Old Befana**. New York: Harcourt Brace Jovanovich, 1980.
Befana is depicted as a quarrelsome old grandmother who becomes a kindly gift-giver through her encounter with the Magi.

De Paola, Tomie. **The Story of the Three Wise Kings**. New York: G.P. Putnam's Sons, 1983.
This simple story of the Magi is illustrated with full-page, colorful drawings.

Franklin, Paula. **The Seventh Night of July**. Agincourt, Ontario: Silver Burdett, 1985.
This magical Japanese tale of Tanabata is illustrated by Ke Ming and Huang Peizhong.

Garthwaite, Marion. **The Twelfth Night Santons**. New York: Doubleday, 1965.
One of his smallest sheep leads Pierre, a French boy, to a bed of clay that is perfect for making santons or crèche figures.

Goldin, Barbara Diamond. **Just Enough is Plenty**. New York: Viking, 1988.
A stranger's visit on Chanukkah reminds a Jewish family that their real wealth is their love.

Hayes, Sarah. **Happy Christmas Gemma**. New York: Lothrop, Lee and Shepard, 1986.
A Jamaican family's special Christmas in England is described with warmth and humor.

Hirsh, Marilyn. **Potato Pancakes All Around**. New York: Bonim, 1975.
This simple Chanukkah folktale describes a peddlar who can make latkes without potatoes, just as stone soup is made without vegetables in another familiar story.

Hughes, Shirley. **Angel Mae**. Vancouver: Douglas and McIntyre, 1989.
While Mae plays an angel in the Christmas pageant, her own baby sister is born.

Kent, Jack. **The Christmas Piñata**. New York: Parents Magazine, 1975.
A cracked pot becomes a beautiful piñata for Los Posados in a Mexican village.

Kimmel, Eric A. **The Chanukkah Tree**. New York: Holiday House, 1987.
Tricked into buying and decorating a "Chanukkah Tree" on Christmas Eve, Jewish villagers rediscover its worth and beauty and make the tree their own village tradition.

Kurelek, William. **A Northern Nativity**. Montreal: Tundra, 1976.
The drawings of a miraculous birth in the Far North are a wonderful inspiration for story-telling, even though the actual text of this book is too difficult for young children.

Laugesen, Mary. **The Chrisamat Tree**. New York: Bobbs-Merrill, 1970.
A Thai boy's living Christmas tree is lit with fireflies and decorated with garlands of frangipani.

Lee, Jeanne M. **Legend of the Milky Way**. New York: Holt, 1982.
This simple adaptation of the Tanabata story, illustrated with full-page color drawings, is ideal for very young children.

Mikolaycak, Charles. **Babushka**. New York: Holiday House, 1984.
This Russian folktale describes Babushka's encounter with the Magi, and her transformation to a generous gift-giver.

Mobley, Jane. **The Star Husband**. New York: Doubleday, 1979.
A girl of the Great Plains People wishes a star were her husband, and has her wish fulfilled with unexpected results.

Robins, Patricia. **Star Maiden**. Don Mills, Ontario: Collier Macmillan, 1975.
This Ojibway legend describes how a star became the first water lily.

Rydberg, Viktor. **The Christmas Tomten**. New York: Coward, McCann, and Geoghegan, 1981.
This Swedish folktale tells of a mysterious tomten who takes a little boy on an exciting Christmas journey.

Solomon, Joan. **Sweet-tooth Sunil**. London: Hamish Hamilton, 1984.
Sunil, a young Indian girl in England, and her brother have fun and enjoy Divali treats.

Speare, Jean. **A Candle for Christmas**. Vancouver: Douglas and McIntyre, 1986.
Tomas, an Inuit boy, lights a candle to guide his parents home on Christmas Eve, and the candle glow extends further than he imagines.

Toye, William. **The Fire Stealer**. Toronto: Oxford University Press, 1979.
This Ojibway legend of how fire came to the earth is illustrated by Elizabeth Cleaver.

Uchida, Yoshiko. **The Birthday Visitor**. New York: Scribner, 1976.
On Emi's seventh birthday he has a special visitor from Japan.

Records and tapes

Children's Television Workshop. **Christmas Eve on Sesame Street**.

Fran Avni, **Latkes and Hamentashen** (Checkmate, 1980).

Manheim Steamroller, **Christmas** (American Gramaphone, 1984).

Raffi. **Raffi's Christmas Album**. (Troubadour, 1983).

Sharon, Lois, and Bram, **Happy Birthday** (Elephant Records, 1988). This album features birthday songs in Greek, Polish, Yiddish, Spanish, French, as well as an "Unbirthday Song."

Suzanne Pinel, **Noël** (Les Editions Clown Samuel, 1983).

CHAPTER FIVE

New Year

New Year: hope for the future

Welcoming the new year and saying good-bye to the old is a tradition everywhere. This is a time for rejuvenation and re-assessment: old troubles, debts, and quarrels are settled, and new resolutions and promises are made. New Year, more than any other holiday of the year, promises hope.

This hope is shown in many good-luck tokens and customs. One such custom is the symbolic burning of problems, debts, and quarrels of the old year: the Mexicans burn a castillo, an elaborate paper castle loaded with messages; the Ecuadorians, a scarecrow called Año Viejo. Other customs include the purchasing of new clothes, rigorous house-cleaning, and the swearing of solemn promises or "New Year resolutions." In Poland on New Year's Eve, it is bad luck to stay at home, so many people plan outings. Special foods are eaten for luck: in Spain and Latin America, 12 grapes or raisins; in Korea, rice-cake soup; in China, Chuen-Hop, a tray of eight preserves.

From the earliest times, loud noise was believed to frighten away the evils of the old year. Today, the celebrations are still noisy: in Japan bells are rung 108 times on New Year's Eve, and in the United States bells chime 12 on the stroke of midnight. In many cities of the world, drivers repeatedly honk their car horns at 12 o'clock on New Year's Eve. Fireworks explode, bands play, and people dance in the streets to welcome in the year.

When the new year is a religious one, the celebration is usually quieter. Rosh Hashanah, for instance, marks the beginning of ten days of contemplation and self-examination, a solemn time for reverence and prayer. Joy is mixed with meditation on the uncertainties of the future. Muharram, the first month of the Moslem year, is a quiet time to remember Mohammed and his companions, and to emulate his life. Greetings are exchanged, but the mood is reflective rather than raucous.

New Year's Day is the first day of the year, but the date itself may vary according to the calendar used. All countries of the world that follow the Gregorian calendar celebrate New Year's Day on January 1. Other ethnocultural and religious groups celebrate New Year at dates specific to their own calendars. When these dates are translated into Gregorian terms, they become variable: New Year may be celebrated in April one year, in May the next.

On the next page is a list of New Year celebrations and their corresponding dates. Dates marked with an asterisk (*) are movable and depend upon either lunar or religious calendars. If a festival is associated with a particular place or people within a country, this is noted in parentheses. Although many of these festivals are celebrated in the United States, the place of origin of each one is keyed by number to a point on the map.

Circle the different New Years on your program calendar, verifying each date with the parents. In a multicultural program this celebration can be held many times during the year, each occasion having a unique secular or religious emphasis.

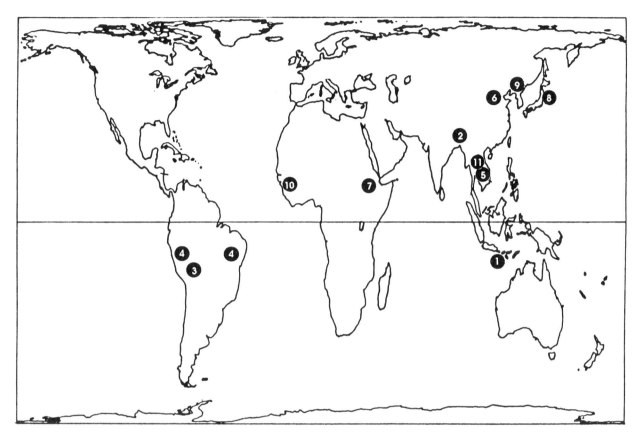

1. Bali	Lela	* December
2. Bangladesh	Bengali New Year	April 15
3. Bolivia	Alacitas	January 1
4. Brazil, Ecuador	Año Viejo	January 1
5. Cambodia	Bon Chol Chhnam	* April
6. China	Yuan Tan	* January
7. Ethiopia	New Year	September 11
8. Japan	Oshoogatsu	January 1
9. Korea	Sŏl	* January/February
10. Sierra Leone	New Year	* March/April
11. Vietnam	Tết Nguyen Dan	* January
Hinduism, Sikhism	Baisakhi	April 13
Islam	Ras-assanah	* July
Judaism	Rosh Hashanah	* September
Zoroastrianism	Navroz	* August/September

Using the New Year theme

GOAL To show the universality of many New Year celebrations

OBJECTIVES To present traditions associated with New Year celebrations

To explain why New Year is at different times for different people

To demonstrate the concept of day and month

To make and use a variety of good-luck tokens

To introduce and use the basic vocabulary of this theme

Measuring time means little to very young children but is important to their parents. Seeing that some special days have their origins in calendars far older than the Gregorian helps parents to further understand the significance of those days. For some Americans, New Year may be more important than Thanksgiving or Christmas, just as Saturday rather than Sunday may be considered a day of rest and prayer.

Share the significance of New Year with the children in a tangible way. Celebrate New Year in the autumn (Rosh Hashanah), winter (Yuan Tan), spring (Baisakhi) or summer (Navroz). Whenever the children are ready for a complete change or a new beginning, introduce New Year activities. The emphasis on parental input and group work makes this an ideal theme to begin the school year as well.

VOCABULARY LIST

first	lunar	luck	bang
day	moon	wish	noise
week	solar	beginning	fireworks
month	sun	pine	bell
year	calendar	bamboo	charm

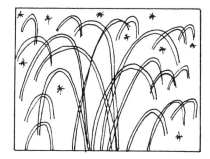

HAPPY NEW YEAR

新 年 快 樂

FELIZ AÑO NUEVO

Vocabulary card, front and back faces

1. Setting the mood

New Year in the United States often marks the time that children return to school after a December holiday. In many programs the walls will have been left quite bare as the children have taken their work home. Rather than rush to redecorate, greet them with a room that is plain and uncluttered. Offer bare walls and bulletin boards, empty tables, and clean floors. Put away some of the dishes, rugs, pots, and utensils used in the previous term; these can be reintroduced later.

Simple, bare spaces create the right mood for starting fresh for a new year. Past themes should not distract the children from the new activities. Make good-luck symbols of the New Year, and hang them in the housekeeping center or over doors and windows. Suggestions follow.

- Pine branches symbolize health, strength, and longevity for many Japanese, and are a traditional Oshoogatsu decoration. Use leftover branches from pine Christmas trees, and arrange them in a vase, or tape them directly on the wall. Before the needles start to drop, use each branch as a paintbrush. When these needles are well-used, wind tissue-paper strips in and out of the twigs on the branch to make a colorful hand-held fan for dramatic play.

- Bamboo is a strong plant used in making baskets, ski poles, umbrellas and chopsticks. In Japan the stalks symbolize uprightness and rapid development, twin hopes for the new year. Buy hollow bamboo stalks and use them to hold pine branches for a table display. The Japanese call such a pine and bamboo arrangement kadomatsu.

- The Chinese call bamboo, pine, and plum the "three friends". Together they signify good luck and long life. Display an arrangement of the three friends on the discovery table.

- The Chinese New Year wishes are: fortune, honor, and longevity. These words are written in Chinese below. Enlarge and photocopy these words, mount them on origami paper, and give them to the parents as New Year cards.

Fortune   Honor   Longevity

- In Venezuela and the Dominican Republic, children wear an azabache or lucky charm. It is usually a gold pin or jet stone mounted on a black backgound. Make an azabache by attaching a gold safety pin to a piece of black cloth or paper. Wind gold string around the pin or hang strands of gold tinsel from it. Pin the azabache on the child's shirt.

- In the Middle East some children wear the lucky hand around their necks to ward off bad luck or the evil eye. In Iran the hand is called the Hand of Fatima or dast. Trace each child's hand on gold origami paper. Cut out the hands, and string them on a clothesline in the room to bring luck in the new year. Alternatively, cut each hand out of plain construction paper, then wrap it in aluminum foil. String the hand on a loop of yarn as a lucky necklace.

- Many people believe that carrying a charm or talisman brings good luck. In Chile and in Canada, a rabbit's foot may be a lucky charm; in El Salvador, a piece of doeskin is considered lucky. Some Peruvians tie a tiny llama hung on a red ribbon around a child's wrist for luck. Shamrocks for the Irish, St Christopher's medals for Catholics, feathers for the Cree, lucky pennies for North Americans — all people have good luck charms or totems that are special to them. Ask the parents to bring in their own lucky charms and display them. Talk about the similarities among these lucky charms.

- Lai-see or lucky red envelopes contain good luck money for children on Chinese New Year. Make lucky envelopes out of a square of red origami paper, following the directions below.

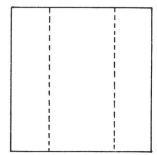

Fold the square so the two sides overlap slightly in the middle.

Glue or tape the two sides together.

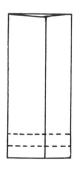

Make a double fold at the bottom and tape it shut. Put a coin inside.

Daruma doll (Japanese)

A Japanese symbol of good luck is the daruma doll. It is named after Bodhidharma (Dharma), an Indian Buddhist said to have founded Zen Buddhism in the sixth century. This branch of Buddhism is a way of life that stresses the practice of meditation. According to legend, Dharma meditated for nine years. When he tried to stand up, his arms and legs were so stiff that he could not move. Instead he was forced to roll from village to village to spread his teachings. The round-bottomed daruma doll represents Dharma. Like him, it shows resistance to physical limitations: when knocked over, it rights itself at once.

Darumas sold at the daruma market in Tokyo are made of many materials. Traditional ones are made of papier mâché decorated with pine, bamboo, and plum blossom designs. In northern Japan, darumas have glass eyes and human hair. Others, made in the form of masks, are used as scarecrows in fields. The "wishing" daruma or hatiman has no eyes. When a wish is made, one eye is painted on the doll. When the wish is fulfilled, the other eye is added.

Make a daruma following the instructions below, then draw on a face, a new year's wish, or the first eye of the hatiman. Tell the story of Dharma, using the daruma as a visual prop. Use several darumas as counters for math games, or as figures for the dramatic play area. Sequence different sizes of darumas. This doll can be part of the learning materials throughout the year.

Time: 20 minutes
Materials: 1 ball of clay per child
           1 lead weight (sinker) per child
           1 disposable cone-shaped drinking cup per child
           markers
Method: 1. Form the clay into an egg shape. Press a lead weight into the bottom of the shape, making sure the weight is in the center and that the shape balances well.
           2. Push the drinking cup over the top of the shape and into the clay.
           3. Draw a face, an eye, or a design on the cup.
           4. Leave the doll to harden overnight.

Daruma doll

2. Music and movement

New Year is often a noisy time. Make musical instruments, using them to scare away the old year, and to wake up the new one.

Horns (Austrian, Jewish, Swiss)

A ram's horn is fashioned to make the Alpine horn, a traditional instrument for accompanying folk dancing in Austria and Switzerland. The horn is also used to make a shofar, the instrument blown at specific intervals during the prayers of Rosh Hashanah. Show the children pictures of a shofar or ask a member of a synagogue to show and play one. Then experiment with similar horns and their sounds.

Time: 5 minutes
Materials: short piece of plastic or rubber hose
             utility knife (for adult use only)
             one 3-in. circle of waxed paper
             elastic band
Method: 1. Cut a small hole near one end of the hose. Hum through that end of the hose, alternately covering and uncovering the hole.
             2. Put the waxed paper over the opposite end and secure it with the elastic. Hum through the hose again.
             3. Play the hose, holding it straight, then bent, noting the differences in tone.

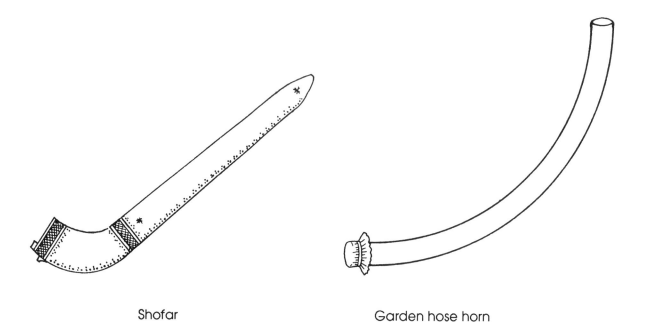

Shofar   Garden hose horn

Ankle bells (Burmese, East Indian, Sri Lankan)

Bells traditionally ring in the new year. Collect and use an assortment of bells: large brass bells, jingle bells, glass bells, china bells, wooden bells, cowbells. Note the differences in sound. Make bells for the wrists or ankles by stringing bells on yarn, knotting each in place. Use a longer piece of yarn to make a bell-headband, and wear the bells just above the eyes. A strip of elastic makes a more durable variety for all the children to use when they ring in the new year.

Time: 20 minutes
Materials: one 10 in. (or 20 in. for headband) strip of 1-in.-wide elastic
            5 small bells
            needle and thread
Method: 1. Knot 5 small bells at regular intervals onto the elastic.
            2. Sew the two ends of elastic together.

Tin bell (Japanese)

Metal bells are hung around cows' necks in many countries. Brass dinner bells are used in the home just as brass bells are used in church. On Oshoogatsu Buddhist priests ring a bell 108 times to summon the new year. Make a simple tin bell and use it to accompany songs, to call the children for snack, or to ring in your own new year.

Time: 10 minutes
Materials: 1 tin can per child
            hammer and nail
            one 4-in. piece of string
            one 20-in. piece of string
            clapper (wooden bead, nail, key)
Method: 1. Punch 3 holes in the bottom of the can: one in the middle and one on either
               side of the middle hole.
            2. Tie the clapper to the end of the 4-in. string. Push the other end of this string
               through the middle hole from the inside, and knot it on the outside of the can.
            3. Thread the 20-in. string through the other two holes, then tie that string to make
               a handle.

Bell songs

One of the most familiar bell songs in the United States is Frère Jacques. Even the very young soon learn this simple song, singing it with big bell-ringing arm movements or with real bells in both hands. Use the New Year bells to ring in this song in many languages. Sing it every day until the English or French version is familiar then, using the same tune, gradually introduce a third language version, and a fourth. In all versions, each line is sung twice. This repetition helps the children become familiar with a second or third language, useful in a multilingual United States.

English:
Are you sleeping,
Brother John?
Morning bells are ringing,
Ding, dang, dong.

French:
Frère Jacques,
Dormez-vous?
Sonnez les matines,
Ding, dang, dong.

Greek:
Kimase,
Athelfe Yanni?
Ee proines kambanes ktipoun,
Ding, dang, dong.

Italian:
Stai dormendo,
Fratello Gianni?
La matina suona la campana,
Din, dan, don.

Arabic:
Khayee Jean,
Inta nayem?
Jraas s-sobh am betren-n,
Ding, dang, dong.

Hoya-hoye (Ethiopian)

In Ethiopia, after sunset on New Year's Eve, small boys traditionally go from door to door singing the Hoya. After the first two verses the housewife offers the boys bread or rolls. The third verse thanks her for this treat, and wishes her good luck in the new year.

Sing the first verse in Amharic to a tune that the children already know. Pronounce the words just the way they look, stressing each syllable equally. Sing the verse again in English. Shake the bells and blow the horn to accompany this song.

Hoya-hoye, hoya-hoye,
Yene mebet atiwhichi gwaro.
Ainish yaberal inde korkoro.
Hoya-hoye, gude,
Dabo dabo yilal hode.

Hoya-hoye, hoya-hoye,
Miss, don't go in your yard.
Your eyes shine like the sun.
Hoya-hoye, listen,
My tummy wants some bread.

Congo Tay (West Indian)

Conga dancing invites everyone to take part in New Year festivities. Use the instruments you have made to set the rhythm. Start the line dance with each child holding the waist of the child in front. Begin by singing only the refrain, "Congo Tay", then sing the other lines. Adapt the words to suit the children in the group.

One day, one day,
Congo Tay,
I went to the bay,
Congo Tay.
I saw Miss .....,
Congo Tay,
With a brood of chickens,
Congo Tay.
I ask her for one,
Congo Tay,
But she gives me none,
Congo Tay.
So I'll take one,
Congo Tay,
Then I'll run,
Congo Tay.

Fizzy (Australian)

Fizzy, an Australian ball-tossing game, expresses well the exuberance of the New Year's celebration. A similar ball game is played by children in Cuba, Ecuador, and Ghana, and is probably common in many American schoolyards too.

Time: 10-20 minutes
Materials: 1 beach ball
Method: 1. In the middle of a small circle of children, one player holds the ball with both hands.
            2. With eyes closed, this player throws the ball up in the air. The person in the circle who catches it is the next to throw the ball.
            3. Form a tight circle around the next player and repeat the game.

3. Art

New Year inspires free and exuberant art, and experimentation with new art media. Put out bright, vibrant colors of paint. Display collage materials such as vinyl and plastic scraps, pine needles, plastic string, plastic lids and caps, and silver and gold mylar.

Miniatures (Bolivian)

In Bolivia on Alacitas miniatures are sold in the marketplace. Some depict Ekeko, the god of prosperity; others depict tiny household scenes in boxes the size of a matchbox. These replicas are fascinating for children. Dollhouses, for example, inspire children to act out situations and manipulate furniture much too large for them in real houses. Use this fascination to introduce children to shrink art and matchbox houses.

Shrink art

Time: 20-30 minutes
Materials: plastic berry baskets, plastic bottles, plastic lids
             hole punch
             markers
             cookie sheet
             yarn
Method: 1. Choose an assortment of plastic items. Use the hole punch to make a hole in the top of the bottles and lids.
             2. Draw designs on the lids and bottles.
             3. Put the items on the cookie sheet and bake for 5 minutes at 400° F.
             4. Take out of the oven quickly and cool. When cool, string 1 or more of the objects on yarn. Tie the ends of the yarn together to make a necklace.

Matchbox house

Time: 20-30 minutes
Materials: 1 empty matchbox per child
             scissors
             glue
             acrylic paint
             fine brushes
             clay

Method: 1. Slide the tray out of the matchbox.
             2. Cut the matchbox front in half right down the middle.
             3. Apply glue to the back and long sides of the tray and press the tray into its original place. Hold the back and sides together for a minute.
             4. Paint all sides of the matchbox.
             5. Shape small clay figures or furniture to put inside the box.

Papercuts (Chinese, Polish)

Papercuts probably originated centuries ago in China. Paper is folded, cut, then opened up and spread flat to reveal an intricate design. Each design is a symmetrical mirror image of the cut: multiple cuts produce multiple images.

Papercuts may be a symbol, tell a story, or depict a special animal or person. A century ago in Poland lacy papercuts or wycinanki were cut out freehand with sheep shears. Even with these unwieldy tools, the intricacy of the tiny designs was astonishing. Papercuts are often made in winter in the United States to depict the many designs and shapes of snowflakes.

Very young children may not be able to fold paper or to cut out a pattern as complex as the one illustrated, but they do enjoy watching their older friends creating papercuts. Give the younger ones a lacy paper doily to fold in half and cut. Even a few small cuts make interesting holes for younger children to feel and look through. Show pictures of Chinese and Polish papercuts, then create some originals by cutting freehand, unrestricted by set designs.

Time: 20-30 minutes
Materials: squares of drawing paper (all colors and sizes)
             scissors
             glue
Method: 1. Fold a sheet of drawing paper in half, then in half again to make a small square.
             2. Cut out triangles and slits along the sides.
             3. Open out the paper to show the cuts.
             4. Repeat this activity, folding the paper just in half, or into a smaller square. Experiment with all sizes of squares, cutting different sides of the square each time.
             5. Glue the paper scraps onto a plain sheet of paper to make another work of art.

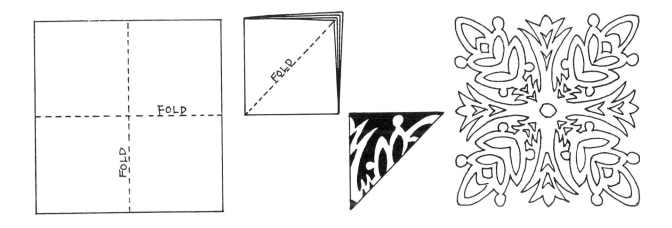

Papercut design for teachers

Fireworks

The noise of fireworks was traditionally supposed to scare away evil spirits; today the noise is frightening only for a moment. Then the beauty of the fireworks against the black night sky takes over. Let the children paint their own bursts of fireworks on paper both to recall this dazzling sight and to experience new painting techniques. Introduce this activity by telling the story on p. 175.

Time: 10-20 minutes per method
Materials: liquid tempera paint
             square pieces of black construction paper
             glitter
             Method 1: 1 pine bough, feather, or nylon brush per child
             Method 2: 1 plastic drinking straw per child
             Method 3: 1 craft stick, pencil, or dowel per child

Method 1:   1. Dip the tips of the pine needles into 1 color of paint, then brush the needles
               lightly upwards on the paper to simulate bursting fireworks.
            2. Repeat, using a second color and so on, until the paper is full of streaming
               color.
            3. Sprinkle glitter on the painting while it is still wet.

Method 2:   Once children are able to use a straw to blow out as well as to suck in, they are
            ready for this activity. Children who are not physically ready may accidentally
            ingest the paint.
            1. Thin the paint with water (1 part paint to 3 parts water). Put a drop of the thinned
               paint on a sheet of construction paper.
            2. Blow this drop all around the paper to make thin streaks of color.
            3. Repeat using a drop of another color of paint.
            4. Sprinkle glitter on the painting while it is still wet.

Method 3:   1. Dip the stick in paint so that it is almost fully covered.
            2. Lay the stick on the paper with the dry end in the center of the page. Twirl the
               stick in a circle so that the paint makes a big circle on the paper.
            3. When this paint is dry, dip half of the stick in a second color and repeat.
            4. When the paint is dry, dip only a quarter of the stick in paint and repeat.

1

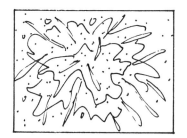

2

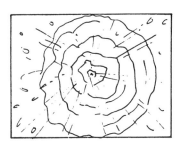

3

The fireworks legend (Vietnamese)

Tell this story to accompany the fireworks activities, or to complement other New Year celebrations. Use simple sound effects as the fireworks. Suggestions follow.

- Clap your hands together loudly
- Blow up several paper bags and pop them
- Bang together foil pie plates or pots and lids

These sound effects are best produced by the children following the word-cue NOISE. This can be their story, and they will love telling it over and over again as long as everyone can stand it! Use Chinese silk bookmarks taped to a dowel as the character puppets.

Long ago in Vietnam there were two wicked spirits who hated everybody. Their names were Na Ong and Na Ba. Na Ong was the husband, and Na Ba was the wife, and they didn't have any children. Maybe that is why they were so unhappy and miserable.

Once a year on Tết, the good spirits went up to the Emperor Jade to report on the people. While the good spirits were away, Na Ong and Na Ba came down to earth. They gave the people bad dreams, stole their food, and took away their toys. They made all the people very unhappy.

Now Na Ong and Na Ba were afraid of only one thing: loud NOISE. What's that? Did I hear a loud NOISE? That's right. That is what they feared most.

When the people saw Na Ong sneaking into their bedrooms at night, they made a loud NOISE. When they saw Na Ba opening up the cupboards in the kitchen to take food, they made a loud NOISE. When they saw Na Ong and Na Ba grabbing their toys, they also made a loud NOISE. Every time the people made a loud NOISE, Na Ong and Na Ba were afraid and ran away.

Soon Na Ong and Na Ba grew weary. They were trying so hard to be bad, and the people were still happy. In fact with all this NOISE, the people seemed to be getting happier! Na Ong and Na Ba left the people just before the good spirits came back.

That is why, once a year on Tết when the good spirits go to the Emperor Jade, the people make lots of NOISE to keep the bad spirits away. What's that? Did you hear anything? I can't hear a thing. I think there is just too much NOISE.

4. Discovery

Throughout the centuries people have devised calendars to keep track of time and to calculate religious and cultural holidays. Some calendars (Chinese, Moslem, Sikh) follow the movements of the moon and are called lunar; others (Coptic, Egyptian, Gregorian) follow the movements of the sun and are called solar; lunisolar calendars take calculations from both. All calendars are divided into days, months, and leap years, and all usually have 12 months with a variable number of days within each month.

The Gregorian calendar used in the United States is one of the youngest calendars. It was devised by Pope Gregory in 1582, and was gradually adopted by countries in Europe, then the rest of the world. Some countries such as Russia and China adopted the Gregorian calendar as recently as the 1920s. The Gregorian calendar measures out a year slightly longer than the solar one, but its relative accuracy has led to world-wide use. Since 1930 in China, for instance, the use of the Chinese calendar has been officially forbidden in favor of the Gregorian one.

The Moslem calendar or Hijra is based on days that run from sunset to sunset rather than from midnight to midnight. The calendar is lunar and the months are either 29 or 30 days long. Because of these shorter months, the whole year is shorter than a Gregorian year. This is why Moslem holy days appear to "move" each year when recorded on the Gregorian calendar.

A Jewish day, like a Moslem one, runs from sundown to sundown; holy days start right after sundown. Days do not have special names except for the seventh day or Shabbat (Sabbath), a day of rest corresponding to the Gregorian Saturday. As in the Moslem calendar, the months are either 29 or 30 days long. There are 12 lunar months. An extra month is inserted within the year periodically so as to keep the holidays seasonally appropriate.

People with a Persian heritage (Afghans, some Arabs, Iranians, Iraquis, and Parsis) may use the Zoroastrian calendar. It consists of 12 months, each with exactly 30 days. Five extra days are added at the end of every year just before Pateti (New Year's Eve). Every four years, the Zoroastrian calendar jumps ahead for one day.

Because all of these calendars either pre-date or post-date the Gregorian one, their numbering of years differs. As the Gregorian is the one commonly used, the other dates are referred to in religious or family gatherings only. For instance, the year 1990 in the Gregorian calendar would be

- 1706 in the Coptic calendar
- 5751 in the Jewish calendar
- 4322 in the Korean calendar
- 1912 in the Sri Lankan calendar
- 1411 in the Moslem calendar.

Classroom calendar

January is an ideal time to introduce calendars to young children. They will have seen new calendars at home, and will have heard adults talking about the new year. Begin with what they already know and make a classroom calendar together, starting with the month of January.

Time: 1-2 hours
Materials: one 21-by-28-in. sheet of bristol board
markers
ruler
calendar pictures (suggestions follow)
glue
Method: 1. On the bottom half of the bristol board draw 31 3-in. squares:
4 rows of 7 squares followed by 1 row of 3 squares. Number the squares from 1 to 31.
2. Write the word "January" in 3 languages at the top of the board.
3. Underneath the name of the month, put an appropriate picture.

- Ask parents for free calendars from grocery stores, community groups, or centers. Use these judiciously to show the month written in many languages, or multi-ethnic pictures of children and families. Avoid using exotic travel calendars that depict holiday pictures of other lands as these may be offensive to refugees from that area.

- Use children's drawings of a January scene. Write the child's name on the picture, and the title they have given that picture.

- Take a photograph of the class and use that photograph for the month of January. This helps to make the calendar personal for every child in the class.

- Use a magazine picture of Japanese children skiing (from the publication **Japan**) or Inuit children snowmobiling (Ministry of Northern Affairs publications). Use pictures of chidren dressed warmly in Peru, China, Lesotho, and other countries usually associated only with warmth and sunshine.

- Use pictures of children across the United States in January. This might include children playing on the grass in Miami, children in a blizzard in Chicago, and children in the rain in Portland, Oregon.

4. Draw pictograms to indicate special days in January such as:

- a child's birthday

- a field trip to a laundromat

- Alacitas

- Yuan Tan

Days-of-the-week card

To reinforce the names of the days of the week, we sing songs and rhymes about them. Extend this program experience by making a pictorial record of one specific week in the form of a card that the children can take home to read with their parents. After a few days, ask the parents how they are using the card. Offer them song or rhyme suggestions. Ask them to make another card with their child, using the drawings and photographs that are special to their family.

Time: 30-60 minutes
Materials: one 2-by-14-in. strip of cardboard per child
markers, crayons
elastic band or 6-in. ribbon

Method: 1. Fold the cardboard strip into seven 2-in. squares.
2. Write a day of the week on the top of each square. Begin with Monday. Write the days in at least 2 languages. English, French, Spanish, Swahili, and Polish days of the week follow:

Monday	Tuesday	Wednesday	Thursday	Friday	Saturday	Sunday
lundi	mardi	mercredi	jeudi	vendredi	samedi	dimanche
lunes	martes	miércoles	jueves	viernes	sábado	domingo
jumatatu	jumanne	jumatano	alhamisi	ijumaa	jumamosi	jumapili
poniedzialek	wtorek	środa	czwartek	piątek	sobota	niedziela

3. Indicate which days of the week the child attends the program.
4. Let the child draw a picture of special activities that take place on each of the remaining days.
5. Fold up the strip and secure it with a band or ribbon.

Days-of-the-week card open

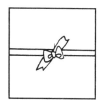

Days-of-the-week card closed

Year-of-birth carousel

Young children may know their own birthday and their age. They may also know their special zodiac sign based on their birth month or their special animal based on their birth year. The latter originates in the Chinese and Vietnamese astrological calendar. In 12 year cycles, each year is assigned an animal's name. Some people believe that all those born in the same year and other years bearing the same animal's name share common qualities.

Use the calendar on p. 180 to find each child's animal. Then use the animal figures on the following pages to make puppets, place cards, name tags, or stickers. In the average single-age program in which most children have a common birth year, this probably involves photo-copying only one or two animals.

Let the children act out the story of the 12 animals. Simple costumes can be improvised: paper ears and a rope tail for the rat; feathers for the rooster; paper-tube horns for the sheep; and so on. Tell the story, letting the children act out the dialogue. Older children may also enjoy making an animal carousel similar to a merry-go-round. This helps them see the relationship between the calendar and the animals.

Time: 60 minutes

Materials: 1 calendar and set of animal figures per child
markers and crayons
scissors
hole punch
glue
2 paper plates
twelve 4-in. strings
2 empty thread spools
1 dowel or pencil to fit inside the spool center

Method: 1. Color the calendar and the animal figures.
2. Cut them out. Punch 1 hole in each animal as indicated.
3. Glue the calendar onto the bottom of 1 paper plate.
4. Punch 12 holes at equal intervals around the rim of that plate, each hole in the middle of a wedge of the calendar.
5. String each animal to the appropriate hole, leaving a 2-in. length of string. between the plate and the animal.
6. Glue a spool to the center of each plate top. Let the glue dry.
7. Insert the dowel in one spool center, then the other, inverting the plate onto the dowel so that the calendar is at the top.

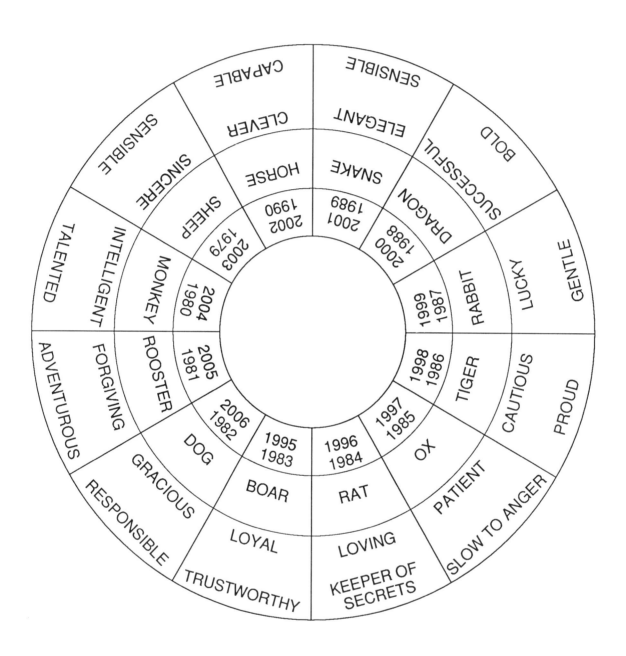

Chinese calendar

Chinese animal figures

Dog

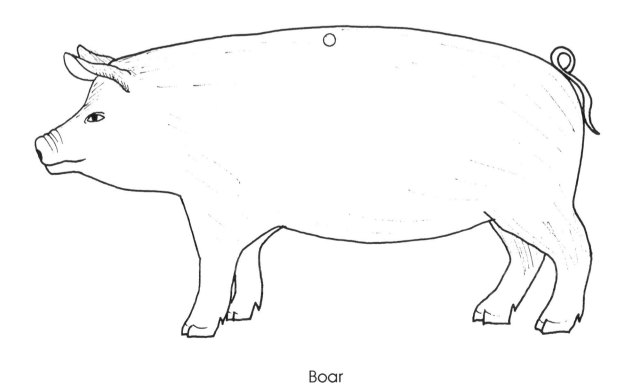

Boar

Monkey

Rooster

Horse

Sheep

Dragon

Snake

Tiger

Rabbit

Rat

Ox

5. Group time

Group time may celebrate any religious or ethnocultural New Year. Chinese New Year is easy to introduce because it involves familiar cross-cultural symbols such as the dragon. It also offers the excitement of loud music, dancing, and games. Use this format for a Chinese New Year celebration and apply it to a New Year that is special to your group.

Dragon mural

Unlike the threatening European dragon, the Chinese dragon is a happy one. Its appearance combines the head of a camel, horns of a deer, neck of a snake, claws of a hawk, and scales of a fish. A symbol of goodness and strength, this dragon leads the way into a good year.

Time: 30-60 minutes
Materials: mural paper
masking tape
newspaper
black marker
triangular sponges
red tempera paint
glue
collage materials: red paper curls, triangular pieces of vinyl cloth, bottle caps, plastic lids, sequins, aluminum-foil scraps
Method: 1. Tape the mural paper to the wall at child height. Lay sheets of newspaper on the floor under the paper.
2. Draw the outline of a large dragon on the mural paper.
3. Print triangles on the dragon's body with the sponges.
4. When the paint is dry, glue red paper curls near the mouth to resemble flames, triangular vinyl scraps on the back for scales, and bottle caps or lids as eyes. Personalize the dragon with other collage materials.

Catch the dragon's tail (Cambodian, Chinese, Indonesian)

This game requires skill, perception, and group awareness. The players stand in a line, single file, each holding onto the waist of the child in front while walking in time to the music. When the music ends the first person, who is the Head of the dragon, tries to tag the last person, who is the Tail. The Tail tries to escape without breaking the line. If the line does break, the game starts again. When the Head catches the Tail, the Tail moves to the front of the line to become Head, and everyone moves down the line. Younger children may enjoy a simpler version that also reinforces the class rope routine.

Time: 10-20 minutes
Materials: 5-6 inflated balloons tied at intervals to the class rope
Method: 1. Show the children how to hold the class rope with 1 hand, and caution them not to drop the rope.
2. Pull the rope through the room. The rope is the dragon's tail.
3. Pull the rope more quickly so that everyone skips to keep in line.
4. Go to the end of the rope and let the next child be the leader.
5. When everyone has had a turn to be the leader, drop the rope and hop on the spot. Try to hop onto a balloon until the whole tail is deflated.

Dragon fingerplay

Celebrate New Year with counting activities during snack, art, games, music, and group time. Build numeracy skills and illustrate one-to-one correspondence by encouraging the children to do the actions and sing the words of this simple fingerplay.

Time: 30 minutes
Materials: one 5-by-8-in. piece of red bristol board
             scissors
             markers
             glue
             glitter or sequins
             one 8-in. square of red construction paper
             masking tape
Method: 1. Photocopy, then cut out the dragon on p. 189. Use it as a pattern to trace a dragon shape onto the bristol board. Cut out the dragon.
           2. Draw features on the dragon.
           3. Apply glue to the scales and mouth of the dragon. Sprinkle on glitter or sequins.
           4. Fold the construction paper twice to make a 2-in. square. Photocopy, then cut out the shoe pattern. Use it to trace a shoe shape onto the paper square. Cut around the shape to make 4 shoes. Write the numbers from 1 to 4 on each shoe.
           5. Give out 1 shoe per child, saying the number as it is given. Hold the dragon by putting a finger through each hole, bending the finger to resemble a foot. Put a masking-tape loop on each foot, sticky side out. Then say or sing the fingerplay:

> *Up climbs the dragon,*
> *Up and around.*
> *Down goes the dragon,*
> *Down to the town.*
> *She's looking for her shoes,*
> *And she's asking you,* (dragon looks at child with shoe 1)
> *Who has one?* (shoe 1 is stuck onto loop)
> *One's no fun.*
> *That won't do!*
> *She needs two.* (dragon looks at child with shoe 2)
> *Let me see.* (shoe 2 is stuck on loop)
> *She wants three.* (shoe 3 is stuck on loop)
> *Roar, roar, roar,*
> *Roar for four.* (shoe 4 is stuck on loop)
> *Now she has her shoes on, she can go.*

           6. Repeat this fingerplay until all the children have a chance to put on several shoes. Then let a child hold the dragon while everyone sings or says the words.

Dragon fingerplay pattern

Dragon costume

The highlight of the Chinese New Year parade is the dragon dance. It sways through the streets accompanied by drums and cymbals. Make a dragon costume and do the dragon dance together. Orchestrate this dance with drums, bells, and cymbals. Remember to photograph the dance, and to bring the dragon dance to other children in the spirit of Chinese New Year.

When making the costume, divide the children into two groups. Let the youngest children block-print the sheet. Let the older ones work together on the dragon's head. This encourages both younger and older children to work together creatively on age-appropriate tasks.

Time: two 1-hour sessions

Materials: 1 cardboard box (large enough for a child's head)
utility knife (for adult use only)
small construction-paper triangles
masking tape
2 paper tubes
red tempera paint
paint rollers
newspaper
double bedsheet
sponges
glue
collage materials: foil pie plates, plastic lids, tinsel, crepe-paper strips or raffia, tissue paper, pipecleaners

Method:
1. Cut a large oval mouth in one side of the box. Tape paper triangles all around the mouth to resemble teeth.
2. Cut 2 tube-size holes near the corners of the bottom of the box. Each hole should be above one side of the mouth. Insert the bottom 1/4 of the tube in the hole, then tape it in place.
3. Use paint rollers to paint the entire box red. Let it dry.
4. While the paint is out, block-print the sheet. Dip a sponge in the red tempera paint, then press the sponge onto the sheet. Repeat until a colorful pattern is formed all over the sheet. Let the sheet dry completely.
5. Use glue to attach collage materials to the box head. Above the mouth glue pie plates or lids as eyes. Glue on tinsel or crepe-paper streamers so that they hang from the mouth. Stuff tissue paper into the tops of the tubes. Poke 2 pipecleaners into the box, one under each side of the nose. Glue on other collage materials as appropriate.
6. When the box head is complete and the sheet is dry, assemble the costume. Have one child wear the box head while the others form a line behind, holding each other's waists. Drape the sheet over the line so that it looks like the dragon's body. Practice moving together in the room or outside.

Dragon costume

Egg-carton dragon

This dragon can be a pull toy, a puppet, a mobile, or an animal in the block area.
By manipulating this dragon, the children become familiar with its body parts and the vocabulary associated with it: teeth, scales, tail, fire, mouth, eyes.

Time: 20 minutes
Materials: 1 cardboard egg carton per child
             scissors
             2 paper fasteners per child
             tempera-sand paint (5 parts liquid paint to 1 part sand)
             wide paintbrushes
             glitter
             one 30-in. piece of string (optional)
Method: 1. Cut the egg carton along its hinge, separating the top piece from the bottom. Working with the bottom piece, cut the 2 rows of egg cups in half to make 2 separate rows of 6.
             2. From the top of the carton, cut out an 8-in. tapered tail. Make the edges of the tail jagged. Use a paper fastener to attach the wide end of the tail to the bottom of a cup at the end of one of the rows of 6.
             3. Cut a cup off the unused row. Cut the edges of this cup to resemble sharp teeth. Use a paper fastener to attach the bottom of this cup to the front end of the dragon.
             4. Paint the egg-carton dragon with the paint-sand mixture.
             5. Before the paint is dry, sprinkle glitter on it so that the surface of the dragon is both gritty and shiny.
             6. If the dragon is to be used as a pull toy, tie the string to the paper fastener in the dragon's mouth.

6. Food to share

Certain foods are considered lucky to eat at New Year. Try your luck preparing and eating them, and tell the story behind each snack.

- Italians, Portuguese, and Spaniards eat 12 grapes or raisins on the stroke of midnight on New Year's Eve. Give each child 12 raisins or grapes in a small cup. Eat them together, counting the numbers as the fruit is enjoyed.

- On New Year many Chinese families offer Chuen-Hop or "a tray of togetherness" to their visitors. Traditionally, it has eight compartments, each with a special food: candied lotus seeds are said to bring sons; candied melon promotes health and growth; watermelon seeds symbolize prosperity. Buy these preserved fruits at a Chinese grocery store, and serve them in an octagonal tin. Suggested fruits are: lotus seed, watermelon rind, watermelon seed, preserved plum, preserved apricot, preserved loquat, candied ginger, and banana chips.

- In Korea rice cake soup is traditionally eaten on New Year's Day. Make your own rice cake snacks by offering a rice cake to each child with a selection of toppings such as red bean paste, humus, cream cheese, or marmite.

- Challah is a traditional braided bread eaten on Shabaat and holy days. On Rosh Hashanah challah is baked as a round loaf. Pieces are dipped in honey so that the new year will be sweet. Serve round rolls or scones spread with honey, and talk about Rosh Hashanah.

- The Vietnamese and Chinese astrological calendar assigns one animal to each year. The zodiac does the same with the 12 months of the year. Buy a box of animal crackers and serve them, saying each animal's name as it is served.

- Traditional fortune cookies are sold year round at Chinese grocery stores. Children can make their own simple version by slipping a lucky message (wrapped in wax paper) into a mini pita.

- In Greece on New Year's Eve many children go from house to house singing the kalanda. They may carry an apple, a paper ship or star, and a green branch. The householder is tapped with the branch, and encouraged to push a coin into the apple. Portuguese children have a similar custom. Imitate this by making wedge-shaped cuts in a number of apples. Insert triangles of cheese in each cut. Serve the cheese to the children, then finish slicing the apples into wedges and serve them.

Lucky apple

Lucky cookies (Belgian, Middle Eastern, Swedish)

Lucky symbols and charms are part of New Year. They are written on banners, cards, and walls. They are even written on cookies! Belgian children give nules or cookies stamped with crosses to their friends on New Year's Day. Many Swedish families use a personal set of carved wooden stamps on cookies or small cakes. Arabs use similar stamps when making special holiday pastries and sweets. Mold playdough or clay stamps, let them dry, then use them on the cookies below.

Ingredients: 2 C butter
1 C sugar
1 t almond extract
4 C flour

Method:
1. Cream together the butter and sugar, then add the almond extract.
2. Add the flour and mix well.
3. Chill the dough for several hours.
4. Form 20 small balls. Stamp each ball with a cookie stamp.
5. Bake at 350° F for 12-15 minutes.

Oliebollen (Dutch)

In many Dutch homes Oliebollen is a New Year's Eve tradition. The name defies translation but this treat is basically a fruit-filled fritter. This recipe makes two to three dozen oliebollen. They can be made in advance and served cold or re-heated.

Ingredients: 2 C milk
1/4 C butter
1 package yeast dissolved according to instructions
1/4 C sugar
2 C raisins
4 C flour
4 apples, peeled, cored, and sliced in rings
4 C cooking oil

Method:
1. Scald the milk and butter together, then let cool to lukewarm.
2. Add all the other ingredients except the apples. Mix together, then let rise in a warm place until the mixture doubles in size.
3. Dip each apple slice in the dough, then drop into the medium-hot cooking oil. Fry until golden brown.

Good-luck milk

Children can easily make some common milk by-products, an experience that gives new meaning to the labels at the dairy counter. For those with lactose intolerance, consider substitutes whenever possible.

Cheese or tofu curds

Ingredients: 4 C whole milk or soya milk
juice of half a lemon
Method: 1. Boil the milk for 1 minute, then add the lemon juice and stir. Leave until warm.
2. Pour the mixture into a fine sieve suspended over a bowl.
3. When drained, spread the curds on crackers.

Butter

Ingredients: 1 C whipping cream
Method: 1. Pour the whipping cream into a clear plastic jar with a tight-fitting lid.
2. Pass the jar around the circle, letting each child shake the jar many times vigorously.
3. After about 30 vigorous shakes, butter should form in the bottom of the jar. Drain off the milk and take out the butter.

Ice cream

Ingredients: 2 C fruit (small pieces, seeded and peeled)
1 C sugar
1 T lemon juice
1 C whipping cream
Method: 1. Sprinkle the fruit with sugar, then stir in the remaining ingredients. Pour into a freezer tray and partially freeze.
2. Remove from the freezer and beat until stiff.
3. Refreeze for 1 hour until firm.

Snow cream

Ingredients: 1 C evaporated milk
1/2 C sugar
1 t vanilla
a large amount of fresh snow
Method: 1. Beat together the first 3 ingredients.
2. Stir in the fresh snow until the mixture looks like ice cream.

Resources for educators

Blackwood, Alan. **Festivals: New Year**. Hove, East Sussex: Wayland, 1985.
Simple text and photographs document New Year festivities everywhere.

Hughes, Paul. **The Days of the Week**. Ada, Oklahoma: Garrett, 1989.
Stories, songs, traditions, festivals, and surprising facts about the days of the week all over the world are presented.

Kelley, Emily. **Happy New Year**. Minneapolis: Carolrhoda, 1984.
This well illustrated book describes the many ways in which New Year is celebrated.

Yoshiko, Samuel. **Twelve Years, Twelve Animals**. Nashville: Abingdon, 1972.
This Japanese folktale of why the years are named after animals can be simplified and the illustrations used for flannelboard stories.

Storybooks for young children (2-6 years)

Anno, Mitsumasa et al. **All in a Day**. New York: Philomel, 1986.
Bright, detailed pictures depict children all around the world on January 1.

Behrens, June. **Gung Hoy Fat Choy, Happy New Year**. Chicago: Children's Book Press, 1982.
A week of festivities surrounding Chinese New Year in San Francisco is described with photographs and simple text.

Brown, Tricia. **Chinese New Year**. New York: Holt, 1987.
This photo essay chronicles the celebration of Chinese New Year in the United States today.

Demi. **A Chinese Zoo**. New York: Harcourt Brace Jovanovich, 1987.
Each animal fable is illustrated with a Chinese motto on a brush-painted fan.

Hou-tien, Cheng. **The Chinese New Year**. New York: Holt, 1976.
Scissor cuts and text by Cheng Hou-tien capture the pageantry and ritual of a traditional Chinese New Year.

Kahukiwa, Robyn. **Taniwha**. Markham, Ontario: Penguin, 1986.
A young Maori boy who sees a legendary monster that looks like a dragon is believed only by his understanding grandfather.

Potter, Dan. **Sun Neen: The Best Time of Year**. Kitchener, Ontario: Edu-Media, 1980.
Genie, a Chinese girl living in Vancouver, describes why she loves New Year best.

Reeves-Stevens, Garfield and Judith. **What Happens First?** Agincourt, Ontario: Gage, 1990.
This multi-ethnic booklet visually introduces time sequencing through practical examples; equally interesting is Reeves-Stevens' **How Old is It**?

Smith, Linda. **Dat's New Year**. London: A & C Black, 1987.
A five-year-old boy talks about his special New Year with colorful photographs to illustrate it.

Solomon, Joan. **Bobbi's New Year**. London: Hamish Hamilton, 1980.
Bobbi, a Sikh boy, celebrates Baisakhi with his family.

Tanaka, Shelley. **Michi's New Year**. Toronto: Northern Lights, 1980.
Michi's first New Year celebration in Canada is not like the last in Japan, but her disappointment changes as she meets new friends.

Wallace, Ian. **Chin Chiang and the Dragon's Dance**. Toronto: Groundwood, 1984.
A young boy in Vancouver learns to overcome fear and perform the difficult Dragon's Dance for Chinese New Year.

Waters, Kate and Madeline Slovenz-Low. **Lion Dancer: Ernie Wan's Chinese New Year**.
New York: Scholastic, 1990.
Ernie, a Chinese-American, participates in a Lion Dance for the first time.

Films

The Fire-flowers of Yet Sing Low (6:00) Sterling
In this animated film a Chinese boy befriends a sneezing dragon on the eve of Chinese New Year.

CHAPTER SIX

Spring

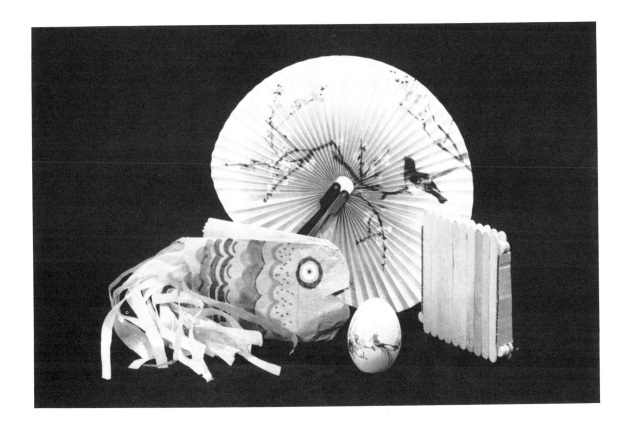

Spring: the awakening of life

Spring signals the beginning of new life and the lengthening of daylight. North of the equator, the first day of spring is usually March 21, the vernal equinox, when the hours of day and night are almost equal. Because of the harshness of winter in northern countries, the vernal equinox is a time for celebration.

In extreme northern regions, spring or "break-up" is the turning point of the year. The tundra changes from an unbroken expanse of frozen land to a spongey marsh where wildlife breed and wildflowers blossom in the short, intense growing season.

Near the equator, the humidity is more variable than the temperature. Here the dry days give way to the rains of spring that are so vital to successful agriculture.

In rural areas spring is a busy time for preparing the soil and planting seeds. Festivals based on traditional planting ceremonies celebrate the return of spring. The old spirit of winter, embodied as collected winter junk (Sweden) or a stuffed figure called Jack Straw (England), is burnt away. This burning is a reminder of the annual burning back of cropland to prepare for planting. Urban dwellers also welcome spring with joy and festivity, expressing this in the fun of April Fool's Day and the squirting of water during Holi.

Each year in almost every country and religion of the world, the renewal of life or the return of spring is celebrated. Following is a list of spring celebrations and their corresponding dates. Dates marked with an asterisk (*) are movable and depend upon either lunar or religious calendars. If a festival is associated with a particular place or people within a country, this is noted in parentheses. Although many of these festivals are celebrated in the United States, the place of origin of each one is keyed by number to a point on the map.

1. Bolivia	Prima Vera	September 21
2. Bulgaria	Prvi Mart	March 1
3. Canada (N.W.T.)	Toonik Tyme	late April
4. China	Li Chun	* February
	Ch'ing M'ing	April 5
5. Colombia	Feria de las Flores	August 1-7
6. Denmark	Pinse	May 18
7. Egypt, Sudan	Shem-Al-Naseem	May 5
8. England	May Day	May 1
9. Finland	Vappu	May 1
10. Ghana	Ngma-Yem	April
11. Italy	Caléndimaggio	May 15
12. Japan	Hana Matsuri	April 8
	Spring Imperial Festival	March 23
	Tango	May 5
13. Korea	Tano	May
14. Lesotho	Tree Planting Day	March 22
15. Mali	Buro	* early June

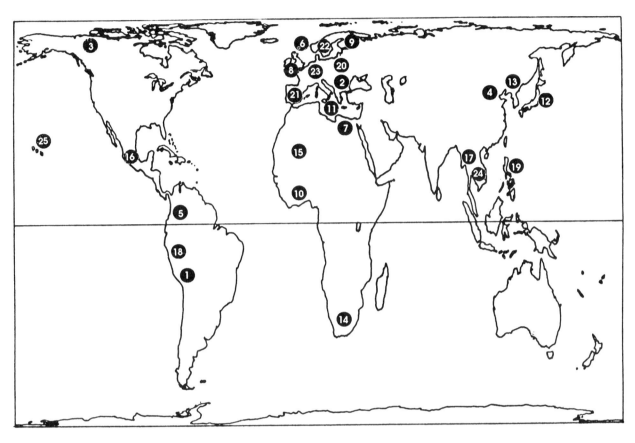

16. Mexico	Cinco de Mayo	May 5
17. Myanmar	Thingyan	April 12
18. Peru	El Desfile de las Flores	* late February or early March
19. Philippines	Santa Cruzen	May 3
20. Poland	Wielkanoc	late March or early April
21. Spain (Seville)	Spring Festival	* April
22. Sweden	Walpurgis Night	April 30
23. Switzerland	Sechselauten	April 19
24. Thailand	Songkran	April 12
25. United States (Hawaii)	Lei Day	May 1
Buddhism	Wesak	2nd Sunday in May
Christianity	Easter	* March/April
Hinduism	Vasanta	* March
	Holi	* March
	Kalpa Vruksha	* April
Islam	Now Ruz	* March/April
Judaism	Tu B'Shevat	* January/February
	Lag B'omer	* May 23
	Passover	* late March or early April
Zoroastrianism	Jamshedi Navroz	March 21

Using the spring theme

GOAL To show the universality of spring celebrations

OBJECTIVES To experience with the children the similarity of springtime rituals in many cultures

To demonstrate that all living things have a beginning from which they grow

To explain the importance of rain and sunshine in the growing of crops

To familiarize the children with the beauty of nature through activities focussing on the rain, the egg and the tree

To introduce and use the basic vocabulary of this theme

Add your own objectives to suit your particular program. For instance, if the tree is chosen as a primary focus of the theme, then another objective would be to learn the parts of the tree (bark, roots, branches, buds, leaves) and the importance of each part.

Depending on your climate, use the spring theme from February to the end of May. It can follow or precede a theme of climate, seasons, baby animals, or maple syrup. Each springtime symbol — the tree, the egg, the rain — can also be used as an environmental theme on its own.

VOCABULARY LIST

The following is a basic vocabulary list for this theme. Try posting these words on your bulletin board or sending a few home to your parents on a vocabulary card. Ask a bilingual parent to translate these words, then send them home in that language to all the families. This is another way to encourage parental participation in a multicultural program.

sun	tree	birth	boots
wind	flower	growing	umbrella
rain	seed	planting	raincoat
cloud	egg	watering	sunhat
sunshine	kite	weeding	sunglasses

 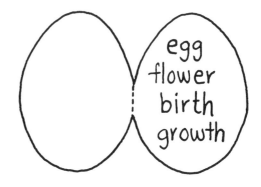

egg
flower
birth
growth

Spring vocabulary card, outside and inside faces

1. Setting the mood

A preliminary to beginning the spring theme is the shared washing and cleaning of the play area. This is both a symbolic and a practical step. Just before Passover, for instance, houses are symbolically cleaned with a feather. In Thailand, on Songkran, houses are cleaned to get rid of unwanted spirits, and ritual baths are taken. In China, on Ch'ing M'ing, family graves are visited and cleaned. Even when the climatic change is not dramatic, spring cleaning seems to be a universal urge. Preparing the room and the activities together can be both satisfying work and co-operative play. It reinforces the children's control over their space, and their personal responsibility for its maintenance.

Preparing the room

- Move the larger pieces of equipment to one side to clear a big floor space. Tape a white paper circle to the middle of the floor. Give each child a whisk, mop, broom, feather or palm leaf duster to sweep the dust onto the circle. Using the circle makes the dust obvious.

- Put a bucket of clean warm water on the floor and give a sponge to each child. Show the children how to wring out their sponges in the clean water. Start together on one side of the room. Let everyone work in a line from one side to the other until the whole floor space is washed. Show the children the dirty water in the bucket. Wring out the sponges for the last time, then leave them out to dry. This is a good opportunity to go outside to play while the floor dries.

- Move the large equipment back into place. Let the children help to push and pull the equipment. If possible, reposition some of the equipment so that the room really appears to be new and fresh.

- Cleaning windows is also gratifying for children, especially in spring when they want to be able to watch the plants growing outside. Fill plastic spray bottles with water and a spoonful of vinegar. Give each child a bottle, a clean cloth, and a small window area to clean.

Beginning the activities

- Wash the toys and the dolls' clothes in warm water. Then use clothespegs to hang them on a line to dry.

- A clean body and a clean spirit are central to most world religions. Even in secular life, daytime communal baths and ritual bathing are daily habits for many. Fill the water table half-full of warm water and let the children put their dolls in it. Put wooden blocks and face cloths around the edge so that the dolls can sit on the "wooden benches" to dry off. Pictures that show children and adults in communal bathing pools and spas reinforce the healthy aspects of this social cleansing ritual.

- Offer a variety of different weights and shapes of plastic buckets. Show pictures of children carrying both light and heavy loads on their heads as they walk to school or home.

- Take one bucket of water for the day and divide it in half, using half for drinking and half for washing. Let the children experience water rationing for one day in this "thirsty activity". Limiting half a bucket of water for communal washing also teaches a new respect for this precious and essential resource.

- Try to balance empty plastic buckets on the head using both hands, one, or none. Make a circlet with a large handkerchief or square of cloth. Twist it into a long cord, then tie the ends together. Put this on the head, then put the bucket on top of the cloth. Feel how much easier it is to carry a bucket this way.

Twist the cloth.

Put it on your head.

Put the bucket on top.

Hats and hair ornaments

Children enjoy being bare-headed after the winter and feeling the wind in their hair. Replace tight-fitting toques and woollen scarves with lighter headgear such as a sombrero, fez, panama, head-band, or conical straw hat.

Leafy hats

Traditional green spring costumes of England, Yugoslavia, New Guinea, and Mali are surprisingly similar. The English Jack-in-the-Green is covered in leaves and branches. Like Green George of Yugoslavia and the Dukduk man of New Guinea, he is a symbol of growth and often leads the May Day processions. The Mali man is dressed in a hood, ruff, and skirt made of leafy branches. He roams through villages in spring, surprising and amusing children.

Time: 10 minutes
Materials: 15 leaves (real or made of crepe paper) per child
           1 green pipe cleaner or plastic-coated wire per child
Method: 1. Holding the leaves by their stems, wrap the pipe cleaner or wire around the stems
              to secure them.
           2. Fan out the leaves to form a conical hat.

Hair-ties

Show pictures of Cree and Algonquin children wearing traditional leather hair-ties decorated with feathers and beads. Although used mainly on special occasions, some Native people like to wear these hair-ties every day. Boys in your group may especially enjoy these hair-ties, and may want to experiment with braiding their hair too.

Time: 10 minutes
Materials: one 2-in. cardboard oval, hole at each end, per child
            small feathers, crepe streamers, beads
            glue
            4 in. of yarn per child
Method: 1. Glue the beads, feathers, and streamers onto the cardboard oval.
            2. Gather a small section of hair in the piece of yarn. Thread one end of the yarn through both holes of the oval. Now thread the other end of the yarn in the opposite direction through the holes. Pull on both ends while pushing up the oval to hold the hair tightly. Tie the ends together in a bow.

Butterfly barrettes

Time: 10 minutes
Materials: one 4-in. square of tissue paper per child
            1 bobby pin per child
            glitter
            glue
Method: 1. Roll or pleat the square so that it looks like a long caterpillar.
            2. Bend the tissue in half. Put the bobby pin through the middle.
            3. Fan out the tissue-paper wings. If desired, tear them slightly at the ends so they appear more feathery and light.
            4. Dab glue on the wings, and sprinkle glitter on the glue. Shake off the excess glitter and let them dry.

Leis

These floral necklaces are worn in Hawaii, Polynesia, and many South Sea Islands. They say "welcome" to visitors, and they are a symbol of friendship and hospitality the world over.

Time: 20 minutes
Materials: one 20-in. piece of string per child
            1 tapestry needle per child
            selection of colored tissue paper, and real flowers
Method: 1. Thread the needle and tie a large knot at 1 end of the string.
            2. Crumple small squares of colored tissue paper into balls.
            3. Thread the balls and real flowers onto the string .
            4. Slip off the needle and tie the 2 ends of string together to make a lei. Use a shorter string to make a floral crown.

Visual props

The tree is a symbol of renewed life. When the first buds appear they proclaim the survival of the tree after yet another winter. Young trees are planted in the spring in China during Ch'ing M'ing and on Arbour Days in Canada, India, Israel, Korea, Lesotho, Spain, and the United States. Celebrate spring by "planting" your own classroom tree.

- Plant a real tree branch firmly in a pot of soil. On the smaller branches hang paper flowers and eggs decorated by the children.

- Shape a nest out of playdough or clay. Press real grass and twigs into the nest. Mold the nest onto a tree branch planted in a pot. Add eggs, birds in branches, tiny animals, insects, grubs, mushrooms, and fungi.

- The pussy willow is a symbol of spring in Central Europe, China, and North America. Make it your classroom tree by planting several pussy willow branches in a hard sponge. Alternatively, put the branches in a water-filled glass vase and watch the roots grow.

- Bring in a branch of a spring flowering shrub such as forsythia. Put it in a jar of warm water in the sun to force it into flower.

- Plant a bamboo ski pole (minus the leather strap) in a pot of sand. Tape green crepe-paper streamers to the top to resemble a copra tree. Large colorful birds like to roost in these trees, and coconuts can grow at the top.

- Two smaller "trees" can support a hammock made of an old mesh onion bag. Rock the dolls to sleep in this hammock.

- Tape a large sheet of laminate, sticky side out, to the wall. In the middle of the sheet press on a big grey construction-paper tree with plenty of small branches. At the bottom let the children press on the maple seeds (keys) they have found. Between the tree trunk and the seeds, string jute, rope, or sisal to indicate roots. On the branches let the children press on small black playdough buds. This visual prop may take weeks to complete. The children can add insects, grass, sand and small stones themselves as no glue is needed: no preparation and no tidying up! To preserve the finished mural, press a large sheet of laminate over it.

- Extend this visual prop by showing trees that produce edible sap such as the maple and the raffia palm. At right angles to the maple attach a toothpick with tape. Poke the toothpick through a plastic creamer as a bucket. If the raffia palm is used, press on a short piece of bamboo at right angles to the trunk. This represents the hollowed-out bamboo tube the tapper connects to the cut trunk. Stick a piece of dried gourd onto the other end as a calabash into which palm wine drips. Sap from the date palm tree, and latex from the rubber tree can also be depicted.

- Use a tree as a permanent part of your visual display. Hang harvest vegetables, carnival masks, valentines, lanterns, woven baskets, or other seasonal symbols on the branches.

Spring banners

Banners and kites fly in the often strong spring winds. Hang a variety of banners, wind chimes, flags, and kites inside and outside, and put out a collection of fans for the children to use for making wind.

In Bulgaria, Haiti, Japan, and Russia red and white spring banners are carried in processions and dances, hung from poles, displayed on buildings and in spring fairs. They carry a message of new life to the people, and are waved proudly by spring celebrants. Let the children make their own spring banner using their favorite spring colors. Here are some suggestions.

- Photocopy and enlarge the Chinese and Inuktitut spring symbols on this page. Cut the shapes out of red cloth and use fabric glue to stick them onto a white cloth backing. Hang this banner on the wall.

- Use the spring symbols on this page as models for block printing. Cut the blocks out of old sponges. Choose paint in fresh spring colors. Then work together to print a banner on a large piece of unbleached cotton.

- With a hot iron, press spring wildflowers between two sheets of waxed paper, protecting the iron by placing a sheet of newsprint between the iron and the waxed paper. When the paper is cool, remove the wildflowers. Glue them to long paper banners (long sheets of computer paper are ideal). Wildflowers can also be preserved between two sheets of laminate. Cut around the edges and hang these suncatchers in the window.

- Make a flag for the Ra-Ra dance (p. 209) by attaching a cloth banner to a pole, broom handle, hockey stick, or dowel.

- In Korea on Tano people make copies of phrases of good luck. Then they post them on pillars and gates. Write your own messages of good luck, then hang them up on the doors or windows.

Spring (Chinese)   Spring (Inuktitut)

Kites

Kites reflect the freedom of spring: the wind, the fresh air, the joy of flying. They originated in India where they were co-operatively flown by groups of flyers who worked together to keep up the kite. Today, kites are usually smaller, varying from the leafy kites of Brazil to the filmy ones of China.

They often tell a story. In Thailand, for instance, kites are flown near the end of the monsoon because of a legend about magical kites that caused the rain clouds to disappear. In Korea, at the end of kite-flying season, the flyers write messages on their kites and fly them high. Then they cut the strings, releasing the kites in a symbolic gesture meant to dispel bad luck for the coming year. On Hallowe'en in Guatemala kites are flown in the graveyard, then set alight to free the souls. The following two kites also represent legends.

Flower kite

Flora was the Roman goddess of spring, and flowers are traditionally associated with spring festivities. The delicate peach and cherry blossoms of Asia, the huge, luscious flowers of tropical regions, the tiny crocus and daffodil of Europe, the pussy willow of North America — all these are welcome messengers of spring. Paper flowers can be strung in rows like the leis of Hawaii and Polynesia, worn in the hair like the floral crowns of Eastern Europe, or offered as tokens of friendship and love. During rural festivals, flowers may adorn the necks of cows and water buffalo.

Time: 2 half-hour sessions: making and flying
Materials: assorted vivid colors of tissue paper
            scissors
            6-in. green pipe cleaners
            1 small bag per child
            one 30-in. string per child
            hole punch
Method: 1. Cut out circles of tissue paper, each one 4 in. in diameter.
            2. For each flower, make a pile of 3 circles. Fold the pile in half, then in half again.
            3. Twist a pipecleaner around the end point to hold the circles in place. Fan out the tissue paper into a flower shape. Make about 5 flowers for each kite.
            4. Push the free end of each pipecleaner into the closed end of the bag. Bend the pipecleaner inside the bag to secure it.
            5. When there are enough flowers on the bag, punch a hole on each side of the open end of the bag. Lace the string through the holes and tie the ends together to form a handle.

Alternative method:
            1. Use 1 large mesh onion bag for the whole group. Weave the pipecleaner stems into it until all the flowers are on the bag. Fly this kite together.

Koinobori (Japanese)

in Japan on Tango (Boy's Day) families with sons fly large carp-shaped kites or koinobori on a pole outside their homes. The carp is chosen for its strength and longevity: some, caught by fishermen, are believed to be over a 100 years old. Each son has a kite, the eldest son's kite being at the top of the pole.

Time: 3 half-hour sessions: painting, decorating, and flying.

Materials: 1 large paper bag per child
            stapler
            scissors
            tempera paint
            wide paintbrush or roller
            white construction-paper circles, 1 in. in diameter
            black construction-paper circles, 2 in. and 1/2 in. in diameter
            glue, tape
            crepe-paper streamers
            one 9-in. piece of string per child
            newspapers

Method: 1. Fold in the corners of the closed end of the bag so that it resembles a fish head. Staple in place.
           2. Cut a triangular hole in the front of the head to resemble a mouth.
           3. Paint the bag, marking on fish scales, then hang up the bag to dry.
           4. Make the eyes by gluing 1 large black circle onto either side of the head. Stick 1 white circle onto each black circle. Stick the small black circle in the middle of each eye.
           6. Tape multi-colored crepe streamers to the open end of the paper bag.
           7. Punch a hole above the mouth. Thread a string through and knot it tightly. Loop the other end of the string over your hand and run against the wind to fly the kite.
           8. Afterwards, bring the kite inside and fill it with newspaper balls so that it is puffy and rigid. Hang it from the ceiling or from the tree or maypole.

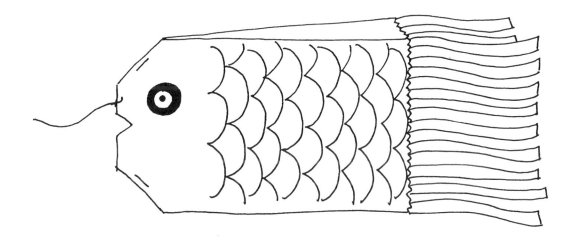

2. Music and movement

Spring is a time of vitality, dancing, and singing outdoors after the long winter. Children are ready now to have at least part of their regular indoor program outside. Make up simple spring songs or use the following suggestions.

In the Spring (Tune: "Sur le Pont d'Avignon")

In the spring, in the spring,
Children playing, children playing.
In the spring, in the spring,
All the children laugh and sing.

Variations: 1. On Ch'ing M'ing, on Ch'ing M'ing (etc.)
     2. On Songkran, on Songkran (etc.)
     3. Use the festival list on pp. 198-199 for further ideas.

De Colores (Raffi, **One Light, One Sun**)

De colores,
De colores se visten los campos
En la primevera.
De colores,
De colores son los parjaritos
Que vienen de afuera.
De colores,
De colores es el arco iris
Que vemos lucir.
Y por eso los grandes amores
De muchos colores me gustan a mi.
Canta el gallo,
Canta el gallo con el quiri, quiri,
Quiri, quiri, quiri.
La gallina,
La gallina con el cara, cara,
Cara, cara, cara.
Los polluelos,
Los polluelos con el pio, pio.

The colors,
The country fields dress themselves
in their spring colors.
The colors,
The little birds are filled with
the colors.
The colors,
The shining rainbow is filled with
the colors.
I love seeing the colors.
I love seeing all these things.
The rooster sings,
with a quiri, quiri,
quiri, quiri, quiri.
The hen sings
with a cara, cara,
cara, cara, cara.
The little chicks sing
with a pio, pio.

Variations: 1. Listen to the song in Spanish first.
     2. Try to learn the Spanish names of the animals.
     3. Act out the actions of the animals.
     4. Dance in a circle to the music.

Dancing

Ra-Ra dancing, maypole dancing, rain dancing, and morris dancing are springtime dances usually performed outdoors. All four make use of bells and ribbons, fast movement, and synchronized action. Music for these dances can come from cassette tapes or the children themselves, the bells on their legs, or the shakers in their hands.

Ra-Ra dancing

Ra-Ra are the spring dancers and dance of Haiti. Each dancer wears a red shirt and carries a red flag. Some of the dancers beat drums; some carry whips to drive out winter; and some wave lanterns. As soon as the crowd sees the group leader or jester, they yell, "Ra-Ra." Try dancing the Ra-Ra over several sessions, doing one or two variations each time. Show the children pictures of dancing, processions, banners, and red clothing. Let the children wear red dress-ups with red streamers tied around their wrists. Let each child also take a turn holding the flag and waving it for the final, "Ra-Ra."

Materials: red dress-ups
              red streamers
              spring flag in red and white (see p. 205)
              tambourines and drums
              tape recording: "Abraham's Children" (Messenjah, **Session**)

Method:
1. Stand in a circle and clap to the rhythm of, "Rain, rain, go away." When the clapping is steady, start the Ra-Ra chant, "Cold, cold, go away. Sunshine come back here to stay." At the end of the chant let the flag-bearer wave the flag and shout, "Ra-Ra."
2. Begin chanting slowly, then repeat the chant a little faster. Increase the tempo again. When the chant reaches a crescendo at "Ra-Ra," let the flag-bearer again wave the flag.
3. A second flag-bearer now takes the flag and leads the group around the room, chanting and clapping as before. Repeat this several times until the chant is steady.
4. Change flag-bearer again. This time, sing the chant and mime the actions:
   "Cold, cold go away" (rub arms vigorously and stamp feet).
   "Sunshine come back here to stay" (arms in a big sunshine circle).
5. Change flag-bearer again. Beat out the rhythm of the chant with a tambourine or a drum.
6. Repeat the chant to the rhythm of feet stamping or drums beating.
7. Continue as above using the suggested tape recording. Many of the songs on this tape can be used with the Ra-Ra dance.

Maypole dancing

The Maypole Dance originated in Europe as a dance of celebration around a tree. As the custom evolved, a tall pole took the place of a tree. Dancers held streamers hung from the top of the pole and wove them into tight, colorful patterns. The dancing continued until all the dancers were exhausted. Today this is still a springtime ritual in many British, American, and European cities.

Spring dancing around a tree is a ritual celebration in other parts of the world too. In rural Korea, for instance, children dance around a rice stack pole early on the morning of Tano. They sing songs calling for a good crop in the coming season. In India on Kalpa Vruksha children dance around a "wishing tree" for good luck.

The maypole dance described below is an outdoor activity. If outdoor space is limited, make individual maypoles by gluing crepe-paper streamers to the top of a drinking straw or cardboard tube. Wave this maypole to the music, then skip in a circle together. If outdoor space is not restricted, make a maypole by taping the top of each streamer to the top of a pole at least 9 ft high. Then double tape all the streamer tops together and plant this pole firmly in the ground. Alternatively, thumbtack the streamer tops high up around a tree trunk and use this real tree as a maypole.

Materials: 1 maypole with a streamer for each child
tape recording: "One Big Family" (Schneider, **Listen to the Children**)

Method: 1. Hold hands in a circle around the maypole. If there are enough adults, alternate adult and child in the circle.
2. Release hands and hold 1 streamer with the right hand. Turn and face left. Skip clockwise together to the sound of the music.
3. Stop and change directions. This time hold the streamer with the left hand, and skip counter-clockwise to the right. Try not to tangle the streamers.

Rain dancing

Just as barefoot dancing in the spring rain is a traditional delight for children, dancing to bring rain is a universal cultural tradition. The Hopi Indians of Central America wear Kachina masks made of shaped rawhide for their rain dance. They impersonate their ancestors as they pray for rain and a good crop. Rain dancers in rural Uganda imitate the sound of the rain with rattles or wooden shakers. The Bobo of Nigeria wear painted masks and fiber costumes representing the god Dwo who brings rain to the parched land. Use the suggestions below to improvise your own rain dance.

Time: 1 hour
Materials: 1 paper plate per child
           scissors
           markers
           dry grass, raffia, or broom bristles (a handful per child)
           tape
           1 craft stick per child
           1 umbrella
           tape recording: "Listen to the Raindrops" (Schneider, **Listen to the Children**)
Method: 1. For each mask cut 2 eye holes out of the plate.
           2. Outline them with a marker.
           3. Tape the dry grass or bristles all around the rim of the plate.
           4. Tape a craft stick to the bottom of the plate as a handle.
           5. Sit in a circle, each child disguised by the paper plate face mask.
           6. Play "Listen to the Raindrops". Try to identify the sounds.
           7. Stand up and begin a rain chant. Turn to the right and begin a slow rhythmic
              march. Keep marching, gradually making the circle tighter and tighter.
           8. When everyone is in a small, tight circle, sit down. Let a person in the middle of the
              circle hold an umbrella over everyone. Crouch under it together while someone
              taps out the rhythm of the rain on the surface of the umbrella.

Bobo rain mask

Morris dancing

In Toronto, Canada, morris dancers get up before dawn on May Day. They gather on the highest hill in High Park to "dance the sun up." This custom dates back to medieval times, to contests between Moors and Christians called Mauresques. It was also seen as a ritual to induce successful crop growing. Today, morris dancing is performed in cities across Austria, the Balkans, the British Commonwealth, Canada, Italy, and Spain. To dance the morris, children should wear white dress-ups, with ankle bells on their legs. They should also hold a white handkerchief or tissue in each hand.

Materials: white dress-ups
large white handkerchiefs or tissues
ankle bells (see p. 169)
tambourines
tape recording: "Oats and Beans and Barley" (Raffi, **Baby Beluga**)

Method: 1. Stand in a circle with the leader in the middle. This position is rotated so that everyone has a turn to be the leader.
2. Listen to the suggested tape recording and follow the actions chosen by the leader. The leader might do low and high jumps or leg kicks, twirling with arms raised to wave the handkerchiefs or twirling with a partner.
3. Sing this song to the tune of "Oats and Beans and Barley":

> *Morris dancers welcome the spring*
> *Morris dancers welcome the spring*
> *Kick your legs, wave your arms,*
> *Twirl around and start to sing.*

Repeat this several times until everyone knows the words.

Spring games

Marbles, hopscotch, and skipping are universal springtime games. Other games that echo from culture to culture are listed below. They can be played indoors or out, depending on the space available and the weather.

Gutera uriziga (Rwandan)

Originally a hunter's game played with spears and a hoop, gutera uriziga was developed to teach young boys skill and accuracy in marksmanship. Try playing this adaptation with a stationary or rolling hoop, or color-code the hoops to match the bean bags.

Materials: 1 hoop
            1 beanbag per child
Method: 1. Stand shoulder to shoulder in a line with 1 person standing in front of the line.
           2. Let that person roll the hoop in front of the line.
           3. Try to throw the beanbags through the hoop.

Takraw (Thai)

This group game depends on co-operation to keep the ball in the air. It also challenges the children to think about using other body parts for batting. Younger children may want to play this game using their hands, concentrating only on keeping the ball up in the air.

Materials: 1 soft ball or balloon
Method: 1. Stand in a circle with hands clasped together.
           2. Let 1 person toss the ball into the air.
           3. Try to keep the ball in the air using the head, elbows, knees, toes, or other body parts.

Flower kick (Indian, Inuit)

This combination game uses the flower kick game of India to practice the Inuit one-foot kick. Children learn balance and co-ordination as they find and practice their own kick level.

Materials: 1 tissue-paper flower with a string attached to it
Method: 1. Suspend the flower so that it dangles at knee level.
2. Try the Inuit 1-foot kick to touch the flower: jump up with both feet, kick the flower with 1 foot, and try to land on this same foot.
3. Raise or lower the flower to suit the kick.

Co-operative hat game (Israeli)

From the Easter bonnets of New York to the new spring clothes of Hong Kong, hats for spring are a universal sight. Challenge the children to find new ways to put on hats, and to work co-operatively in pairs. Plastic or paper hats can be used, although incorporating a variety of hats enriches this game. Put all the hats on the floor in the middle of the circle. Tie the ribbon together so that it makes a loop as big as your circle.

Materials: 1 hat per child
Method: 1. Sit in a circle holding the ribbon loop with both hands.
2. Try to get a hat onto someone else's head without dropping the loop. Use mouth, feet, or elbows instead. Continue until everyone is wearing a hat.
3. When everyone has a hat to wear, drop the loop. Listen to "Got a Hat Hat" (Bob Schneider, **Having a Good Time**). Follow the directions to tilt the hat forwards, tilt the hat backwards, twirl the hat around, and so on. Listen to the song several times and learn the words.

3. Art

Springtime presents an opportunity to use natural materials such as eggs, branches, flowers, sand, leaves, and wool, materials that remind us of the earth's continual renewal. Use them in art activities that communicate with nature in a special way, weaving spring magic for the children.

The egg

The oldest of all spring customs is that of giving and receiving eggs. The egg symbolizes both the return of life and the wholeness of the universe itself. The following are various methods of preparing, painting, dyeing, and filling eggs. They are listed from the simplest to the more difficult so that they can be matched to the ability level of young artists.

Preparing the egg

- In place of a fresh egg, consider a clay ball, wooden egg, or oval rock.
- Use a duck or goose egg for a larger decorating surface, or a quail egg for a smaller surface. Grocery stores and outdoor markets often sell these special eggs in the spring.
- Hard-boil an egg by cooking it in boiling water for 10 to 12 minutes. Keep this egg in the refrigerator and eat it within a week.
- Ask parents to help by bringing in blown-out eggs.
- Blow out an egg by carefully making a hole in either end of the egg, then blowing the raw egg into a dish (beat them later to make scrambled eggs).

Painting the egg

- Put the egg into an egg cup. Imitate the Chinese style of egg people by painting the top half as a face, leaving the bottom half of the egg covered by the egg cup.
- Use a discarded eggshell from the kitchen. Paint a face on the shell. Then fill the empty shell with potting soil and sprinkle in some grass, cress, or parsley seed. Watch the hair grow.
- Thread a string through a blown-out egg and knot the string at one end. Drag the egg through a tray of water in which there are a few drops of baby oil mixed with tempera powder. This produces "marbleized" eggs.
- Use waterproof markers to draw on a design suggested by the Ukrainian pysanka eggs (see designs below).
- To preserve the painted eggs, spray them with varnish after the children have left the room. This gives the eggs a glossy, finished appearance.

Pysanka symbols of life,   fertility,   health,   and love.

Dyeing the egg

- On the prepared egg print the child's name with a white wax crayon. Dip the egg into natural or commercial dye. The name will remain white.
- Make a design on the egg with small pieces of masking tape. Dip the egg into dye. When the egg is dry, remove the tape to expose the design.
- Use a glue stick to stick leaves or grass onto the egg. Put the egg inside old pantyhose. Knot the pantyhose to keep the leaves in place. Dip the egg into dye. When the egg is dry, remove the pantyhose, leaves, and grass to expose the pattern.
- Wrap the egg in a small piece of brightly patterned (not colorfast) cloth. Boil the egg in water for 10 minutes. Remove the cloth to uncover an equally brightly patterned egg.
- Wrap the egg in several layers of onion skins, then in cheesecloth. Boil it in water for 10 minutes. Remove the cloth and skins to uncover a marbleized egg. The egg may be red, orange, or yellow depending on the type of onion (red, Spanish, or cooking) and the type of egg (brown or white).
- Crack a hard-boiled egg gently all over, then soak it in beet juice for a day. Take the egg out and let it dry. Then peel the egg to reveal a purple egg etched with tiny white lines.
- Use natural dyes rather than commercial ones. Boil 4 cups of onion skins in water for an orange-brown dye. Boiled beetroot tops make a purple dye, and dandelion flowers make a yellow dye.
- Make suncatchers by putting each color of used dye in a separate clear glass bottle.

Filling the egg

- Very carefully enlarge the hole in the top of a blown-out egg. Then stuff confetti into the hole. Glue paper over the hole. During Los Posados such a confetti-stuffed egg or cascarone is symbolically cracked over the head of a sweetheart. In Nicaragua and Guatemala children toss these eggs as part of spring festivities.
- Stuff tiny paper or dried flowers into a blown-out egg. Paste layers of colored tissue-paper strips over the hole and around the egg. Let the egg dry into a hard, colorful spring piñata.
- Pour colored water into a blown-out egg. Then seal the hole with playdough to make a trick cascarone. Use this egg in an outside game like Raindrops (p. 225). Toss it back and forth, taking a step backward each time until the cascarone breaks.

Using broken eggshells

- Combine painted or dyed eggshells with playdough or clay for a different textural experience.
- Make a mosaic by gluing eggshells onto a pattern drawn on cardboard.
- Put a combination of plain white and brown eggshells into the sensory bin for children to grind, sieve, crack, roll, or hammer.

Spring magic

Sandpainting (Australian, Central American, North American)

The Native People of British Columbia say that long ago the gods taught their healers how to make pictures in the sand, pictures with the power to cure an illness or lift a curse. But the pictures had to be made and destroyed on the same day; otherwise, they would bring bad luck. The Aborigines in Australia and the Indians in Central America also made sandpaintings with symbolic patterns.

Before Easter in Central American cities, a type of sandpainting is done on the road. Colored sawdust, rather than sand, is used. During the night the sawdust is sprinkled onto the road through stencil cutouts. The sawdust is continually dampened to keep it in place. Patterns and floral designs are formed, stretching like a carpet for many city blocks. The next day religious processions march the entire length of this temporary carpet, destroying it at the same time.

Show pictures of Central American road paintings or some of the symbols used in Navajo sandpaintings (see below). Then take the children outside to rediscover their sand play area. Do the paintings in one session as suggested, or over several days so that the paintings gradually grow in color. If you believe in magic, though, it is best to make the sandpainting and destroy it in one day!

Time: 1 hour
Materials: 1 square piece of cardboard per child
           crayons
           sand
           grated colored chalk or powdered tempera
           plastic squeeze bottles
           glue
Method: 1. Use crayons to draw a design on the cardboard square.
         2. Mix sand with 1 color of paint or grated chalk to make colored sand. Then put 1 color of sand into each squeeze bottle.
         3. Begin on 1 section of the design. Cover it with glue, then squeeze colored sand onto the glue.
         4. Repeat this on another section of the design, using a second color of sand, and so on, until the design is completely painted with sand.

 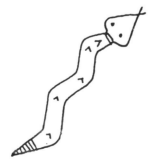 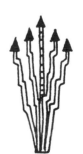 

Navajo symbols of the sun,   a snake,   lightning,   and an eagle.

Ojo de Dios (Central American, Mexican)

The Huichol Indians of Mexico originated this woven charm or talisman. Nowadays, the Ojo de Dios (God's Eye) is planted in both Central American and Mexican cornfields. Its traditional colors are said to secure the protection of the gods of the east (red) so that they will send sun (yellow) and rain (blue) to help the crops. It is also meant to protect children, to give them the strength and power of the Aztecs.

Try making an Ojo de Dios with the children. Tie the red yarn to the blue, and the blue to the yellow, to make one long piece of yarn that is easier to use. Work individually with each child until the rhythm of over-under is established. Younger children may just want to wrap up a stick, then wrap up the next one, until the four sticks are wrapped in yarn.

Time: 1 half-hour session
Materials: one 3-ft length of red, yellow, and blue 3-ply yarn per child
            2 small sticks tied into 1 cross shape per child
            scissors
            one 20-in. piece of yarn per child
Method: 1. Tie a knot around any 1 of the 4 sticks. Push the knot to the center of the
               cross to start.
            2. Wind the yarn around each stick in succession, circling over 1 stick,
               and circling under the next. Keep circling the yarn over and under,
               winding around and around until the yarn is finished. Then tie a knot to end it.
            3. Thread the 20-in. yarn through one point of the God's Eye to make a necklace.
               Wear it as a lucky charm in the spring.

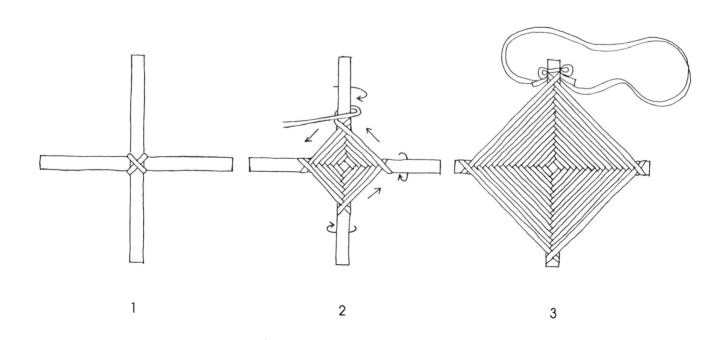

1   2   3

4. Discovery

In the discovery area the children can examine signs of new and renewed life: nests, pictures of newborns, spring flowers. This is a time to grow plants in the classroom. Chinese cress and parsley grow very quickly in potting soil, and radish seeds sprout in a jar if kept moist. Magnifying glasses invite the children to look closely at the seeds, the soil, and a drop of water. A prism on the table splits the sunlight into a rainbow of colors. Caterpillars and silkworms show the renewal and vitality of life. Springtime is exciting, so bring the outdoors into your discovery area.

Oware

Oware is played by young and old alike. The game board has two rows of six cups called houses, and small seeds are rotated around the board until there is a winner. In Mali the game is called Star Play or the Game of the Universe. In Nigeria the game is Mankala or Oware, two words that mean transferring. In Cambodia it is called Bykom, in Somalia, Shax. In Malaysia the game is Chongkak and stones are used rather than seeds. A simpler version is described below.

Materials: 1 cardboard egg carton
scissors
markers
12 pairs of seeds or beans (see suggestions below)
bowl

Method: 1. Cut off the top of the egg carton and save it for another use, then decorate the bottom half. This is the game board.
2. Put all 24 seeds or beans in the bowl. Suggested varieties: pumpkin, squash, melon, mango, peach, papaya, orange, and apricot seeds; corn kernels; black-eyed peas; chickpeas; mung, fava, lima, kidney, pinto, soya, black turtle, navy, and great northern beans; coffee beans. Larger seeds and beans are easier for very young children to handle.
3. Try to find a pair of seeds or beans for each cup. This is a self-correcting game.

Extend the experience by matching the seeds or beans to 12 corresponding pictures of the fully-grown plant. When the game is no longer used, remember to wash, cook, and eat the beans.

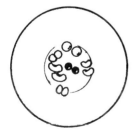 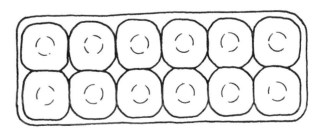

Flower card game

Japanese flower or hanafuda cards are smaller and thicker than Western playing cards. The deck of 48 is divided into 12 suits of four identical cards each. Each suit represents one of the twelve months of the year, and shows a tree or a plant associated with that month. These cards can be bought at Japanese stores. Make a simpler set of 24 cards with the help of the illustrations on the next page.

Materials: markers or crayons
2 pieces of bristol board 71/2 by 10 in. each.
glue stick
laminate
scissors
cardboard box

Method: 1. Make 2 photocopies of the following page, then color the pictures. Suggested colors:

Iris	blue, purple, cream
Dandelion	yellow
Buttercup	yellow
Pussy willow	grey
Poppy	red
Crocus	yellow, purple, white
Tulip	red, orange, yellow, cream, purple
Daffodil	yellow, cream
Orchid	white (outlined with purple or pink)
Cherry blossom	pink
Lilac	purple
Peony	pink, cream, purple

2. Glue the picture sheet to one side of a piece of bristol board, and the corresponding name sheet to the opposite side. Laminate.
3. Cut out along the solid black lines.
4. There are now 12 pairs of flowers. Find the pairs and identify them. Turn the cards over for a game of memory. Find the pairs. For other card games, see p. 53 and p. 63.
5. Store the cards in a sturdy cardboard box, suitably decorated.

Myths and healing properties are often associated with spring flowers.

- When the Empress of China ordered all the flowers to bloom in winter, only the peony refused. For this the Empress burned her to ashes. The Queen of Flowers, however, rewarded the peony for her wisdom by making her the most luscious of all the spring flowers in China.

- In Japan the iris symbolizes integrity because of the rigid way it sits on the stem. Wooden toy swords sold on Tango are also called iris swords.

- Crocus leaves were used by the Blackfoot as a poultice for rheumatism. The Blackfoot also used pussy willow branches boiled in water to reduce fever or alleviate pain.

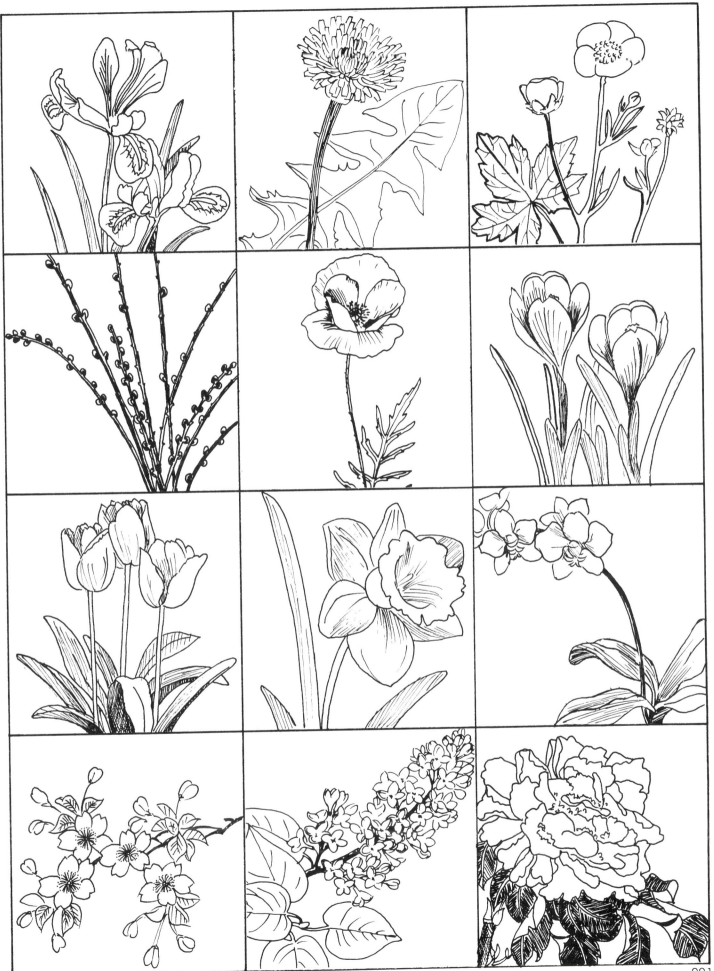

Buttercup	Dandelion	Iris
Crocus	Poppy	Pussy willow
Orchid	Daffodil	Tulip
Peony	Lilac	Cherry blossom

5. Group time

Children understand and remember environmental concepts best when they learn from direct personal experiences. That was Jim Eagle's message when he told me a story of his childhood on the reserve. When he would walk through the woods with his grandparents, his hands would push the leaves aside, sometimes needlessly snapping a branch. This same branch would be used to punish him for such thoughtless damage.

Although punishment is not an ideal teacher, love and respect for our living earth are feelings we all want our children to share. Enjoy the first two group activities either in your yard (provided there are trees and grass) or in a park beyond it. Model respect for nature by being sensitive to its delicate ecological balance.

Tree rubbings

Rubbing is a modern word for the Chinese art of T'ai-pen or ink-squeezing. The earliest recorded Chinese rubbings were done in 7 AD, using dampened rice paper pressed onto an object. These rubbings were used to duplicate and preserve a pattern. By preserving the intricacy of a tree bark pattern in a rubbing, children can begin to appreciate the textural beauty and individuality of each tree. Remind them that the bark is part of the tree just as skin is part of our bodies.

Time: 15-30 minutes
Materials: 5 sheets of lightweight white paper per child
            brown or black chalk or charcoal
            masking tape
Method: 1. Walk to a wooded area. Let the children find a comfortable tree to hug and let them feel its bark: is it rough or smooth?
            2. Find a tree with rough bark. Tape a sheet of paper over the bark and rub chalk over the paper until a pattern emerges.
            3. Do another rubbing with a second sheet of paper on another part of the bark. Compare rubbings. Note that each pattern is as individual as a fingerprint.

Birchbark patterns

Perhaps because of its color and because it comes into leaf early, the birch tree is often called the tree of spring. Years ago, birchbark canoes and baskets were made from the bark of fallen trees, and today these crafts are still practiced by Native Americans. Let the children try painting these birchbark designs, ideally outdoors near the birch trees that inspired them.

Time: 15-30 minutes
Materials: 1 circle of white construction paper per child
            1 pine tree branch per child
            black tempera paint
            clear adhesive tape
Method: 1. Dip the needles of the branch in the paint, then drag the needles across the paper. This produces a striped effect that makes the paper resemble birchbark.
            2. When the paper is dry, roll it into a cone and tape it closed like a muhkuk, the Ojibwa birchbark cone. Use this cone to hold rocks, sand, or pinecones.

Making recycled paper

Paper as we know it was developed in China around the year 105 AD. Early paper was made by soaking rags, rope, bark, and other materials, then adding glue to this mixture. This paper was then pressed into sheets. Making paper with children has a threefold purpose: it demonstrates paper-making as a skill and art; it shows another use for paper waste; and it illustrates that substance is constant despite changes in form. Hopefully, this activity will also encourage recycling on a daily basis, a necessary activity for all of us.

Time: 30 minutes
Materials: used paper: newsprint, computer paper, or paper towels
            1 blender
            1 old window screen
            1 pan or tub that is slightly larger than the screen
            sponges, dry paper towels
            iron, rolling pin (optional)
Method: 1. Tear up the paper into tiny pieces. Put the pieces in a blender that is 3/4 full of hot water. Process to make pulp.
            2. Put the wire screen over the pan and empty the contents of the blender onto the wire screen.
            3. Press down and smooth the pulp by hand or with a rolling pin. Sponge the excess water off the pulp until it feels dry.
            4. Put a paper towel over the pulp, then invert the screen so that the pulp is on top of the paper towel. Sponge dry. For quick results put a second towel over the pulp and iron the pulp dry with a warm iron.
            5. Produce a second batch of colored (orange, red) paper by adding vegetable scraps (carrot skins, beet peels) to the pulp.
            6. Older children may want to personalize their paper by laying flower petals, small strips of colored paper, or colored threads on the screen before the pulp is poured.

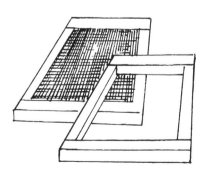

Water play

In India during Holi people spray one another with colored water, just as they do in Eastern Europe the day after Easter Sunday. In Thailand on Songkran people sprinkle water on Buddhist monks, statues of the Buddha, and one another. In the United States on April Fool's Day the squirting pen or flower sprays unsuspecting victims. These water games are universal springtime rituals well worth imitating. Play them outdoors on the soft grass or sand, or indoors with a plastic wading pool.

Candle spray

Time: 15 minutes
Materials: 6 short, fat candles
            matches (for adult use only)
            snowbank, sandbox, or a plastic wading pool of water
            plastic spray bottles full of water
            skipping rope or string
Method: 1. Plant the candles upright in a snowbank or sandbox, or float them in a wading
               pool of water.
            2. Light the candles.
            3. Stand behind the rope at a safe distance (6 ft) from the candles. Use
               a spray bottle full of water to squirt out the candles.

Raindrops

Time: 15 minutes
Materials: vinyl flowers (cut from old shower curtains or rainwear)
            skipping rope or string
            durable colored balloons full of water and tied at the top
Method: 1. Scatter the flowers on the grass outdoors, or in a plastic wading
               pool indoors.
            2. Standing in a line behind the rope, toss the balloons on the flowers.

Holi spray

Time: 15-30 minutes
Materials: 1 large plastic sheet (preferably white)
            assorted colors of tempera powder in shakers
            plastic spray bottles full of water
            fingerpaint paper
Method: 1. Shake different colors of tempera powder on the sheet.
            2. Spray the powder with water until it is soft like paint.
            3. Mix the colors by hand and make handprints on the paper.

Spring folktales

Beginning in mid-May the countries of South Asia await the monsoon wind and the heavy rain it brings from the tropical oceans. The arrival of the monsoon is greeted with joy because it means water for plants, crops, flowers, and grass.

To prepare the children for the water activities, tell one or all of the folktales that follow. Patterns for the characters, P'eng and Hanuman, follow on pp. 228-229. Use the patterns to make puppets or feltboard figures.

How P'eng brought the rain (a Chinese legend)

In spring, when the day is as long as the night, a big bird called P'eng flies out of the sea. With his big golden wings he covers the whole sky. He spreads his wings to blot out the sun, and the whole sky darkens. Then he flies faster, and the winds begin to blow. He flies faster, and the waves roll up as high as the trees. The sky is dark, the winds blow, the waves roll, and the people run into their houses. "P'eng is here!" they shout. "P'eng is here!" They stay inside until the big bird flies away. Then they go outside to feel the sun and the soft, wet earth. The rains are over and P'eng is gone for another year.

The rain dance (a Brazilian legend)

Once the sun, the moon, and the water lived on earth just as people do. The sun kept the people warm, the moon lit their nights, and the water quenched their thirst. But the people grew spoiled with this good life and chased them away — the sun because it was too hot; the moon because it was too bright and kept them awake at night; and the water because it drenched their homes. The earth became cold and cheerless. The plants and animals began to die for lack of water.
Then the people turned to the Wise One, old Na-ma-ka-ra-ne, for help. "What can we do? We have no warmth, no water, and our children are dying!" He told them, "Drum without pause until the old man Rain hears you and sends you water for your thirst." So the people drummed and danced for days and days in their first rain dance until drops of rain fell to moisten the earth again.

The sun, the moon, and the water (a Zimbabwean legend)

Once the sun, the moon, and the water all lived in Africa. The sun and the moon shared one hut and the water lived alone. Now the sun and the moon felt sorry for their friend the water, and invited the water to share their home.
"You wouldn't want me," said the water. "I am too big."
"Nonsense," said the sun and the moon. "You are always welcome."
"But I will take up too much room," said the water.
"Nonsense," said the sun and the moon. "You don't take up too much room. We insist."
"All right," said the water. "If you insist, I will come and stay with you."
So in came the water. All day long the water moved into their home, all day and all night, and all the next day. The water filled the hut right up to the roof, and sent the sun and the moon whirling into the sky. The sun went one way, the moon another high up into the sky, and neither one has ever come back to live in Africa again!

Hanuman, the Monkey God (an Indian legend)

Hanuman, the Monkey God, once had a craving for hot, spicy food. He became so hungry for it that he turned to the sun and swallowed the sun whole. With the sun inside him, Hanuman grew hotter and hotter, while the people on earth became colder and colder. The flowers died and the trees lost their leaves. Snow fell during the dark days and the dark nights. The birds went away for there was no sun to warm them, and the animals hid in their caves. The people grew sad and wondered what they could do to bring back the sun.
Then a child suggested, "Let's make Hanuman laugh! He will laugh until he spits out the sun. Then we will be warm again."
The people thought about this and said, "Yes, that is a good idea! But how can we do this?"
They thought. Someone suggested telling Hanuman a funny story, but they knew he was too hot to listen. Someone else suggested painting a funny picture, but they knew he wouldn't look. Then a child said, "I know. We can paint one another!"
"What?" said the people. "That is a silly idea." Then they began to laugh. Someone picked up some red dirt and put it on a neighbor's head. Someone else threw blue powder over all the adults. Oh, how funny they looked. The colors flew and mixed, and the people laughed and laughed so loudly that Hanuman looked down.
"What is this?" he bellowed. Then he saw the blue, orange, purple, and green people and he smiled. He giggled. One huge laugh fell out and another, until Hanuman was rolling with laughter. He laughed so hard that tears came to his eyes. At last, out popped the sun.
"Hurrah!" said the people. "The plan worked." Then they, too, started to laugh as they felt the world become warm and sunny. Every year on Holi they remember Hanuman and throw colored powders over one another to make the Monkey God laugh again!

P'eng

Hanuman

6. Food to share

In Iran on the 13th day of Now Ruz, called Sizdar-Bedah, it is considered unlucky to stay indoors, so the entire family goes outside for a picnic. In Egypt on Shem-Al-Naseem, families pack up a picnic to "smell the spring." Throughout the world in spring, food is bundled up as the extended family gathers outdoors to eat fresh food. Certain foods are associated with spring. Eggs are symbols of life and fertility in the Jewish Seder meal, and red eggs are exchanged in the Middle East, the Ukraine, China, and Egypt. Tree fruits such as dates, figs, nuts, and St John's Bread are eaten on Tu b'Shevat in Israel. Fiddleheads, rhubarb and asparagus announce the spring to many North Americans.

Remember some of these foods when packing your picnic, or prepare easy snack foods with the children. Print the recipes clearly or use pictograms. Laminate the recipe cards and hang them above the work area so that everyone can follow the directions. Each recipe serves 10.

Portable picnic (Italian)

Ingredients:
1 loaf of Italian bread
4 lettuce leaves
1 T olive oil
dash of vinegar
6 slices tomato
8 slices salami or pastrami
8 slices provolone or mozzarella cheese

Method:
1. Cut the bread in half lengthwise.
2. Place the washed lettuce leaves on the bread. Sprinkle with the oil and vinegar.
3. Lay the other ingredients on top.
4. Cover with the top of the bread and press down. Cut into 10 slices for serving.

Pickled eggs (Ukrainian)

Ingredients:
5 eggs
2 C pickled beetroot juice

Method:
1. Boil the eggs for 10 minutes. Cool and shell.
2. Cover the eggs with the beetroot juice and refrigerate them for a week.
3. Remove the eggs and drain well. The eggs are now purple.

Egg drop soup (Chinese)

Ingredients:
5 chicken bouillon cubes
5 C boiling water
1 beaten egg (from blown-out egg)
chopped chives or parsley or radish sprouts

Method:
1. Boil the water with the cubes until the cubes dissolve.
2. Whisk the beaten egg into the mixture.
3. Take off the heat and serve immediately, topped with chives.

Lassi (Indian)

Ingredients: 2 C yogurt
2 C water
2 T fresh fruit and sugar, or 1 t salt
dash of cumin/nutmeg

Method:
1. Whip the yogurt, water, and fruit or salt until the mixture is frothy and thick.
2. Top the salt mixture with a dash of cumin, the sweet with nutmeg.
3. Drink this with a straw as if it were a milk shake. Try comparing the taste of savory (salt) lassi to sweet (fruit) lassi.

Matzot meal chremslach (Jewish)

Ingredients: 1 egg, separated
1/4 C water
1/4 C matzot meal
dash of salt and pepper
1 T vegetable oil

Method:
1. Beat the egg white until stiff.
2. Combine the yolk, water, meal, salt and pepper. Fold in the egg white.
3. Grease a griddle with the oil. Drop the matzot mixture by tablespoons onto the griddle and brown on both sides.

Global salad

Ingredients: fiddleheads
young dandelion leaves
red and yellow peppers
snow peas
red cabbage
bean sprouts
tzatziki (see below)

Method:
1. Wash and dry the vegetables thoroughly. Cut the peppers and cabbage into strips.
2. Place a bowl for the tzatziki in the centre of a large plate, and arrange the vegetables around this bowl.
2. Put the tzatziki into the bowl and enjoy dipping the vegetables.

Tzatziki (Greek)

Ingredients: 1 C yogurt or sour cream
1/2 t garlic powder
1/2 cucumber, chopped

Method:
1. Combine all the ingredients and serve as a dip.

Special springtime meals

During many spring festivals special meals are eaten. In the Now Ruz meal the seven dishes have changed over the years but they usually include vinegar for preservation, fruit for happiness, flowers for productivity, sugar for sweetness, and spices for the spice in our life. At Passover the Seder meal includes salt water for tears, green vegetables for spring, hard-boiled eggs for fertility, horseradish for bitterness, charoset for binding (recipe below), bone for sacrifice, and wine for sweetness. The meals are eaten in a prescribed way with the family, and the symbolism of each dish is explained so that even the youngest child can understand. In Poland and the Ukraine Easter begins in the church with the blessing of the pasky (bread), pysanky (decorated eggs), butter, lard, cheese, sausage or smoked meat. Then this blessed food or sviachene is taken home for the the family to eat.

Prepare a special springtime meal and invite all the families to participate. It can be a pot-luck lunch with each family bringing a dish and an explanation of its springtime significance. It can also be a meal prepared beforehand by the children. Use the Jewish, Moslem, or Ukrainian menus described above or compose a simpler menu with the following symbolic foods:

sesame butter on matzot (seeds of spring)
celery sticks and green pepper strips (greens of spring)
radish flowers (flowers of spring)
dates, figs, and raisins (sweetness)
lemon tea or lemonade (sunshine)
chives, cress, sprouts, and parsley (grown by the children)
Easter bread such as christonomo or hot cross buns

Charoset (Jewish)

Charoset is eaten at the Seder meal as a symbol of the mortar used by the Jewish slaves who built pyramids for the Egyptian pharaoh. It is usually made with red wine, but grape juice can be substituted.

Ingredients: 1 apple
              1/3 C chopped walnuts
              1/4 t cinnamon
              2 T grape juice
Method: 1. Peel and chop the apple.
              2. Add the nuts, cinnamon, and grape juice. Mix well.

Resources for educators

Behrens, June. **Fiesta! Cinco de Mayo**. Chicago: Children's Book Press, 1978.
Beautiful color photographs and simple text document Mexican children celebrating the spring.

Linton, Marilyn. **The Maple Syrup Book**. Toronto: Kids Can, 1983.
Recipes and activities for sugaring-off are simply described and illustrated.

Kalman, Bobbie. **We Celebrate Spring**. Toronto: Crabtree, 1985.
The clear pictures and simple text explain spring celebrations across cultures.

Storybooks for young children (2-6 years)

Aardema, Verna. **Bringing the Rain to Kapiti Plain**. New York: Dial, 1981.
This Nandi (African) tale written in cumulative rhyme tells the story of young Ki-Pat who shoots down rain from the clouds when the land is dry.

Ahenakew, Frank. **How the Birch Tree Got Its Stripes**. Saskatoon: Fifth House, 1988.
George Littlechild illustrates this exciting Cree legend of the origin of the stripes on birchbark.

Anno, Mitsumasa. **The King's Flower**. Toronto: Collins, 1979.
A king learns that small is also beautiful in this multi-ethnic fable.

Baker, Jeannie. **Where the Forest Meets the Sea**. New York: Greenwillow, 1987.
A boy plays in the tropical rain forest of Australia and wonders how long the forest will still be there. Collage illustrations depict this visual journey through the threatened wilderness.

Beavon, Daphne "Odjig". **Nanabush and the Spirit of Winter**. Toronto: Ginn, 1971.
Nanabush, a Native Spirit, tricks Winter into bringing warmer weather to the people.

Bonnici, Peter. **The First Rains**. Minneapolis: Carolrhoda Books, 1985.
A young Indian boy waits impatiently for the monsoon, his anxiousness captured by Lisa Kopper's drawings. This delightful story is simple, but prepare the children beforehand with visual explanations of sugarcane, banyan tree, and kites (birds).

Cleaver, Elizabeth. **How Summer Came to Canada**. Toronto: Oxford University Press, 1969.
This is a beautifully illustrated story of Glooskap, the legendary creator of the Micmacs, who chased Winter from the land; supplement the book with the film, **Summer Legend** (NFB, 1986).

Clifton, Lucille. **The Boy Who Didn't Believe in Spring**. New York: Dutton, 1973.
King Shabazz and his friend Tony Polita find spring in a garbage dump and describe it with inner city humor.

Dalby, Lois. **Grandma Knows**. Winnipeg: Peguis, 1972.
A Native grandmother teaches her young grandson how to make a simple basket out of birchbark so he can help to collect blueberries.

Dunham, Meredith. **Picnic: How Do You Say It?** New York: Lothrop, Lee and Shepard, 1987.
Colorful picnic items are named in four languages: English, Spanish, French, Italian.

French, Fiona. **Aio the Rainmaker**. London: Oxford University Press, 1975.
Full-page color drawings enhance this exciting African tale of a rain dance.

Fujikawa, Gyo. **Let's Grow a Garden**. Tokyo: Zokeisha, 1978.
A multi-ethnic group of children plant a co-operative garden in this simple, colorful story.

Iwasaki, Chihiro. **Momoko's Lovely Day**. London: Bodley Head, 1970.
Momoko, a Japanese girl, spends a rainy day indoors enjoying herself.

McKissack, Patricia C. **Mirandy and Brother Wind**. New York: Alfred A. Knopf, 1988.
Mirandy, a black American of the early 1900s, wants the wind to be her partner in the cakewalk.

Munsch, Robert. **Millicent and the Wind**. Scarborough, Ontario: Firefly, 1984.
This is a delightful, multi-ethnic tale of a mountain girl and a boy who is brought by the wind.

Polacco, Patricia. **Rechenka's Eggs**. New York: Philomel, 1988.
This tale set in old Russia tells of Rechenka, the goose who laid pysanka eggs for her kindly keeper, Babushka.

Sachs, Dorothea M. **Baby Sister**. New York: Golden, 1986.
A black American, Benito, learns to love his baby sister when he too finds a baby, a little kitten.

Spalding, Andrea. **The Most Beautiful Kite in the World**. Red Deer, Alberta: Red Deer College, 1988.
A Canadian Prairie girl learns the value of homemade fun when she creates a dazzling kite with the help of her Ukrainian neighbors and her father.

Takeshita, Fumiko. **The Park Bench**. Brooklyn, New York: Kane/Miller, 1988.
This beautifully illustrated book in Japanese and English describes the children and adults who use the park bench in the spring.

Waterton, Betty. **Petranella**. New York: Vanguard, 1980.
In pioneer days, a Scandinavian girl drops her seeds on the wagon trail and rediscovers them later as gay spring flowers.

Wettasinghe, Sybil. **The Umbrella Thief**. Brooklyn, New York: Kane/Miller, 1987.
This amusing tale describes a Sri Lankan man who uses banana or yam leaves in the rain until he buys an umbrella which then mysteriously disappears,

Yashima, Taro. **Umbrella**. New York: Viking, 1958.
Selected Japanese characters explain key points of this story of Momo and her new umbrella.

Yolen, Jane. **The Emperor and the Kite**. New York: Philomel, 1988.
This is a touching Chinese legend about an emperor's daring rescue by his tiniest daughter, and the new respect he feels for her.

Zusman, Evelyn. **The Passover Parrot**. Rockville, Maryland: Kar-Ben Copies, 1983.
This amusing story describes a family's preparation for Passover and the chaos caused by their parrot on the first night of the holiday.

Records and tapes

Messenjah, **Session** (WEA, 1984), especially "Abraham's Children."

Raffi, **Baby Beluga** (Troubadour, 1980), especially "Oats and Beans and Barley."

Raffi, **Corner Grocery Store** (Troubadour, 1979).

Raffi, **Everything Grows** (Troubadour, 1987).

Raffi, **One Light, One Sun** (Troubadour, 1985).

Bob Schneider, **Having a Good Time** (Capitol, 1983).

Bob Schneider, **Listen to the Children** (Capitol, 1982), especially "Listen to the Raindrops" and "One Big Family."

Bob Schneider, **When You Dream a Dream** (Capitol, 1982).

Bill Usher, **Drums** (Kids Records, 1986), especially "Haitian Ra Ra" and "Haitian Playground Chant."

A SELECT BIBLIOGRAPHY

Arora, R.K. and C.G. Duncan. **Multicultural Education: towards good practice**. London: Routledge and Kegan Paul, 1986.

Bennett, Christine. **Comprehensive Multicultural Education: Theory and Practice**. Boston: Allyn and Bacon, 1986.

Chud, Gyda and Ruth Fahlman. **Early Childhood Education for a Multicultural Society: a Handbook for Educators**. Vancouver: University of British Columbia, 1985.

Derman-Sparks, Louise. **Anti-Bias Curriculum: tools for empowering young children**. Washington: NAEYC, 1989.

Hendry, Joy. **Becoming Japanese: the World of the Preschool Child**. Manchester, England: Manchester University Press, 1986.

Kehoe, John. **A Handbook for Enhancing the Multicultural Climate of the School**. Vancouver: University of British Columbia, 1984.

Kendall, Frances E. **Diversity in the Classroom: a Multicultural Approach to the Education of Young Children**. New York: Teachers College Press, 1983.

Lee, Enid. **Letters to Marcia: a Teacher's Guide to Anti-racist Education**. Toronto: Cross Cultural Communication Centre, 1985.

Lynch, James. **Prejudice Reduction and the Schools**. London: Cassell, 1987.

McLeod, Keith A. **Multicultural Early Childhood Education**. Toronto: University of Toronto, 1984.

Mock, Karen. **Multicultural Early Childhood Education in Canada: a Cross Canada Survey**. Ottawa: Secretary of State, 1986.

Parry, Caroline. **Let's Celebrate! Canada's Special Days**. Toronto: Kids Can, 1987.

Pedersen, Paul. **A Handbook for Developing Multicultural Awareness**. Alexandria, Virginia: American Association for Counseling and Development, 1988.

Ramsey, Patricia G. **Teaching and Learning in a Diverse World: Multicultural Education for Young Children**. New York: Teachers College Press, 1987.

Samuda, Ronald J. and Shiu L. Kong. **Multicultural Education: Programmes and Methods**. Kingston, Ontario: Intercultural Social Sciences, 1986.

Saracho, Olivia N. and Bernard Spodek. **Understanding the Multicultural Experience in Early Childhood Education**. Washington: NAEYC, 1983.

Tiedt, Pamela L. **Multicultural Teaching: a Handbook of Activities, Information, and Resources**. Boston: Allyn and Bacon, 1986.

Tshabalala-Mogadime, Goodie. **Creativity and Self-Discovery in Every Child**. Concord, Massachusetts: Belsten, 1988.

Williams, L. and Y. de Gaetano. **ALERTA: A Multicultural Bilingual Approach to Teaching Young Children**. Menlo Park, California: Addison-Wesley, 1985.

Music and movement

Butler, Gwynneth and Joe Karetak. **Inuit Games**. Rankin Inlet, NWT: Keewatin Inuit Association, 1980.

Cass-Beggs, Barbara. **A Musical Calendar of Festivals**. London: Ward Lock, 1983.

Chanan, Gabriel and Hazel Francis. **Toys and Games of Children of the World**. Paris: UNESCO, 1984.

Fralick, Paul. **Make it Multicultural: Music Activities for Early Childhood Education**. Hamilton, Ontario: Mohawk College, 1989.

Nelson, Esther L. **Holiday Singing and Dancing Games**. New York: Sterling, 1980.

Walther, Tom. **Make Mine Music**. Toronto: Little, Brown, 1981.

Art

Jefferson, Louise. **The Decorative Arts of Africa**. New York: Viking, 1973.

Conaway, Judith. **Manos: South American Crafts for Children**. Chicago: Follett, 1978.

Fowler, Viriginie. **Folk Toys Around the World and How to Make Them**. Englewood Cliffs, New Jersey: Prentice-Hall, 1984.

Schuman, Jo Miles. **Art from Many Hands: Multicultural Art Projects for Home and School**. Englewood Cliffs, New Jersey: Prentice-Hall, 1980.

Discovery

Gryski, Camilla. **Super String Games**. Toronto: Kids Can, 1987.

Kee, Lorna. **The Toy Box**. Ottawa: National Museum of Man.

Temko, Florence. **Folk Crafts for World Friendship**. New York: Doubleday, 1976.

Group time

Andrews, Jan, ed. **The Dancing Sun**. Victoria: Porcépic, 1981.

Canadian Hunger Foundation. **Let's Try to Understand**. Ottawa: Canadian Hunger Foundation.

Gibson, Jane and Yvonne Hebert. **Folk Rhymes: from Kids to Kids. A Teacher's Guide**. Vancouver: University of British Columbia, 1986.

Pellowski, Anne. **The Story Vine: a Sourcebook of Unusual and Easy-to-tell Stories from Around the World**. New York: Macmillan, 1984.

Rosenberg, Maxine B. **Living in Two Worlds**. New York: Lothrop, Lee and Shepard, 1986.

Food to share

Barer-Stein, Thelma. **You Eat What You Are**. Toronto: McClelland and Stewart, 1979.

Cooper, T. and Marilyn Ratner. **Many Friends Cooking: an International Cookbook for Boys and Girls**. New York: Philomel, 1980.

Crookshanks, Carol, et al. **Multiculturalism through Foods**. Vancouver: Vancouver School Board, 1984.

Tharlet, Eve. **The Little Cooks**. Toronto: UNICEF Canada.

PRONUNCIATION GUIDE

After each of the non-English words below is a guide to its pronunciation. Within words, vowels are pronounced as follows:

a   h**a**t
á   g**a**te
ä   c**a**rt
e   s**e**t
é   p**e**anut
i   h**i**m
í   k**i**te
o   p**o**t
ó   h**o**pe
u   j**u**nk
ú   **u**niverse
ü   ch**oo**se
H   as in the German **ach**. Pronounce K without closing the breath passage.
N   as in the French m**on**. Pronounce O at the back of the mouth.

In each word, stressed syllables are underlined. Where no stress is indicated, give equal emphasis to all of the syllables. In this way, "memory" would be written in the guide, "m_em_óré."

adire eleko	ad_ér_ elekó	choinka	h_á_énka
akuaba	a_kw_äbä	chremslach	remslä
akwadu	a_kw_ädü	chuen-hop	chenhop
Alacitas	alas_é_tas	chullo	h_ü_yó
amauti	am_ót_é	Ch'usok	chüsuk
Año Viejo	anó vy_á_yó	Cinco de Mayo	s_incó_ dá m_íó_
Apokreis	apók_ré_as	daruma	da_ru_ma
azabache	azab_a_xá	Deeyah Diwali	déwa divalí
Babushka	bab_ü_shka	dhalang	daläng
baguette	bag_et_	dias	d_é_as
Baisakhi	bes_a_ké	didgeridoo	d_i_jurédü
Basanth	basänt	dipa	d_é_pa
bashiki	ba_shé_ké	Divali	dé_va_lé
Befana	bef_ä_na	dousha	dósha
berritta	ber_i_ta	douyung	dóyeng
bindie	b_in_dé	Dozynki	dójinké
boleadoras	bóléa_d_óras	El Día del Maiz	ela d_éa_ dá del máz
bolero	bó_le_ró	El Día de Los Reyes	ela d_éa_ dá lóz ráz
Bon Chol Chhnam	bon jól chinam	Eyo	áyó
calendimaggio	calendem_a_jéó	Farsang	farshong
cascarone	cascároné	Fasching	väshing
chadar	_ch_ader	Fasnacht	väsnaH
challah	h_ä_lä	Gaghant	gaHant
chanukiyah	hänü_k_íyä	gamelan	gamelan
chanukkah	_hä_nükä	Gawai Dayak	gawí díyak
chapati	chapaté	getas	gétas
charoset	h_ä_róset	gi	gé
cheng dwah	chen dwä	Giang Sinh	gang sin
chima	chéma	goosh va damagh	g_üsh_ va da_ma_
chogori	chógóré	gregger	_g_reger

238

Term	Pronunciation
gubytra	gübéträ
guk	guk
gutera uriziga	gütera üzéga
gutra	gütra
Hana Matsuri	hana matsüré
hanetsuki	hanétsüké
Hanuman	hanumän
Hidrellez	hidrelez
hijra	hejra
Holi	hólé
hora	hóra
injera	njera
Janmashtemi	janemmestémé
jubba	jüba
Junkanoo	junkanü
Kadomatsu	kadomatsu
kaffiyeh	kaféá
kamaj	kmaj
kameez	käméz
kathakali	katakalé
kente	kenté
kitsune	kitsun
klaben	kläben
koinobori	koynobóré
kolo	kóló
koliadnyky	kóliadniki
krathong	kratón
kufi	küfé
kuma	kuma
kumandori	kumadoré
kurta	kürta
Kwanzaa	kwänzä
Lag B'omer	lag bó ómer
lai-see	lisé
Lan Khoong	lan kóng
lassi	lasé
li chun	lé chün
lien p'u	len pú
lienyung	lenyen
Los Posados	los pósadós
loz-e-nargil	lózánargélé
mao gwa	mowkwa
matracas	matracas
matrioshka	matrióshka
matzot	matzót
mendhi	mahendé
Milad-an-Nabi	meladanabé
moises	moyzes
mola	móla
Momowo	hómówó
moteca	móteka
Navroz Jamshedi	nórüz jamshédé
Ngma-yem	míyem
Now Ruz	no rüz
Objinki	objinké
Obon	óbon
Ojo de Dios	óhó dá déós
oshiroi	óshiró
Oshoogatsu	óshógätsü
oware	ówaré
papassi kawan	papasi kawän
Pinse	pinsé
Pongol	pengol
Prvi Mart	vé märt
pysanka	pisanka
Ramnavmi	ramnamé
rebozo	rebózó
Réveillon	reváyN
rotis	róté
Samhain	sawen
Sechselauten	seHseloyten
shalwar	shalwar
shawaro	shäró
shofar	shófar
Songkran	sóngkran
sukkah	sükä
Sviaty Vechir	svaté vekér
Tanabata	tanabata
Tango	tangó
Tano	tanó
Têt Nguyen Dan	tet nwin däng
Têt Trung-thu	tet trung tü
Thingyan	tingyan
tlukere	tlükere
Toonik Tyme	tünik tím
tortilla	tortéyas
trullas	trülas
Trung-thu	trungtü
Tu B'Shevat	tü béshvat
tzatziki	satséké
ulu	ülü
vaccine	vaxén
Vappu	vapü
Vasanta	vasanta
vibersko	viberskó
wayang kulit	wayäng külit
Wesak	vésak
Wielkanoc	vélkanots
Wigilia	végelya
wycinanki	wisinanké
Yuan Tan	yun tan

INDEX